Distributed and Parallel Systems
From Cluster to Grid Computing

T0189482

Distributed and Parallel Systems
From Cluster to Grid Computing

edited by

Péter Kacsuk
MTA SZTAKI
Computer and Automation Research Institute
Hungary
Thomas Fahringer
Universität Innsbruck
Austria
Zsolt Németh
MTA SZTAKI
Computer and Automation Research Institute
Hungary

 Springer

Péter Kacsuk
MTA SZTAKI Research Institute
Lab. Parallel and Distributed Systems
Victor Hugo u. 18-22
1132 BUDAPEST
HUNGARY
kacsuk@sztaki.hu

Thomas Fahringer
Universität Innsbruck
Institut für Informatik
Technikerstr. 21a
6020 INNSBRUCK
AUSTRIA
Thomas.Fahringer@uibk.ac.at

Zsolt Németh
MTA SZTAKI Research Institute
Lab. Parallel and Distributed Systems
Victor Hugo u. 18-22
1132 BUDAPEST
HUNGARY
zsnemeth@sztaki.hu

Distributed and Parallel Systems:
Cluster and Grid Computing
Edited by Péter Kacsuk, Thomas Fahringer, Zsolt Németh

ISBN-13: 978-1-4419-4348-4   e-ISBN-13: 978-0-387-69858-8

Printed on acid-free paper.

9 8 7 6 5 4 3 2 1

springer.com

Contents

Part III: Grid and web services

Part IV: Grid infrastructure

Part V: Advanced grid techniques

Contents

Preface

The sixth Austrian-Hungarian Workshop on Distributed and Parallel Systems is organized jointly by University of Innsbruck and the MTA SZTAKI Computer and Automation Research Institute. The series of workshops started as a small regional meeting early in the nineties, and since then it evolved a lot and became an acknowledged international scientific event. The scope of the workshop has changed as well during the years following the new trends in technology. The first workshop was dedicated to transputers whereas in recent years, just like this year, it is tagged with cluster and grid computing.

This year the workshop attracted authors from Europe, North-America, Africa and Asia. To continue the recent trends in improving the quality of the workshop, around 52% of the submitted papers were accepted after a thorough review process. These papers are presented in this volume and give a good overview of recent advances in various aspects of parallel and distributed computing. The proceedings is composed of five parts according to the major topics of the workshop – albeit they cover a much broader range in this field. Part I is devoted to general algorithmic aspects of parallel and distributed computing. Communication is a fundamental issue in distributed computing addressed in Part II. The rest of the papers are directly or indirectly related to grid computing: Part III introduces its service oriented questions; Part IV raises various crucial questions tied to the infrastructure whereas Part V presents the most abstract papers introducing advanced problems and challenges of grid computing.

There were two invited talks at the workshop delivered by Leif Laaksonen introducing grid computing in Finland and Nordic collaboration and by Peter Coveney about attracting computational scientist to grid computing by middelwares that simplify user interaction.

We would like to express our gratitude for the generous support of Hewlett-Packard, Intel, Sun Microsystems, Bundesministerium für Bildung, Wissenschaft und Kultur and University of Innsbruck.

We would like to thank the members of the Program Committee and the additional reviewers for their work in refereeing the submitted papers and ensuring the high quality of DAPSYS 2006. Special thanks to those who helped us beyond their duties. We are grateful to Susan Lagerstrom-Fife and her assistant, Sharon Palleschi at Springer for their endless patience and valuable support in producing this volume. The conference could have never been realized without the devoted work of the local organizers: Michaela Lechner, Wolfgang Kausch and the tireless omnipresent almost-PC-chair Stefan Podlipnig. Special thanks to the webmasters Attila Csaba Marosi and Csaba Kujbus and Philippe Rigaux for providing the MyReview system.

Péter Kacsuk	Thomas Fahringer	Zsolt Németh
Workshop Chair	Program Co-chair	Program Co-chair

Program Committee and Additional Reviewers

Workshop Chair

Péter Kacsuk (MTA SZTAKI, Hungary)

Program Chairs

Thomas Fahringer (Univ. of Innsbruck)
Zsolt Németh (MTA SZTAKI, Hungary)

Program Committee Members

Artur Andrzejak (ZIB, Germany)
László Böszörményi (University Klagenfurt, Austria)
Marian Bubak (CYFRONET, Poland)
Alois Ferscha (Johannes Kepler University Linz, Austria)
Günter Haring (University of Vienna, Austria)
Ladislav Hluchy (II SAS, Slovakia)
Zoltán Juhász (University of Veszprem, Hungary)
Károly Kondorosi (Technical University of Budapest, Hungary)
Gabriele Kotsis (University of Vienna, Austria)
Dieter Kranzlmüller (Johannes Kepler University Linz, Austria)
Domenico Laforenza (CNUCE-CNR, Italy)
Erwin Laure (CERN, Switzerland)
Evangelos Markatos (FORTH-ICS, Greece)
Ludek Matyska (Univ. of Brno, Czech Rep.)
Jarek Nabrzyski (PSNC, Poland)
Thierry Priol (INRIA, France)
Radu Prodan (Univ. of Innsbruck)
Rizos Sakellariou (U. Manchester, UK)
Wolfgang Schreiner (University of Linz, Austria)
Domenico Talia (Univ. Calabria, Italy)
Gábor Terstyánszky (Westminster University, UK)
Marek Tudruj (IPI PAN / PJWSTK, Poland)
Jens Volkert (Johannes Kepler University Linz, Austria)
Ramin Yahyapour (U. Dortmund, Germany)

Additional Reviewers

Jan Astalos
Marian Babik
Zoltán Balaton
Mehmet Ceyran
Miroslav Dobrucky
Rubing Duan
Gianluigi Folino
Xaris Gikas
Christian Glasner
Balázs Goldschmidt
Gábor Hermann
Miklós Kozlovszky
Bartosz Kryza
Róbert Lovas
Attila Marosi
Carlo Mastroianni
Monika Moser
Farrukh Nadeem
Christos Papachristos
Christian Perez
Stefan Plantikow
Stefan Podlipnig
Christian v. Prollius
Jun Qin
Viera Sipkova
Gergely Sipos
Csongor Somogyi
Marek Wieczorek
Henan Zhao

I

PARALLEL AND DISTRIBUTED ALGORITHMS

THE WANDERING TOKEN: CONGESTION AVOIDANCE OF A SHARED RESOURCE

Augusto Ciuffoletti
CoreGRID Institute of Grid Information, Resource and Workflow Monitoring Services
INFN/CNAF – Via Berti Pichat – 40127 Bologna

augusto@di.unipi.it

Abstract
In a distributed system where scalability is an issue, the problem of enforcing mutual exclusion often arises in a *soft* form: the infrequent failure of the mutual exclusion predicate is tolerated, without compromising the consistent operation of the overall system. For instance this occurs when the operation subject to mutual exclusion requires massive use of a shared resource.

We introduce a scalable *soft mutual exclusion* algorithm, based on token passing: one distinguished feature of our algorithm is that instead of introducing an overlay topology we adopt a random walk approach.

The consistency of our proposal is evaluated by simulation, and we exemplify its use in the coordination of large data transfers in a backbone based network.

This algorithm is studied in the frame of the CoreGRID Institute of Grid Information, Resource and Workflow Monitoring Services, in cooperation with the FORTH Institute, in Greece.

Keywords: congestion avoidance, random walk, token circulation, self-stabilization, soft mutual exclusion.

1. Introduction

In an ideal distributed system all resources are equivalently able to play any role. However, in practical applications, it is often the case that the introduction of a centralized resource may be appropriate, in order to reduce the cost, or to improve the performance. The loss of scalability and fault tolerance, which is inherent to the introduction of a centralized resource, is accepted as a tradeoff.

In order to avoid congestion, an appropriate access control mechanism must be provided. It is a well known fact that locating such mechanism at resource-side exhibits several drawbacks: the resource must be designed to negotiate services, using an appropriate protocol which consumes a share of available resources, and clients should make appropriate use of such negotiation. Here we propose a client-side mechanism especially suited for environments where resource and networking infrastructure are legacy.

A congestion avoidance mechanism coordinates the access to the centralized resource. The basic requirement is that resource performance, as observed by the client, must be nominal as long as the overall load does not exceed resource capacity. When requests overtake the capacity of the resource, it should reproduce at client side the effect of an overload, but without stress for the resource. The mechanism must not introduce bounds on system size, other than those enforced by resource capacity: this excludes the adoption of centralized algorithms, that are not scalable, as well as distributed algorithms based on deterministic consensus, that have an heavy footprint.

As a case study, we consider a "Video on Demand" environment where video streams at $650Kbps$ (appropriate for low resolution movies) are delivered to a group of subscribers. The shared resource in a $200Mbps$ backbone, which saturates with 300 subscribers. We want that subscribers coordinate their access to the infrastructure in order to limit their access to the stream source, thus keeping the overall used bandwidth below $200Mbps$. Only exceptionally such limit can be exceeded: the Service Agreement states that bursts up to $400Mbps$ are delivered with an additional cost, and that packet delivery is not guaranteed over that further limit. This might justify a flexible control over the number of subscribers, that might go over the theoretical maximum of 300 subscribers.

Summarizing, unlike traditional mutual exclusion modeled by a concurrent write on a shared register, our problem statement includes the occasional occurrence of simultaneous access to the resource. This is due to the nature of the resource whose performance may degrade (in the case study, degradation is initially only financial) when many are executed simultaneously, but without damage for the consistency of the system. This is formally translated in the following definition:

REQUIREMENT 1 *A* soft mutual exclusion *algorithm for the* protected operation **A** *ensures that at any time, with high probability, there is just one agent enabled to perform* **A**. *The probability that more than one agent is enabled falls exponentially in the number of enabled agents.*

We propose a distributed algorithm that implements soft mutual exclusion. The algorithm falls into the *peer to peer* family, since there is no centralized agent, and all participants run the same code. It is *randomized*, in the sense that the algorithm is controlled by decisions affected by a random bias, injected in order to improve the performance, and *probabilistic*, in the sense that the performance of the algorithm is itself a random variable, with a favorable distribution.

The basic idea is the circulation of a token ensuring that, with high probability, exactly one token is present in the system. The token will visit each *peer agent*, granting exclusive access to the resource to the agent that holds the token. This random process can be modeled using the cover time of a random walk in the system graph: in Jonasson, 1998 the authors prove that the distribution of token interarrival time on a peer is characterized by a small probability after a value that grows with $O (N \log N)$, where N is the number of agents in the system. We do not assume a fixed topology or a preliminary *overlay design* phase (as in Kwon and Byers, 2003, aimed at multicast). We evaluate its performance in a full mesh that represents the transport level of the Internet. Formal results (see Jonasson, 1998) justify the claim that our algorithm may be of interest also in networks with an average degree comparable with $\log N$.

The algorithm relies on the knowledge of the *membership* that can execute the protected operation by each agent. Here we do not introduce a solution for membership management, but propose a way to regulate access to a shared resource once the membership is established. We insist on the fact that, on each agent, the knowledge of the membership may be limited to $O (\log N)$ other agents, randomly selected.

The relationships with (deterministic) *self-stabilization* in Dijkstra, 1974 are evident: however, instead of using the knowledge of neighbor's state, we enforce mutual exclusion using time constraints computed locally. We share with some *randomized* self-stabilizing algorithms the basic idea of performing random moves in order to compensate lack of information. Our approach may be regarded as an evolution of Israeli and Jalfon, 1990: with respect to that work, we introduce a probabilistic definition of closure, since the token management scheme may itself induce divergence from the legal state.

Divergence is represented by two kinds of events: the loss of the token and the generation of spurious tokens. The former is induced by a system failure, the second is an inappropriate response of our algorithm. Both events occur with low probability, and the algorithm autonomously recovers. We exclude token duplication (spurious tokens are distinct) using a 3-way token passing protocol (see Ciuffoletti, 2006).

Although many topics discussed in this paper have been individually treated in formal papers, here we prefer a simulation approach: this option is motivated by the fact that the solution we introduce uses a combination of randomization techniques which makes unapproachable a formal evaluation. Whenever appropriate, we indicate formal works that motivate the framework of our approach. Simulation results are summarized in section 3.

2.   System model and the wandering token idea

The system is composed of a set of N *peer agents*, whose clocks are loosely synchronized, interconnected by a complete mesh of *links*: for each couple of agents (c_i, c_j) there is a link $l_{i,j}$ that connects them, as in a *transport level* view of the Internet.

The resource sharing problem is defined by two parameters: N_{max} the number of agents that saturates the resource and Δ_{op} the time during which access is granted to the resource, once the agent holds the token.

The algorithm, described in figure 1, is a probabilistic self-stabilizing algorithm, according with Afek and Brown, 1993. Let us first examine the stable behavior, that corresponds to the case where there is exactly one circulating token.

In that case the behavior of the agent consists of receiving the token, performing an action associated to the presence of the token, and passing the token to a randomly selected peer. The associated action consists in a simple delay of Δ_{skip} time units in case the agent already performed the protected operation less than Δ_{min} time units ago; otherwise the agent holds the token for a time Δ_{op}, while the protected operation is performed. We assume Δ_{skip} to be significantly smaller than Δ_{op}.

Given N_{max} and Δ_{op} we compute a reasonable value for Δ_{min} as

$$\Delta_{min} = \frac{\Delta_{op} * N_{max}}{2}$$

which is half the access period that would saturate the resource. Such simple rule of thumb is appropriate in many cases.

A token loss event, which has a probability that is significantly reduced by the 3-way token passing protocol, breaks the *stable* behavior. The *token regeneration rule* is triggered when the agent does not receive one within a timeout that is obtained incrementing Δ_{min} of a random quantity. A randomized rule guarantees the absence of *synchronization* effects that might degrade the performance. To this purpose, the Poisson distribution is regarded as a convenient candidate.

The $\gamma_{generate}$ parameter corresponds to the γ parameter of such distribution, and a reasonable value is:

$$\gamma\,generate = \Delta_{min} * N_{max} = \frac{\Delta_{op} * N_{max}^2}{2}$$

comment: Compute algorithm parameters
$\Delta_{min} = \Delta_{op} * N_{max}/2$
$\gamma_{generate} = \Delta_{min} * N_{max};$
$lasttoken = \{timestamp = 0, id = NULL\}$
while (**true**)
    do
        comment: Receive token or trigger regeneration timeout
        $select(receive(token), \Delta_{min} + poisson(\gamma_{generate}))$
        if $(defined(token))$
          then
              comment: Apply sandwich token removal rule
              if $(\exists i, j, i < j \wedge$
                $history(j).id = token.id \wedge$
                $history(i).timestamp < token.timestamp)$
                then
                    comment: Silently remove the token
                    $discard(token)$
              fi
              comment: Decide whether to execute the protected operation
              if $(time - (lastaccess.timestamp)) \leq \Delta_{min}$
                then
                    comment: Just skip an early token
                    $sleep(\Delta_{skip})$
                    $send(token)$
                else
                    comment: Execute protected operation
                    $execute(A)$
                    $lastaccess = \{timestamp = time, id = token.id\}$
                    $send(token)$
              fi
          else
              comment: On timeout, generate a new token
              $token = \{timestamp = localclock, id = newid()\}$
              $execute(A)$
              $lastaccess = \{timestamp = time, id = token.id\}$
              $send(token)$
        fi
        $push(history, token)$
od

Figure 1. The Wandering token algorithm

If we *rescale* such distribution in order to have N_{max} events per time unit, we obtain a distribution with an interarrival time of Δ_{min} time units. Therefore, in our system, where N_{max} agents run in parallel, the timeouts will expire, on the average, every $2 * \Delta_{min}$ time units, which corresponds to the requested access period and is considered as a reasonable setup. Although the value of this parameter determines the behavior of the algorithm, significant variations do not modify its basic properties, and can be adjusted to tailor the system to specific environments.

The token generation rule does not exclude that a new token is created even if the old one is not really lost: in that case, such rule may induce the simultaneous presence of multiple, but distinct, tokens in the system. Therefore the token generation rule, which is introduced in order to recover from an unlikely token loss event, most times has the effect of disrupting the stable property by introducing *spurious* tokens.

In order to remove spurious tokens, we apply to a *token removal rule*: for this we require that tokens are timestamped when they are generated, using a coarse grain clock. The agent discards a token with id x when two conditions hold: i) the token was already received in the past at time T_{last} and ii) another token with lower timestamp was received after time T_{last}. Visually, the three tokens of which one is hold form a sandwich, and the agent silently discards the token it holds.

Such rule is justified considering that if an agent receives a token with a timestamp lower than a previously observed token y, it can conclude that token y is spurious. It does not have any convenient way to remove token y at once, since it has been already passed elsewhere, but, the next time it observes token y, it will have a chance to remove it, and nobody in the system might have removed token x as a consequence of the existence of token y.

The timestamping of the token does not require accurately synchronized clocks. In case two tokens have inconsistent timestamps, the application of the *sandwich* rule will remove the one generated before, instead of the other. This fact has no side effects on our protocol, so we conclude that, in principle, timestamps could be generated randomly.

The *sandwich* rule has two minor weaknesses. One is that the removal operation has a latency that corresponds to the a complete roundtrip, which is of the order of $2 * \Delta_{min}$: during that time the state of the system is not legal, and multiple accesses can be executed concurrently. The other is that token x, in the meanwhile, might be lost: in that case token y, although generated as a spurious token, might have become the new unique token. Such drawbacks have a minor impact on system operation, and do not diminish the practical interest for the algorithm: they indicate directions for its improvement.

The problem of token elimination is well studied in theory, and is often referred as a solution to the leader election problem (see Bshouty et al., 1999). However our setting disencourages a formal approach for the validation of our proposal: a complex random process controls both token generation, and token collision (or *meeting*). These two facts make smart theoretical results, that are based on an initial population of tokens, and on exact collision of tokens for token elimination, useless for our purpose. However, we note that, with respect to Israeli and Jalfon, 1990, the probability of collision is augmented by widening the *collision window* so that recovery is substantially improved.

3.   Simulation results

The simulation results summarized in this section reflect the case study described in the introduction: agents of our algorithm correspond to *subscribers* that require the availability of 650 Kbps over a 200 Mbps channel, fairly distributed in time. From the definition of the problem we derive that the system supports approximately 300 subscribers, which corresponds to N_{max}. We carried out a series of experiments using a simple (a few hundreds Perl lines) *ad hoc* discrete event simulator, which is available upon request. Each experiment lasted 10^5 time units, corresponding to approximately one day operation in our case study. The simulation takes into account token regeneration and token removal as well as token loss, controlled by a parameter that represents token loss interarrival. We do not simulate variable durations of the token passing operation, which is assumed to be negligible with respect to Δ_{skip}, the minimum time a subscriber holds the token.

We assume each subscriber is granted exclusive access to the channel for a time slot of a fixed size, that corresponds to Δ_{op}: it is set to 4 seconds, considering that the subscriber application can cache information locally.

To have a sort of reference, we introduce a simplistic solution to the problem: each subscriber issues a service request randomly, without any form of coordination. The interval between two successive requests is $4 * 300 = 1200$ seconds, incremented by a random bias, chosen in the interval $[-600, +600]$, that breaks synchronous behaviors.

Observing simulation results summarized in figure 2 (dashed line only) we understand that such algorithm is a *low end* solution to the soft mutual exclusion problem: since the number of time units during which more than one protected operation is running falls exponentially with the number of simultaneous operations. However it is not applicable as a solution to our case study: the share of time when the resource is idle is 40% (not shown in figure), while during 8% of the time three or more subscribers are simultaneously active, thus falling in the "delivery not guaranteed" region.

N_{max}	300	peer agents	from case study
Δ_{skip}	0.1	time units	from case study
Δ_{op}	4	time units	from case study
Δ_{min}	600	time units	$(\Delta_{op} * N_{max}) / 2$
$\gamma_{generate}$	$180 * 10^3$	time units	$\Delta_{min} * N_{max}$
γ_{loss}	$10 * 10^3$	time units	mean time between packet loss events

Table 1. Parameters used in the simulation. One time unit correspond to one second in our case study

The simulation of a system controlled using the wandering token algorithm requires the definition of three further parameters: Δ_{skip}, which is required to be significantly less than Δ_{op}, is set to $0.1 secs$, while Δ_{min} and $\gamma_{generate}$ are set according to the formulas given previously. Their values are summarized in table 1.

The comparison with the benchmark solution is clearly favorable, as shown in figure 2: the system controlled with the wandering token exhibits only 0.2% percent of the time with more than two subscribers concurrently downloading a video chunk, and the extra-billing zone (exactly 2 concurrent downloads) takes only 7% of the time.

Another relevant parameter to evaluate the quality of our solution is the distribution of the time between successive accesses to the resource.

In the case of the benchmark algorithm this is uniformly distributed between 600 and 1800 time units, and we may assume the time between successive accesses is adapted so that the stream playback never experiences buffer underruns (unless an high number of concurrent transfers determines packet drops, which is an event that is likely to occur).

In the case of the wandering token algorithm the evaluation is more complex, since the token interarrival time is ruled by a non-deterministic law. In figure 4 we see that 80% of the times the token interarrival time falls below $1200 secs$, which means in time to download the next chunk of video. A moderate buffering can be appropriate to accommodate cases when the interarrival time is longer.

It is interesting to see how this performance changes when the number of subscribers does not correspond exactly to N_{max}. In figure 3 and 4 we observe that figures change smoothly varying the number of subscribers from 70% to 120% of N_{max}: the probability of concurrent access (in figure 3) does not exceed 10%, and the interarrival time (in figure 4) in case of overbooking, tends to have a longer tail, although more than 50% of the interarrival times are below 1200 seconds.

Based on the above results, we can figure out the behavior of the system. As long as the number of subscribers is N_{max} or less, concurrent

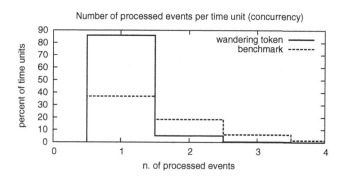

Figure 2. Benchmark algorithm vs. wandering token: distribution of the number of concurrent operations for memberships of 300 (full load) subscribers (simulation lasted 10^5 time units)

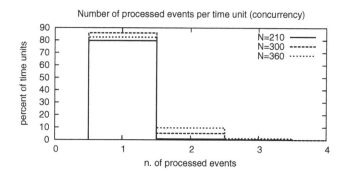

Figure 3. Wandering token: distribution of the number of concurrent operations on a shared resource for membership size from 210 to 360 (simulation lasted 10^5 time units)

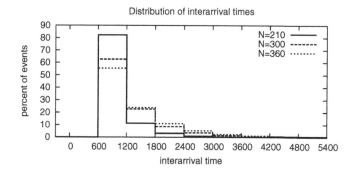

Figure 4. Wandering token: distribution of intervals between successive firing of the protected operation (simulation lasted 10^5 time units)

access of two subscribers occurs during less than one percent of the time, and 80% of the times the applications have access to the backbone within $2 * \Delta_{min}$. When the number of subscribers grows over resource saturation, the chance of concurrent execution increases, but the event that more than 2 data transfers are occurring simultaneously is rare. The application will be aware of the problem, since it is able to measure interarrival times, that will increase linearly with the number of subscribers: this may induce the negotiation of lower quality of service, reducing the stream bitrate.

4.   Conclusions

The *wandering token* algorithm is proposed as a solution for an architecture where moderating the concurrent access to a shared resource can improve performance. Its cost, in terms of communication and computation, is negligible.

The algorithm is fully scalable: the algorithm does not induce any bound on the number of agents exchanging the token. When such number overtakes the capacity of the shared resource, the *wandering token* algorithm gradually reduces the resource share granted to each agent, thus shielding the shared resource from the consequences of the overload.

References

Afek, Y. and Brown, G. (1993). Self-stabilization over unreliable communication media. *Distributed Computing*, 7(1):27–34.

Bshouty, N. H., Higham, L., and Warpechowska-Gruca, J. (1999). Meeting times of random walks on graphs. *Information Processing Letters*, 69(5):259–265.

Ciuffoletti, A. (2006). Scalable accessibility of a recoverable database using a wandering token. Technical Report TR-06-02, Università di Pisa, Largo Pontecorvo - Pisa -ITALY.

Dijkstra, E. W. (1974). Self-stabilizing systems in spite of distributed control. *Communications of the ACM*, 17(11):643–644.

Israeli, A. and Jalfon, M. (1990). Token management schemes and random walks yield self stabilizing mutual exclusion. In *Proceedings of the Ninth Annual ACM Symposium on Distributed Computing*, pages 119–129, Quebec City, Quebec, Canada.

Jonasson, J. (1998). On the cover time of random walks on random graphs. *Combinatorics, Probability and Computing*, (7):265–279.

Kwon, G. and Byers, J. (2003). ROMA: Reliable overlay multicast with loosely coupled TCP connections. Technical Report BU-CS-TR-2003-015, Boston University.

A LOCALITY OPTIMIZING ALGORITHM FOR DEVELOPING STREAM PROGRAMS IN IMAGINE

Jing Du, Xuejun Yang, Canqun Yang, Xiaobo Yan, Yu Deng
School of Computer, National University of Defense Technology, Changsha 410073, China

Abstract: In this paper, we explore a novel locality optimizing algorithm for developing stream programs in Imagine to sustain high computational ability. Our specific contributions include that we formulate the relationship between streams and kernels as a Data&Computation Matrix (D&C Matrix), and present the key techniques for locality enhancement based on this matrix. The experimental results on five representative scientific applications show that our algorithm can effectively improve the computational intensiveness and avoid the utilization of index streams to achieve high locality in LRF and SRF.

Key words: locality; Imagine; D&C Matrix; computational intensiveness; basic stream.

1. INTRODUCTION

Imagine is a programmable stream processor that implements an efficient memory hierarchy including several local register files (LRFs) with a 256-word scratchpad unit (SP), a 128 KB stream register file (SRF) and off-chip DRAM to sustain high computations[1,2]. The stream applications on Imagine are structured as some computation kernels that operate on sequences of data records called streams[3]. Imagine achieve high performance when the stream applications[4,5] present the fine locality in LRF and SRF to fully utilize so many ALUs. However, the straightforward coding of scientific programs does not exhibit sufficient locality to effectively exploit the tremendous processing power of Imagine. Therefore, in this paper, we explore a novel locality optimizing algorithm for developing stream programs in Imagine to achieve high memory performance. Our specific contributions include that we formulate the relationship between streams and kernels as the Data&Computation Matrix (D&C Matrix), and present the key techniques for locality enhancement based on this matrix. We implement our algorithm to five representative scientific applications on the ISIM simulation of Imagine. The results show that our algorithm can effectively improve the computational intensiveness and avoid the utilization of index streams to achieve high locality in Imagine.

2.   D&C MATRIX

Loops and arrays are fundamental structures of most scientific applications. Thus our approach is based on building a matrix called the Data&Computation Matrix (D&C Matrix) for a given program shown in Fig. 1. Each raw of the D&C Matrix represents an array and each column of this matrix describes the access pattern of a loop. The item in the ith row denoted D_i and the jth column denoted L_j position of the D&C Matrix corresponds to a mapping denoted as m_{ij}: $D_i \rightarrow L_j$. We define the computation distance Cdistance(x,y) as the number of iterations between x and y such that Cdistance(x,y)=y-x and the data distance Ddistance(c,d) as the interval between the two data layouts such that Ddistance(c,d)=d-c.

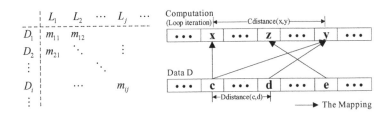

Figure 1. The D&C Matrix and the mapping in the matrix

Furthermore, we treat loop iteration spaces unrolling as the stream organization pattern. We formulate this approach as follows, where ORG(i,j) denotes the stream organization, the symbol " ゟ$^{+}$" denotes the connection of different data sequences, max(x) is the maximum iteration of the loop body.

$$ORG(i,j) = \sum_{x=0}^{max(x)} {}^{+} m_{ij}^{-1} \left(x \mid x \in L_j \right)$$

Thus, the layout of the basic stream[6] is important for it affects the stream organization. By analyzing the D&C Matrix, form the basic streams according to the least common array region of the most time-consuming loops. We formulate the basic stream layout of each array as follows, where f is the time-consuming factor that presents the importance of each loop for basic stream layout.

$$BS(i) = \forall j \left(\cap \left(ORG(i,j) \cdot \frac{1}{f} \right) \right)$$

3. PROGRAMMING OPTIMIZATION FOR LOCALITY ENHANCEMENT

3.1 Improving LRF Locality

The enhancement of LRF locality can reduce wire delay between clusters, improve computational intensiveness and increase the utilization of LRF[7]. Thus we present the locality optimizations of LRF for shortening the computation distances and the data distances in the D&C Matrix.

3.1.1 Enhancing temporal locality in LRF

Enhancing LRF temporal locality can increase the computational intensiveness to sustain high computational ability. We provide the following formula for the fine temporal locality in LRF.

$$\forall i \forall j \left(\forall x \in L_j \left(m_{ij}^{-1}(x) = m_{ij}^{-1}(x \pm 1) \right) \mid D_i \in D(K) \cap L_j \in L(K) \right)$$

First, aiming at producing computational intensive kernels, we centralize all the computations that perform on the same stream into a large kernel based on the following formula, and yield a new computational intensive matrix.

$$\forall j_1 j_2 \in L_j \left(\exists a \in D_i \left(\left(m_{ij_1}(a) \cap m_{ij_2}(a) \right) \neq \phi \right) \right)$$

Second, we consider reducing the computation distance in the new D&C Matrix as follows.

1. Avoiding wire delay between clusters

Due to wire delay becoming increasingly important in locality enhancement, we can't assign the dependent data to different clusters but to the same cluster. There is no influence of wire delay when the following formula is satisfied, where cluster$_i$ denotes the records in the ith cluster.

$$\forall i \forall j \left(m_{ij}^{-1} \left(m_{ij} (cluster_x) \right) \right) \cap \{ cluster_y \mid y = 0 \cdots 7 \ \& \ y \neq x \} = \phi$$

2. Shortening the computation distance between loops

Data dependence tells us that two references point to the same LRF location, thus the computation distance can be shortened by eliminating the loop-carried dependence[8]. If the dependence can't be eliminated, we consider tiling the computation space[9]. Thus the dependences just exist within inner loops. The left part of Fig. 2 shows the optimizations.

3. Reducing the dependent threshold in the inner loop

To achieve fine-grained optimization, we need reduce the computation distance in the innermost loop, that is, reduce the dependent threshold. We can eliminate the intermediate variables to centralize the computations on the same record as many as possible.

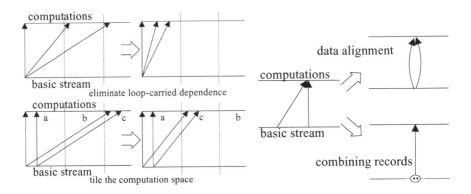

Figure 2. Enhancing temporal and spatial locality in LRF

3.1.2   Enhancing spatial locality in LRF

Since LRF can't make random access, the spatial locality in LRF is successive and limited to the LRF capacity and the overhead caused by SPs[10]. We provide the following formula for fine kernel spatial locality.

$$\forall i \forall j \big(\forall a \in D_i \big(m_{ij}(a) = m_{ij}(a \pm 1)\big)\,|\, D_i \in D(K) \cap L_j \in L(K)\big)$$

1. Enhancing spatial locality of long stream

We must avoid the very latter part of a long stream reusing the previous data due to the limited LRF capability and SPs. One side, the loop-carried dependence need be eliminated for avoiding the LRF reuse[11]; on the other side, tile the data space and restructure the data stream in LRF so that a single strip length fits in LRF and reduce the utilization of SPs.

2. Shortening the data distance in the inner loop

The iterations of the inner loop need to be placed into a cluster to enhance high spatial locality. First, we can align different records referenced by the same computation or combine these records to a big record[12], and thereby the data distance can be reduced so that achieve fine spatial locality in LRF, which is shown in the right part of Fig. 2. Second, we can apply loop interchange to reduce the data distance according to the access pattern of the basic stream. Last, we need to reduce the intermediate variables to utilize the fewest SPs. We formulize the number of SPs kept before iteration y, where NUM(X) denotes the number of sequence X.

$$\sum \text{NUM}\left(m_{ij}^{-1}(z)\right) \mid \forall i \left(\forall z > y\right)\left(\exists z\left(m_{ij}^{-1}(z) < m_{ij}^{-1}(y)\right)\right) \cap \left(D_i \in D(K)\right)$$

3.2   Improving SRF Locality

The locality in SRF is exposed by forwarding the streams produced by one kernel to subsequent kernels[13].

3.2.1   Unifying streams between kernels

First, we alter the streams' region to make the streams in successive kernels uniform shown in the left of Fig. 3. Then we can transfer some computations to the next kernel to reduce the intermediate results given in the right of Fig. 3. Last if some parts of a long stream can be reused between kernels, we consider strip-mining the stream to enhance SRF locality.

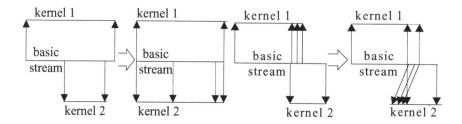

Figure 3. Unifying streams between kernels

3.2.2   Make full use of the SRF capacity

Above all if some loops in the successive kernels exist data dependency, we can transfer the loops in the previous kernel to the next kernel. This idea can reduce the intermediate results to make full use of the SRF capacity and enhance SRF reuse. Second, if some parts of a long stream can be reused between multiple kernels, we consider strip-mining the stream to enhance SRF locality and reduce off-chip memory access overhead.

3.2.3   Avoiding the utilization of index stream

The usage of index streams makes stream organization flexibly, but it also loses the SRF locality owing to too much extra overhead of DRAM reordering. So we must avoid using index stream as follows.

1. Organizing streams as the basic stream

To avoid using index stream that reduces SRF locality, we need select successive basic streams as operation objects of kernels by using loop interchange etc. transformations.

2. Data-centric loop splitting

We bring forward a new transformation to avoid index stream for higher locality, which is data-centric loop splitting. We can distill the computations that reuse data with large temporal span as self-governed loop.

3.3   A locality optimizing algorithm

In this section, we develop a locality optimizing algorithm for stream program generation denoted LOA shown in Fig. 4.

ALGORITHM: LOA
INPUT: The serial program P
OUTPUT: A stream program with fine locality
form the D&C Matrix of P, denoted M
ProgramLocality(M)
for each L_j
    KernelLocality($\forall i(M_{ij})$)

ALGORITHM: ProgramLocality(M)
INPUT: The D&C Matrix of P, denoted M
OUTPUT: A new D&C Matrix
for each j
    for each c and d
        if $M_{cj} \circ 0$ & $M_{dj} \circ 0$
            distribute(L_j)
for each i
    for each x and y
        if $M_{ix} \circ 0$ & $M_{iy} \circ 0$
            merge(L_x, L_y)
for each j and i
    if output($M_{ij}^{-1}(L_j)$) ˇ input($M_{ij+1}^{-1}(L_{j+1})$) $\circ$ ⁊
        schedule(D_i, L_{j+1})
for each j and i
    common= $M_{ij}^{-1}(L_j)$ ˇ $M_{ij+1}^{-1}(L_{j+1})$
    if common $\circ$ ⁊ then begin
        if common > T
            unify($M_{ij}^{-1}(L_j), M_{ij+1}^{-1}(L_{j+1})$)
        else
            stripming($M_{ij}^{-1}(L_j)$, common)
            stripming($M_{ij+1}^{-1}(L_{j+1})$, common)
for each i and j
    $BS(i) = \forall j \left(\cap \left(\sum_{x=0}^{max(x)} {}^+ m_{ij}^{-1}\left(x \mid x \in L_j\right) \cdot \frac{1}{f_i} \right) \right)$

ALGORITHM: KernelLocality($\forall i(M_{ij})$)
INPUT: $\forall i(M_{ij})$ is the jth column of M
OUTPUT: the kernel with fine locality
for each i
    if $\sum_{x=0}^{max(x)} {}^+ M_{ij}^{-1}\left(x \mid x \in L_j\right) \neq BS_i$
        avoid the utilization of index streams
for each c, d ‾ D_i
    if $M_{ij}(c) = M_{ij}(d)$
        put c and d on the same cluster
judge if the dependence can be eliminated
if success then
    eliminate the loop-carried dependence
    InnerLoopLocality($\forall i(M_{ij})$)
else
    tiling the loop
    InnerLoopLocality($\forall i(M_{ij})$)

ALGORITHM: InnerLoopLocality($\forall i(M_{ij})$)
INPUT: $\forall i(M_{ij})$ is the jth column of M
OUTPUT: the loop with fine locality
for each i
    for each c ‾ D_i then
        reduce the intermediate variables
        between two computations on c
        for each d ‾ D_i & d $\circ$ c then begin
            if $M_{ij}(c) = M_{ij}(d)$
                combine c and d to a big record
                or data alignment
    for each x, y ‾ L_j
        if $M_{ij}^{-1}(x) = M_{ij}^{-1}(y)$
            reduce Cdistance(x,y)

Figure 4. The LOA algorithm

First, **LOA** algorithm forms the D&C Matrix of the program that need to be expressed as stream program. Then apply **ProgramLocality** algorithm for data-centric program restructuring to enhance the locality and computational intensiveness between kernels. Afterward it employs the routine **KernelLocality** to optimize the locality of each kernel.

ProgramLocality first analyze the profile information to find the most time-consuming parts that need be streaming. And increase the computations per words by loop distribution and loop fusion based on the D&C Matrix transformations. Then schedule partial computations to the next kernel and reuse the same data region between kernels by unifying stream or strip-mining stream to enhance the SRF locality. Last, form the basic streams according to least common array region of high access frequency by profiling.

KernelLocality first avoids the utilization of index streams to enhance the SRF locality. Then optimize the LRF locality. It assigns the dependent data to the same cluster to avoid the wire delay between kernels. And increase the locality of long streams by eliminating the loop-carried dependence between loops or tiling the computation space. Finally, invoke **InnerLoopLocality** to reduce the computation distance and data distance in the inner loop by eliminating the intermediate variables, enlarging the records, aligning different records and reducing the dependent threshold.

4. EXPERIMENTAL RESULTS AND ANALYSIS

Five representative scientific programs are used to evaluate our LOA algorithm on ISIM simulator[14] that is a cycle-accurate simulator of Imagine, including Swim, Dfft, Transp, Vpenta and N-S. Swim is a weather prediction program for comparing the performance of current supercomputers in SPEC2000. Dfft and Transp are the most time-consuming subroutines in Capao that is an application on the field of optics. Vpenta is one of the kernels in nasa7. N-S is an application of solving partial differential equation of fluid dynamics for the flow of an incompressible viscous fluid.

Fig. 5 shows the computational intensiveness that is a significant representation of LRF locality by applying our LOA algorithm. Groups of bars represent the original version (Orig) of each application and the version optimized with LOA algorithm (LOA). We can observe the LOA optimization improves the computations per memory accesses of the five programs. However Swim and Transp achieve a little varying, because Swim has too many data and irregular access pattern so that the loops are difficult to be distributed or combined, and all the arrays in Transp are referenced rarely leading a little variety of computational intensiveness compared with original stream program. The LOA optimization can centralize all computations in Vpenta, Dfft and N-S to a kernel due to repetitive references to each array in these programs.

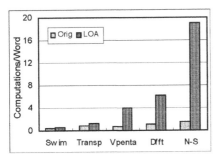   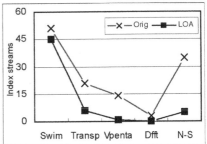

Figure 5. Computational intensiveness   *Figure 6*. The reduction of index streams

Fig. 6 shows the reduction of index streams by applying LOA to present the variety of SRF locality. One of the key techniques in LOA is to form appropriate basic streams so that the number of index streams can be reduced. But in Swim, the choice of basic stream has little effect on stream forming owing to complex data access pattern. Dfft has a few data in original stream program, so the index streams are lessened a little too. The index streams of Transp, Vpenta and N-S reduce observably for achieving higher performance. In Transp, lessening the scale of original basic streams at the beginning of this program can avoid a great deal of index streams. The index stream can be eliminated in Vpenta by applying MBO when stream is short due to regular data access pattern by using SPs in kernel. In N-S, the basic stream reorganization plays an important role of reducing index streams.

Fig. 7 presents the variety of computation rate of these applications measured in the number of operations executed per second by applying LOA optimization. Our LOA optimization assigns all dependent data to a cluster, avoiding communication delay and memory access latency. However Swim optimized by LOA still presents overfull index steams so that memory delay can't be overlapped, resulting in low computation rate. Despite Transp and Vpenta both achieve higher LRF locality by eliminating loop-carried dependence between inner loops and shortening dependent threshold in inner loop, their computation rate are increased a little, because both low computational intensiveness of Transp and the usage of index streams in Vpenta when streams are long make overlapping memory latency difficultly. N-S also presents high computational density by applying LOA optimization, however the computation rate of N-S is slow because it invokes inefficient mathematical kernels for many times. The high computation rate of Dfft indicates that the stream programming system delivers high computational density on this application.

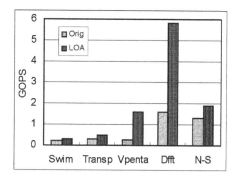

Figure 7. The variety of computation rate

Table 1 illustrates the efficiency of the program yielded by our optimization (LOA) compared with original stream program (Orig). It is obvious that our optimization provides high speedup of Dfft, Transp, Vpenta and N-S due to fine locality. And compared with highly sensitive to memory latency of general processor, these applications can hide latency to achieve good performance. But for data intensive applications such as Swim, the speedup is low due to irregular access pattern so that our optimization can't hide memory access latency. In conclusion, Swim is not well suited for the Imagine architecture.

Table 1. Comparison of different scientific applications by applying LOA

	Swim	Transp	Vpenta	Dfft	N-S
Cycles(Orig)	8.10E+09	1.98E+07	4.97E+07	5.07E+11	1.68E+08
Cycles(LOA)	6.69E+09	9.28E+06	1.69E+07	9.71E+10	4.36E+08
Speedup	1.21	2.13	2.94	5.22	2.60

5.   CONCLUSION AND FUTURE WORK

In this paper, we explore a novel locality optimizing algorithm for developing stream programs in Imagine to fully sustain high computational ability. Our specific contributions include that we formulate the relationship between streams and kernels as the Data&Computation Matrix (D&C Matrix), and present the key techniques for locality enhancement based on this matrix. The results show that our algorithm can achieve high locality in LRF and SRF.

One future work is to research more programming optimizations to exploit more architectural features of Imagine. Another is to search more scientific applications suited for stream architecture by applying our algorithm.

ACKNOWLEDGEMENTS.

We gratefully thank the Stanford Imagine team for the use of their compilers and simulators and their generous help. We also acknowledge the reviewers for their insightful comments.

REFERENCES

1. Saman Amarasinghe, William. Stream Architectures. In PACT03, September 27, 2003.
2. Brucek Khailany. The VLSI Implementation and Evaluation of Area-and Energy-Effcient Streaming Media Processors. Ph.D. thesis, Stanford University, 2003.
3. Ola Johnsson, et al. Programming & Implementation of Streaming Applications. Master's thesis, Computer and Electrical Engineering Halmstad University, 2005.
4. B. Khailany et al. Imagine: Media processing with streams. IEEE Micro, 21(2):35–46,March 2001.
5. Saman Amarasinghe et al. Stream Languages and Programming Models. In PACT03, September 27, 2003.
6. Peter Raymond Mattson. A Programming System for the Imagine Media Processor. Dept. of Electrical Engineering. Ph.D. thesis, Stanford University, 2002.
7. Nuwan S. Jayasena. Memory Hierarchy Design for Stream Computing. Ph.D. thesis, Stanford University, 2005.
8. M. J.Wolfe. High Performance Compilers for Parallel Computing. Addison-Wesley, 1996.
9. J. Xue. Loop Tiling for Parallelism. Kluwer Academic Publishers, Boston, 2000.
10. Jinwoo Suh, Eun-Gyu Kim, Stephen P. Crago, Lakshmi Srinivasan, and Matthew C. French. A Performance Analysis of PIM, Stream Processing, and Tiled Processing on Memory-Intensive Signal Processing Kernels. In ISCA03, 2003.
11. M. E.Wolf and M. Lam. A loop transformation theory and an algorithm to maximize parallelism. IEEE Transactions on Parallel and Distributed Systems, 2(4):452 – 471,October 1991.
12. Jing Du, Xuejun Yang, et al. Scientific Computing Applications on the Imagine Stream Processor. In ACSAC06, September 6-8, 2006.
13. Jung Ho Ahn, William J. Dally, et al. Evaluating the Imagine Stream Architecture. In ISCA04, 2004.
14. Abhishek Das, Peter Mattson, et al. Imagine Programming System User's Guide 2.0. June 2004.

GRANULAR SSOR PRECONDITIONING PLACED ON DYNAMIC SMP CLUSTERS WITH COMMUNICATION ON THE FLY

Boguslaw Butrylo[1], Marek Tudruj[2,3], Lukasz Masko[2]

[1]Białystok Technical University, Faculty of Electrical Engineering, ul. Wiejska 45D, 15-351 Bialystok, Poland; [2]Polish Academy of Sciences, Institute Of Computer Science, ul. Ordona 21, 01-237 Warszawa, Poland; [3]Polish-Japanese Institute of Information Technology, 86 Koszykowa Str., 02-008 Warsaw, Poland

Abstract   The paper presents a comparative analysis of parallel implementation of the preconditioned conjugate gradient method with symmetric successive over relaxation preconditioner. Two parallel implementations are compared. The first one is a message passing version that turned out to be inefficient when executed on a typical cluster of workstations. The other one is an efficient version simulated on a novel architecture of dynamically reconfigurable shared memory clusters with a new paradigm of inter-processor communication called communication on the fly. The presented example shows high suitability of the proposed architecture for fine grain numerical computations what can be very useful in simulation of physical phenomena described as numerical problems for fine grain parallel execution.

Key words: matrix computation; finite element method; distributed processing; cluster of workstation; dynamically reconfigurable system.

1.   Introduction

Modeling realistic devices with a finite element (FE) method requires solution of a large either linear or nonlinear matrix equation, which arises from the formulation of partial differential equations. The form and properties of the matrix equation depend on type of implemented finite elements (FE). Different kinds and mixed formulations of the FE method are especially useful in computational electromagnetics (CEM) (Jin, 1993; Lee et al., 1997). Spatial decomposition of the computational domain, as well as inherent interdependencies between distributed threads are the hardest and the most problematic constrains in high performance analysis of electromagnetic fields.

An efficient formulation of the distributed, in core matrix subroutine is extremely important in the time domain electromagnetic computations. The principle, most significant constraints of the FE method is a sparse, positive defined (e.g. time domain methods) or bad conditioned (e.g. some time-harmonic problems), and diagonal dominant form of the matrix. A wide spectrum of physical phenomena and various properties of materials in the analyzed model require some smart, black-box solver, which can be easily implemented in different problem formulation. It must be flexible and adoptable to different problem formulation as well as hardware platform. The conjugate gradient (CG) method with different, well-adopted preconditioners (PCG) fulfils these requirements (Van der Vorst 2003). A preconditioned conjugate gradient algorithm (PCG) with properly selected preconditioner is one of the most suitable methods in CEM (Vollair et al., 1998). Since the data (i.e. extremely large matrices) and task (e.g. dot product, matrix-vector multiplication, vector updates) are partitioned in parallel implementation, some specific properties of hardware platform cannot be negligible.

The formulation of the SSOR preconditioner presented in the paper, enables to tune the relation between calculation and data transfer operations. Two steps domain and task decomposition paradigms are used in the SSOR subroutines. The granulation of the algorithm can be flexible matched even during execution. In this way performance of this stage can be adjusted to current available computational power and specific properties of the communication network. From the general point of view, this form of the algorithm can be applied on any hardware multicomputer/multiprocessor platform with distributed memory. The COW platform, as a common, popular tool in practical, real simulation, was used to check the performance of the elaborated algorithm. Next, the algorithm is ported to the system of runtime configurable, shared memory multiprocessor clusters (SMP). The multiprocessor platform with on the fly communication facilitates new class of hardware. Its architecture, should be particularly helpful in computationally and data transfer demanding algorithms. The idea of this platform enables to overlap data processing and data access commands. In this system, a new method for data exchange (communication on the fly) is applied. It is based on a combination of porting data in caches of processors switched between clusters with distribution of data in target clusters by means of simultaneous reads into many processor data caches by snooping data exposed on the cluster shared memory bus (Tudruj et al., 2004). Such architecture can be used to build a dynamically configurable parallel embedded subsystem aimed in speeding up time consuming numerical computations in particular oriented to fine grain numerical simulation. Specific rules of the platform coincide with the presented structure of the SSOR preconditioner and the PCG algorithm. Simulation experiments with implementation of the distributed SSOR preconditioner confirmed strong advantages of the proposed architecture over a classical cluster of workstations.

2.   Numerical problem formulation

According to mathematical background of the finite element method (FEM), the investigated model of electromagnetic phenomena is translated to its discrete form. The spatial discretization of the analyzed model and the unconditionally stable backward Euler time integration scheme lead to large size matrix equation

$$\left(\mathbf{T} + \Delta t \mathbf{R} + \Delta t^2 \mathbf{S}\right) \cdot \mathbf{e}_\tau = \left(2\mathbf{T} + \Delta t \mathbf{R}\right) \cdot \mathbf{e}_{\tau-1} - \mathbf{T} \cdot \mathbf{e}_{\tau-2} \tag{1}$$

where $\mathbf{e}_\tau$, $\mathbf{e}_{\tau-1}$, $\mathbf{e}_{\tau-2}$ describe the investigated time dependent spatial distributions of the electric field intensity in succeeding time steps $\tau = n\Delta t$ ($n \in \mathbb{I}$). By analogy to structural dynamics problems, the $\mathbf{T}$, $\mathbf{R}$ and $\mathbf{S}$ are called mass matrix, damping matrix, and stiffness matrix, respectively, $\dim(\mathbf{T}) = \dim(\mathbf{R}) = \dim(\mathbf{S}) = N_{DOF} \times N_{DOF}$.

The presented implementation of the distributed solver is based on the domain decomposition paradigm. In natural way, the row-wise decomposition of matrices $\mathbf{A} = \mathbf{T} + \Delta t \mathbf{R} + \Delta t^2 \mathbf{S}$, $\mathbf{B} = 2\mathbf{T} + \Delta t \mathbf{R}$, and $\mathbf{C} = -\mathbf{T}$ is used. The non-overlapped sub-matrices $\mathbf{A}_n$, $\mathbf{B}_n$, $\mathbf{C}_n$ are stored in the appropriate computing units P_n ($n=1,..., N$), $\dim(\mathbf{A}_n) = (N_{DOF}/N) \times N_{DOF}$. The geometrical binding of the sub-matrices creates comprehensive and coherent representation of the FEM model. According to mathematical formulation of the problem, any analyzed model is decomposed into non-overlapping sub-matrices $\mathbf{A} = \mathbf{A}_1 \cup ... \cup \mathbf{A}_n \cup ... \cup \mathbf{A}_N$.

The presented algorithm was executed for a three dimensional model with sinusoidal high frequency wave (2GHz) propagated in an open space (Butrylo et al., 2004). The implementation of the solver requires complete representation of the common data structures both in the preconditioner and in the conjugate gradient algorithm. The vectors of projection, displacement, correction and others structures are decomposed, but they must be exchanged and concatenated in each step of the PCG and the SSOR algorithms. That decides on the fine grain character of the involved inter-processor data exchange.

The development of distributed preconditioning algorithms is aimed at decreasing communication cost as well as improving convergence of iterative calculation. The diagonal (i.e. Jacobi) preconditioner is the simplest preconditioner. Its implementation in parallel environments can reach ideal speedup, since distributed form of this preconditioner is a set independent, simple matrix-vector multiplications in each sub-domain. Unfortunately, extremely simple structure of operations is not consonance with convergence of CG algorithm with diagonal preconditioner. Therefore the SSOR algorithm, taking into account number of iterations and absolute elapsed time of CG algorithm, has better properties. This fact appears in sequential form as well as in parallel formulation. The distributed version of the SSOR lost some advantages, since the matrix-vector multiplication must be made in each iteration. This is the main reason to propose new algorithms or some modifications of this preconditioner.

The constraints related to the section of the algorithm critical in respect to the excessive size of data were taken into account in the final, efficient version of the parallel algorithms. Initial decomposition of the **A, B, C** matrices and some related data structures are crucial for algorithm. The data critical section consists of the operations on the largest data structures in the PCG algorithm, i.e. sub-matrices $\mathbf{A}_n$. In a distributed memory systems, locally available sub-matrices cannot be efficiently transferred between processors, because this task decreases performance of the algorithm. Simultaneously, in a typical case, the size of the FEM model, and the distributed sub-models are too large to create and copy some redundant data structures in processors.

3.   Message passing implementation

The construction and performance of the stages of conjugate gradient algorithm are modified by the row-wise domain decomposition of the matrices. The form and final properties of the forward calculation, formulation of diagonal matrix, and backward substitution are changed in a different way. The **A** matrix is processed by columns in the forward calculation stage, while the backward substitution is made by rows. The partial results of these stages, the **u** and **v** vectors respectively, are placed in the separated memory spaces of computing units P_n. They are processed separately, but finally the sub-vectors $\mathbf{u}_n$ and $\mathbf{v}_n$ must be moved between the computing nodes, and concatenated, e.g. $\mathbf{u}=\mathbf{u}_1\cup\ldots\cup\mathbf{u}_n\cup\ldots\cup\mathbf{u}_N$. The backward and forward calculations (including calculation and transfer of $\mathbf{u}_n$

and $\mathbf{v}_n$ sub-vectors) consist of some inherently sequential parts. They limit performance of the algorithm in the message-passing environment.

The formulation of the diagonal matrix does not require data transfers. Thus, the second step of the preconditioner is fully parallel with no communication. The forward and backward stages are only partially distributed. The flexible adjustment of relation between sequential and distributed parts of these stages enables the optimal and hardware independent formulation of the preconditioner.

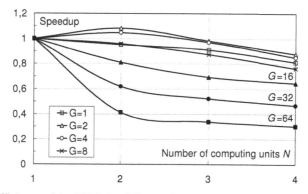

Figure 1. Efficiency of the SSOR for different G and N against $G=1$ with message passing.

Therefore, the second order domain decomposition is introduced in the algorithm. The locally defined sub-matrices $\mathbf{A}_n$ are decomposed into some column-wise sub-matrices. This decomposition results in varying the computation grain in processors between subsequent data communications. We call it granulation. The granulation degree is determined by granulation coefficient G. For $G>1$, a computation sub-domain $\mathbf{A}_n$ in any processing node is decomposed into G square sub-matrices. Reordering of some matrix operations enables to overlap data transfers with distributed processing of sub-matrices. In such a way, for $G>1$, processors obtain earlier input data for their computations and more frequently than in the case $G=1$, when they stay idle a longer period of time. Larger G corresponds to a finer-grain decomposition of the algorithm into shorter computations and communication, where a processor performs relatively few computations between consecutive data transfers. In the forward calculation (stage 1) and backward substitution (stage 3) the processors perform computations one after another and distribute the results to other processors. With larger G, the parallelism degree in phases (1) and (3) increases.

The algorithm was tested on the cluster of Xeon 2,6 GHz processors interconnected by a Gigabit Ethernet network with MPI communication library. This system did not provide any parallel speedup versus execution on 1 processor for $G=1$. The speedup as a function of N and increasing G, against execution with the same N but $G=1$, is presented in Figure 1. The maximal speedup improvement (equal to 1.1) is obtained for $N=2$ and $G=2$. Further increase of G and N produces bad results, since data transfer costs in this typical message passing system eliminate potential speedup improvement due to applied finer grain and more intensive parallelization.

4.   Implementation in shared memory dynamic clusters

The presented formulation of the SSOR preconditioner has been ported to a parallel system based on dynamic switching of processors between shared memory clusters and data reads on the fly inside clusters (Tudruj et al., 2004). The elementary module of the subsystem is composed of N processor nodes PE_n and N memory modules M_n. Processor nodes connected to a memory bus under control of a bus arbiter constitute an SMP cluster. The system can contain a number of such elementary modules connected by a common global data network.

Communication on the fly eliminates shared data exchange through multiple memory transactions. Processor nodes are switched between SMP clusters with data in their data caches (DC_n). The shared data brought by a switched processor node are written to the target cluster memory module. At the same time other processor nodes in the cluster simultaneously read on the fly the data to their data caches by means of snooping the cluster memory bus under control of their Bus Request Controllers (BRC). In this way, multiple data reads (otherwise performed sequentially over the memory bus) are overlapped with data writes, which speeds up communication. Such data exchange takes place directly between processor data caches, which is another source of communication speedup since it eliminates memory-data cache transactions and transactions by the global bus that also exists in the system to implement. Each processor's P_i data cache is connected at the same time to two memory modules: with one module permanently during program execution and with another module that can be changed dynamically according to the program needs. The permanent connection is meant for communication with large data sets. In the case of the discussed PCG-SSOR algorithm, this module is used to store sub-matrices $\mathbf{A}_n$ and the results of $\mathbf{A}_n$-relevant operations. All other processors that want to use the results, have to get connected to the respective memory bus dynamically, shortly before the relevant data will be sent by a producer to its permanent memory module. While a processor - the producer of data writes them to the memory module through the memory bus, other processors fetch the data they need to their data caches.

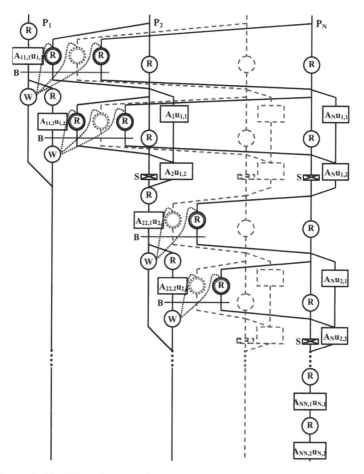

Figure 2. The EMDFG graph of the distributed SSOR preconditioner (stage 1) with reads on the fly commands.

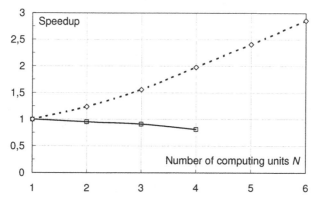

Figure 3. SSOR preconditioner speedup (*G*=1) as a function of number of processors: in the SMP dynamic SMP clusters (*dotted line*), in the message passing (COW) system (*solid line*).

The elaborated SSOR algorithm with different degrees of granulation has been analyzed by simulation of execution of program graphs expressed by an extended macro data flow graph (EMDFG) (Tudruj et al., 2004). EMDFG (Figure 2) contains special kinds of nodes: read nodes (R) from memory to processor's data cache, write nodes (W) from data cache to memory, the processor switch nodes (crossed rectangles with S) and barriers (B). The experiments that evaluated the efficiency of SSOR preconditioner execution in the described system architecture were performed using a simulator (written in C\C++) of symbolic program (EMDFG) graph execution. In dynamic SMP clusters, parallel speedup versus execution on 1 processor was obtained even for $G=1$ with efficiency about 0,5 (Figure 3). Increasing G (making computation grain finer) gives in this case positive results, Figure 4. The algorithm is reasonably sensitive to the rise of G only in the range of up to 10-15, giving the improvement of up to 1.35 for small number of processors. Both mentioned characteristics are incomparably better than in the classic cluster of workstations. The relatively low speedup improvement with G is due to the rather sequential character of the preconditioner program, where processors have to wait for results of directly preceding computations to start new ones.

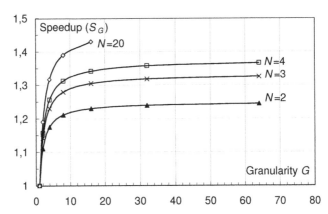

Figure 4. Changes of the speedup for SSOR in dynamic SMP clusters versus $G=1$ as a function of granularity (G) and number of processors (N).

5.   Conclusions

The paper deals with parallel implementation of the PCG-SSOR algorithm in two executive environments: classic cluster of workstations and system of dynamic shared memory clusters with communication on the fly.

A classic cluster of workstations with MPI communication library appeared to be inadequate for parallelization of the SSOR preconditioner. Two level task decomposition and variable number of independently processed sub-matrices applied in the forward calculations and the backward substitution of the SSOR algorithm did not enable a noticeable speed up improvement in the classical system.

The proposed new architecture based on dynamic SMP clusters and communication on the fly can be efficiently applied for the discussed PCG algorithm in a parallel accelerator of the SSOR preconditioner. Simulation experiments have shown that the new architecture provides good parallel execution of the analyzed programs providing parallelization efficiency of 0,5. Dynamic reconfiguration of shared memory clusters enables adjusting system structure to SSOR algorithm needs. The finer parallel computations by decreasing the computations and communications size and increasing their mutual overlapping in time can provide further improvement of speedup.

The experiments presented in the paper show that the dynamic SMP cluster architecture can be successfully employed in problem solving including parallel simulation based on fine grain numerical problem modeling. The described architecture can be fully implemented today and is convergent with the emerging technology of systems on chip - SoC (Benini et al., 2002).

6.   References

Benini, L., and De Micheli, G., 2002, Networks on chips: a new SoC paradigm, *IEEE Computer,* pp. 70-78.

Bertozzi, D. et al., 2005, NoC synthesis flow for customized domain specific multiprocessor Systems-on-Chip, *IEEE Trans. on Parallel and Distributed Systems*, No.2, **16**:113-129.

Butrylo, B., Vollaire, C., and Nicolas, L., 2004, Stability and fidelity of the finite element time domain method with distorted mesh, *IEEE Transactions on Magnetics*, IEEE Press (2004), no. 2, **40**:1424-1427.

Jin, J., 1993, *The Finite Element Method in Electromagnetics*. John Wiley & Sons, New York.

Lee, J. F., Lee, R., and Cangellaris, A., 1997, Time-domain finite-element methods, *IEEE Trans. Antennas Propagat.,* IEEE Press, no. 3, **45**:430-441.

Tudruj, M., and Masko, L., 2004, Fine-grain numerical computations in dynamic smp clusters with communication on the fly, *Proceedings of International Conference on Parallel Computing in Electrical Engineering, PARELEC 2004*, Dresden, IEEE CS Press, pp. 386-389.

Van der Vorst, H. A., and Chan, T. F., 1997, Linear system solvers: sparse iterative methods, in *Parallel numerical algorithms*, ed. D. E. Keyes, A. Sameh, V. Venkatakrishnan, Kluwer, pp. 91-118.

Van der Vorst, H. A., 2003, *Iterative Krylov methods for large linear systems*, Cambridge University Press.

Vollaire, C., and Nicolas, L., 1998, Preconditioning techniques for the conjugate gradient solver on a parallel distributed memory computer, *IEEE Trans. on Magnetics*, IEEE Press, no. 5, **34**:3347-3350.

BULK SYNCHRONOUS PARALLEL ML WITH EXCEPTIONS

Louis Gesbert[1], Frédéric Gava[1], Frédéric Loulergue[2]
and Frédéric Dabrowski[3]

[1]*Laboratory of Algorithms, Complexity and Logic, University Paris XII, France*

[2]*Laboratoire d'Informatique Fondamentale d'Orléans, Université d'Orléans, France*

[3]*Institut de Recherche en Informatique et Automatique, Sophia-Antipolis, France*

Abstract   Bulk Synchronous Parallel ML is a high-level language for programming parallel algorithms. Built upon OCaml and using the BSP model, it provides a safe setting for their implementation, avoiding concurrency related problems (deadlocks, indeterminism). Only a limited set of the features of OCaml can be used in BSML to respect its properties of safety: this paper describes a way to add exception handling to this set by extending and adapting OCaml's exceptions. The behaviour of these new exceptions and the syntactic constructs to handle them, together with their implementation, are described in detail, and results over an example are given.

Keywords: Parallel programming, exception handling, functional programming, BSP, syntax of languages

1.   Introduction

The Bulk Synchronous Parallel ML (BSML) language [9] is a parallel extension of ML (a family of functional programming languages). BSML aims at providing the right balance between the two opposite approaches to parallel programming, low-level and subject to concurrency issues, and high-level with loss of flexibility and efficiency. In the former, we find libraries such as MPI [12] generally used with Fortran or C; these approaches are unsafe and leave the programmer responsible for deadlock or indeterminism issues. In the latter stand traditional algorithmic skeletons [3] where programs are safe but limited to a restricted set of algorithms.

BSML follows the BSP (Bulk Synchronous Parallel [1, 11]) paradigm to structure the computation and communication between the processors in a data-parallel fashion. All communications in BSML are collective (require all processes) and deadlocks are avoided by a strict distinction between local and global computation; BSP also provides BSML with a simple and efficient cost model.

Exception handling is a traditional and natural mechanism to manage errors and events that disrupt the normal flow of instructions of a program. It can also be used purposefully to extract the results in the course of some recursive algorithms. Widely used languages or libraries for data-parallel programming are mostly imperative like C or Fortran [2, 7]. These languages do not provide exception mechanisms. In the case of Java [6], the interaction of parallel constructions with exceptions is not studied. Exception handling is accordingly an issue in parallel languages and efficient, simple and expressive solutions to this problem are a current research topic [10]. To our knowledge, there exists no related work on exception mechanisms for data-parallel languages.

BSML is implemented as a library for Objective Caml [8], which enables it to benefit from the advanced, general-purpose features of this language. A few of these features however, among which exception handling, do not provide the desired safety when used in parallel. In this paper, we adapt and extend the exception handling mechanism of OCaml to respect the constraints of parallel programming in BSML. The approach we define is not specific to OCaml though, and it could be applied to any strict language with exceptions. In particular, Java behaves very similarly to OCaml regarding exceptions and we think there would be little work involved in adapting our system to this language.

In section 2, we introduce the BSP model and Bulk Synchronous Parallel ML (BSML). In section 3 we study issues related to OCaml-style exception handling in a parallel setting, and our solution is presented in section 4. The implementation of this solution for BSML is described in section 5, followed by an example of use and results in section 6. We conclude and introduce future work in section 7.

2.   Functional Bulk Synchronous Parallel Programming

2.1   The BSP Model

In the BSP model, a computer is a set of uniform *processor-memory pairs*, a *communication network* allowing inter-processor delivery of messages and a *global synchronization unit* which executes collective requests for a synchronization barrier (for the sake of conciseness, we refer to [11] for more details). A BSP program is executed as a sequence of *supersteps*, each one divided into (at most) three successive and logically disjoint phases: (a) Each processor uses its local data (only) to perform sequential computations and to request data transfers to/from other nodes; (b) the network delivers the requested data transfers; (c) a global synchronization barrier occurs, making the transferred data available for the next super-step.

The performance of the machine is characterised by 3 parameters: p is the number of processor-memory pairs, L is the time required for a global synchronization and g denotes the speed of the network. Using these and the structure of the execution, it is possible to predict the performance of a program.

2.2   The BSML Language

bsp_p: unit→int
bsp_g: unit→float
bsp_l: unit→float

mkpar: (int →α) →α **par**
apply: (α →β) **par** →α **par** →β **par**
put: (int→α option) **par** →(int→α option) **par**
proj: α option **par** →(int →α option)

Figure 1.   Primitives

The BSML language is based on seven primitives, three of which are used to access the physical parameters of the machine. A BSML program is built as a sequential program on a parallel data structure called parallel vector. Its type is α **par**, which expresses that it contains a value of type α at each of the p processors, where type α may be any type not containing an occurrence of **par** (this point is discussed in detail in [4]). We adopt the notation $\langle x_0, \ldots, x_{p-1} \rangle$ to denote the parallel vector with value x_i at processor i.

BSML programs use the four parallel primitives **mkpar**, **apply**, **put** and **proj** for the creation and manipulation of parallel vectors. The asynchronous computation phase is programmed using the two primitives **mkpar** and **apply**.

mkpar creates a parallel vector from a sequential function.
$$\text{mkpar:} \quad f \ \mapsto \ \langle f\ 0, \ldots, f\ (p-1) \rangle$$

This primitive induces *local* computation that will be resolved differently on each processor. We call in comparison *replicated* top-level sequential execution, which is in fact replicated at every one of the processors, and *parallel* execution that involves different values at different processors (*e.g.* parallel vectors and primitives).

The primitive **apply** applies a parallel vector of functions to a parallel vector of arguments:
$$\text{apply:} \quad \begin{matrix} \langle f_0, & \ldots, & f_{p-1} \rangle \\ \langle x_0, & \ldots, & x_{p-1} \rangle \end{matrix} \ \mapsto \ \langle f_0\ x_0, \ldots, f_{p-1}\ x_{p-1} \rangle$$

Unlike BSPlib [7] or PUB [2] we do not distinguish between communication phase and synchronization barrier. The two primitives **put** and **proj** both end implicitly with a synchronization barrier, putting an end to the current super-step.

put is the first communication primitive. It takes as argument a parallel vector of functions which should return, when applied to i, the value to be sent to processor i. **put** returns a parallel vector with the vector of received values at each processor.

$$\mathbf{put}:\quad \langle f_0, \ldots, f_{p-1} \rangle \quad \mapsto \quad \left\langle \begin{array}{ccc} f_0\ 0 & & f_0\ (p-1) \\ \vdots & , \ldots, & \vdots \\ f_{p-1}\ 0 & & f_{p-1}\ (p-1) \end{array} \right\rangle$$

The second communication primitive, **proj**, allows to get replicated values back from locally computed ones. It projects a parallel vector to a standard, replicated vector.

$$\mathbf{proj}:\quad \langle x_0, \ldots, x_{p-1} \rangle \quad \mapsto \quad x_0 \ \cdots \ x_{p-1}$$

3.   Exceptions and BSML

Exceptional situations and errors are handled in OCaml with a powerful system of exceptions. There are two major reasons to use exceptions: first, as a way to quickly get out of a computation and return some parameters. This is specially useful when doing an in-depth search for example, as it saves the trouble of returning the results manually at every level while climbing back in the stack. In parallel, this is at least as relevant since you get the trouble of gathering the results from the different processors. The second reason is error recovery: an unexpected error in OCaml raises an exception. If one processor triggers a Stack_overflow exception during the course of a parallel computation, BSML has to deal with it, like OCaml would, and prevent a crash. This section describes how OCaml handles exceptions and what could get wrong if OCaml exceptions are used in BSML without special care.

exception Exc **of** τ declares a new OCaml exception Exc that encloses data of type τ. Exceptions are considered an extensible variant type, e.g. for matters of pattern-matching. The above-defined exception would be triggered with the syntax **raise** (Exc x), where x is of type τ. Once an exception is raised, it is propagated up the stack until it meets an enclosing **try**...**with** Exc x →t block that pattern-matches against the exception. The exceptional behaviour t is then followed and returns a value of the type expected for the expression without exception.

When using this scheme in parallel with BSML, we face three different cases:

1 If, during a parallel computation, a single processor raises an exception but catches it before the end of the local section, no global operations or communications are hindered and the function that catches the exception returns a result as expected.

2 Exceptions may be raised during a replicated section. In that case, all processors follow the same path of execution and catch the exception or fail together: no inconsistency appears either.

3 When an exception is raised locally, but not caught immediately, however, the processor concerned is not going to execute any of the replicated code that might occur until the end of the superstep: the system gets into an inconsistent state. Worse, the concerned processor is most likely not to meet the expected synchronisation at the end of the superstep and cause a deadlock when the other processors reach the barrier.

Let's take a closer look at the last case with an example:

```
let f pid = if pid=0 then raise (Failure "0") else (fun _ →Some pid)
in let v = mkpar f
in put v
```

Evaluation at processor 0	Evaluation at processor 1
let v = <**raise** (Failure "0"),..> **in put** v	**let** v = <..,**fun** _ →Some 1,..> **in put** v
*** Exception raised ***	**put**: trying to send "Some 1" to 0

Here, an exception is raised locally on processor 0 but processor 1 continues to follow the main execution stream, until it is stopped by the need for a synchronisation. Then, a deadlock occurs. If the same code had been enclosed in a **try**...**with** Failure →..., processor 0 and 1 would have branched into different global execution streams, the normal one and the exceptional one, leading to a global inconsistency: they could have a different number of super-steps which is not possible in the BSP model.

The solution we provide intends to stay as familiar as possible to the programmer. We explain in the next parts how to extend it to manage the problematic case.

4. An Exception Mechanism for BSML

4.1 Syntax

The missing piece to a parallel exception system is a way to catch globally exceptions that are raised locally. Exceptions are defined and raised in the usual way from the user side, using the keywords **exception** and **raise**. Only the catching of local exceptions in a replicated setting is changed. Below is an example of use of exceptions in BSML.

```
trypar                                 withpar
  let f pid = match pid with             eset →Exception_set.iter
    | 0 →raise (Failure "0")                (fun e →prerr_endline
    | x →x                                     (Printexc.to_string e.exc))
  in mkpar f                              eset
```

The parallel execution of f in this example raises a local exception on processor 0 only. The structure **trypar...withpar**, which is similar to **try...with** in OCaml is then used to safely recover this local exception, globally. Globalised local exceptions caught this way are implemented as sets (of type Exception_set.t) of records containing the standard OCaml exceptions raised and their originating processor number. Here, **withpar** binds the name eset to a set containing the Failure raised by processor 0. The exceptional code provided after the arrow iterates on this set and prints the exception on standard error.

The new structure **trypar...withpar**, somehow similar to the standard one, is needed mainly for two reasons: first, a formerly-local exception and a standard replicated exception may exist at the same time and need to be distinguished. Second, it deals with *sets* of exceptions and not with single exceptions.

4.2   A new mechanism

We will consider this two points carefully: (a) a local exception should never prevent replicated code from being executed, or the system becomes inconsistent (replicated code is not executed by all the processors anymore). (b) at the end of the super-step, a local exception has to be treated replicatedly.

Since replicated and local code may be juxtaposed in the same super-step, we need to get aside from the standard exception handling techniques to ensure that replicated code is run normally even after a local exception. During a super-step, there might be local and replicated exceptions coexisting and they must be treated at different levels: a replicated exception, since it is raised by all processors, is treated immediately in the OCaml way. A local exception, on the other hand, must not hinder the global behaviour of the processor yet, so it is kept silent to replicated code until the end of the super-step. This means, in particular, that a processor in a state of exception may not perform any local computation until the next synchronisation.

At the end of a super-step (**put** or **proj**), the exception state is communicated to all processors to allow a global decision to be taken. In such a situation, the local results obtained are partial, inconsistent or nonexistent. Although we are discussing a way to enable the program to recover them afterwards, we currently adopt the standard approach and discard them, switching to the exceptional treatment specified by the user.

Local exceptions are thus *deferred* until the end of the super-step. However, it is undesirable that an exception escapes the scope of the **trypar...withpar** it was raised in. For this reason, communications (and barrier) must be forced at the **withpar**.

This behaviour is described formally and in more detail in the semantics presented in [5].

5. Implementation

Keeping local exceptions hidden from replicated execution is made possible by the strict distinction between local and replicated execution in BSML: by enclosing local execution in a **try...with** safety net in the implementation of the parallel primitives, we are sure to catch every exception raised on a single processor. These exceptions can't be ignored in further local computation on that processor though, so they are retained in a local variable status: (Fine | Stopped of int * exn) ref. The second role of the safety net is then to prevent any local operation on that processor until the end of the super-step, since these operations may use results that failed to compute; replicated code will continue to execute normally.

At the end of the super-step, initiated by the **put** or **proj** primitives or by **withpar**, the communication phase starts with an exchange of data sizes. We take the opportunity to communicate processor states: in case there is any exception, normal communication is replaced by a total exchange of the exceptions and their parameters. We then get back to a consistent replicated state with the same set of exceptions raised everywhere. The propagation of exceptions drives out of the normal execution flow and can't be implemented in OCaml (without exceptions) outside of the compiler, it is therefore piggy-backed onto the OCaml exception Global_exn of Exception_set.t.

To implement the extension in the language, in particular the new keywords **trypar** and **withpar**, we chose to use OCaml's generic precompiler, camlp4. The core of **trypar...withpar** is a **try...with** catching exceptions of the kind Global_exn, but several other problems must be taken into account:

- A barrier must be done before the **with**.
- The super-step may end at an imbrication level different from the one the exception was raised at.
- Local exceptions and global exceptions may conflict. A native global exception has to meet the **withpar** barrier before jumping further in the stack.

- Our Global_exn must be protected from being caught by the user with a normal **try**...**with**.

6.   Experiments

6.1   A generic parallel backtracking algorithm

Backtracking consists in searching for a solution by exploring a tree of possibilities depth-first. If a recursive function doing this search raises an exception whenever a solution is found, it can be caught directly by the calling function without the need to switch cases and return a solution if it exists, or continue exploring otherwise. The parallelisation of this process explores the children of several different nodes at the same time, making the gathering of solutions even more difficult without using exceptions.

To assess the usability of exceptions in BSML, we present a simple implementation of generic parallel backtracking. It takes as argument a sequential function that returns all the children of a given node in the tree and raises a specific exception on a solution. The function exploring the tree proceeds in three steps:

1 the list of current nodes is split into a parallel vector
2 the function returning the children is run in parallel on a limited amount of the nodes at each processor
3 the resulting children nodes are gathered globally, and these three steps are processed recursively on them.

If no solution has been found at the third step (no exception raised), new nodes from step 2 are tried. If there are none left, the algorithm backtracks to the caller. This recursive function is enclosed into a **trypar**...**withpar** that gathers and returns any solution found.

Another version, without any use of exceptions, was implemented. The main descending function had to gather the results of all processors and check if there was a solution at one of them. Accordingly, the size of the core part of the algorithm was increased from 26 lines of code to 44 – exceptions made us save 40% in code size on that example.

6.2   Results

As an example of use, we implemented a brute-force sudoku solver. Sudoku is a fashionable game that consists in filling a $n^2 \times n^2$ grid with integers from 1 to n^2 according to constraints that ensure, given some initial numbers, that only one solution is possible. We generate the children by trying every possibility for each free square and checking for validity. A mild optimisation consists in composing the children function

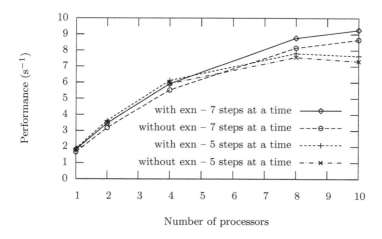

Figure 2.   Sudoku of dimension 9 solved with and without exceptions

several times to obtain enough nodes for an even distribution between processors, which becomes mandatory when increasing the size of the machine.

We solved a given grid of dimension 9 on a cluster of PC (using native-code execution) linked with a gigabit network, for a number of processors varying from one to ten. Figure 2 shows the performance in seconds^{-1} depending on the number of processors (so that a linear speedup would be a straight line), for two different levels of the latter optimisation. This results are the median of a large number of experiments. We notice little impact on performance between the versions with and without exceptions, which is sound since the algorithm is not changed; better, the difference is very stable and in favor of the version with exceptions: we explain it by the added checks that have to be made to extract the possible results at every step of computation.

7.   Conclusion and Future Work

Hardware is heading massively towards parallel architectures. Advanced programming paradigms, however, are still trying to find the best expression for the adapted programs. In this paper, we tackled the problem of exception handling for the functional, OCaml-based BSML language, pushing it one step further to that goal.

We defined global sets of locally raised exceptions and dedicated handlers which offer a natural way to deal with them. A realistic implementation was presented, together with a test program and promising benchmarks.

The work presented here is tightly related to the BSP model, but the exception scheme it bases on is not specific to OCaml. Hence, we reckon there would be little work involved in translating it to, for instance, Java. Future work includes recovery of partial results, a full type system, and automated performance prediction.

References

[1] R. Bisseling. *Parallel Scientific Computation. A structured approach using BSP and MPI*. Oxford University Press, 2004.

[2] O. Bonorden, B. Juurlink, I. von Otte, and O. Rieping. The Paderborn University BSP (PUB) library. *Parallel Computing*, 29(2):187–207, 2003.

[3] M. Cole. *Algorithmic Skeletons: Structured Management of Parallel Computation*. MIT Press, 1989.

[4] F. Gava and F. Loulergue. A Static Analysis for Bulk Synchronous Parallel ML to Avoid Parallel Nesting. *Future Generation Computer Systems*, 21(5):665–671, 2005.

[5] L. Gesbert and F. Loulergue. Semantics of bulk synchronous parallel ml with exceptions. In Zoltán Horváth, editor, *Draft proceedings of the 18th International Symposium on Implementation and Application of Functional Languages (IFL'06)*. to appear, 2006.

[6] Yan Gu, Bu-Sung Lee, and Wentong Cai. JBSP: A BSP programming library in Java. *Journal of Parallel and Distributed Computing*, 61(8):1126–1142, August 2001.

[7] J.M.D. Hill, W.F. McColl, and al. BSPlib: The BSP Programming Library. *Parallel Computing*, 24:1947–1980, 1998.

[8] X. Leroy, D. Doligez, J. Garrigue, D. Rémy, and J. Vouillon. The Objective Caml System release 3.09, 2005. web pages at www.ocaml.org.

[9] F. Loulergue, F. Gava, and D. Billiet. Bulk Synchronous Parallel ML: Modular Implementation and Performance Prediction. In Vaidy S. Sunderam, G. Dick van Albada, Peter M. A. Sloot, and Jack Dongarra, editors, *International Conference on Computational Science, Part II*, number 3515 in LNCS, pages 1046–1054. Springer, 2005.

[10] Alexander B. Romanovsky, Christophe Dony, Jørgen Lindskov Knudsen, and Anand Tripathi, editors. *Advances in Exception Handling Techniques (the book grow out of a ECOOP 2000 workshop)*, volume 2022 of *Lecture Notes in Computer Science*. Springer, 2001.

[11] D. B. Skillicorn, J. M. D. Hill, and W. F. McColl. Questions and Answers about BSP. *Scientific Programming*, 6(3):249–274, 1997.

[12] M. Snir and W. Gropp. *MPI the Complete Reference*. MIT Press, 1998.

II

NETWORKING AND COMMUNICATION

A NEW APPROACH TO MPI COLLECTIVE COMMUNICATION IMPLEMENTATIONS

Torsten Hoe er,[1,4] Jeffrey M. Squyres,[2] Graham Fagg,[3] George Bosilca,[3] Wolfgang Rehm,[4] and Andrew Lumsdaine[1]

[1] *Indiana University, Open Systems Lab, Bloomington, IN 47404 USA*

{htor,lums}@cs.indiana.edu

[2] *Cisco Systems, San Jose, CA 95134 USA*

jsquyres@cisco.com

[3] *University of Tennessee, Dept. of Computer Science, Knoxville, TN 37996 USA*

{fagg,bosilca}@cs.utk.edu

[4] *Technical University of Chemnitz, Dept. of Computer Science, Chemnitz 09107 Germany*

{htor,rehm}@cs.tu-chemnitz.de

Abstract

Recent research into the optimization of collective MPI operations has resulted in a wide variety of algorithms and corresponding implementations, each typically only applicable in a relatively narrow scope: on a specific architecture, on a specific network, with a specific number of processes, with a specific data size and/or data-type – or any combination of these (or other) factors. This situation presents an enormous challenge to portable MPI implementations which are expected to provide optimized collective operation performance on *all* platforms. Many portable implementations have attempted to provide a token number of algorithms that are intended to realize good performance on most systems. However, many platform configurations are still left without well-tuned collective operations. This paper presents a proposal for a framework that will allow a wide variety of collective algorithm implementations and a flexible, multi-tiered selection process for choosing which implementation to use when an application invokes an MPI collective function.

Keywords: Collective Operation, Message Passing (MPI), Automatic Selection, Framework, Open MPI

1. Introduction

The performance of collective operations is crucial for the runtime and scalability of many applications [Rabenseifner, R., 1999]. Decades of collective communication research have yielded a wide variety of algorithms tuned for specific architectures, networks, number of participants, and message sizes. The choice of optimal algorithm to use therefore not only depends on the system that the application is running on, but also the parameters of the collective function that was invoked (e.g., number of peers, data size, data type). The sheer number of algorithms available becomes a fundamental problem when optimizing a portable Message Passing Interface (MPI) library – how should it choose which algorithm to use at runtime?

Our work aims at providing the capability to automatically select the optimal collective implementation for each system and MPI argument set. Such an approach can potentially result in a large performance gain for each collective function invocation [Pjesivac-Grbovic, J. et. al., 2005; Hoefler, T. et. al., 2005; Mitra et al., 1995].

Predictive performance models of point to point communications (such as LogP [Culler, D. et. al., 1993] or LogGP [Alexandrov, A. et. al., 1995]) can return a reasonable approximation of collective communication performance upon which we can base the selection of the collective implementation. Hence, invoking modeling functions at runtime to estimate the algorithm performance is one approach to determine which should be used.

However, such modeling techniques are not necessarily relevant for hardware-assisted collective operations (or other implementations not based on point-to-point operations). Indeed, hardware-based collectives typically outperform even the best software-based algorithms; it is a reasonable optimization to directly invoke available hardware-based collectives and bypass any modeling evaluation.

Based on these considerations and the ideas proposed in [Squyres, J. M. et. al., 2004], we present the design of a next-generation collective framework with the following goals:

1. Enable fine-grained algorithm selection such that a selection atom is an individual function.
2. Perform efficient run-time decisions based on the MPI function arguments.
3. Enable a "fast path" for trivial decisions (e.g., hardware implementations).
4. Enforce a modular approach, preserving the simplicity of adding (and removing) algorithms – especially by third parties.
5. Enable *all* algorithms – even those added by third parties – to be automatically used by user applications, testing, and benchmarking tools.

The rest of this paper is divided as follows: Section 2 discusses related work. Section 3 describes the architecture of our approach. The logic for selecting which algorithm to use is described in Section 4, followed by an analysis of its applicability to a set of real world applications. The last section draws conclusions and points out further work.

2.   Related Work

Many research groups inherently limit the selection problem by implementing only a subset of the standardized collective operations to fit their particular needs and assume that those algorithms are globally applicable [Huse, 1999; Chan, E.W. et. al., 2004]. Some MPI implementations (as MPICH [Gropp, W. et. al., 1996], MPICH2 [MPICH2 Developers, 2006], LAM/MPI [Burns, 1994]) do their selection of the collective implementation to use either statically at compile time or based on a limited number of arguments at runtime. The selection decision is typically based on the communicator and/or data size and does not take into account network characteristics (such as bandwidth and/or latency) and ignores the physical network topology.

FT-MPI [Fagg, G.E. et. al., 2004] and current generations of Open MPI [Gabriel and et al., 2004] base their decisions on an augmented set of parameters which include the network characteristics. However, in order to make the right selection, a decision table must be built prior to the execution by a benchmarking tool. This input file has to be generated by an external tool after running intensive set of benchmarks. The cost of building the decision table on the full set of possible combination of arguments can be prohibitive (especially for large clusters); a subset of all available nodes and/or algorithms may need to be used, leading to the selection of a sub-optimal algorithm in some cases. Even though this approach can provide an increase in performance, it is difficult to add a new algorithm since both the decision function and the benchmark tool have to be modified in order to include the new algorithm.

Similar modular approaches were described by Vadhiyar et. al. [Vadhiyar, S.S. et. al., 2000] and Hartmann et. al. [Hartmann, O. et. al., 2006]. Both propose methods and show the potential benefits of selecting between collective algorithms during runtime. However, these approaches are limited to a small set of implemented algorithms and not easily extensible by third party implementers.

3. Framework Architecture

We propose a hierarchical framework architecture composed of collective components, collective modules and collective functions. A collective component is the software entity which is provided by the module implementer and it generates communicator specific modules on request (called query in the following). Each component is loaded, queried and unloaded by the framework. A collective module is a software instance of a collective operation bound to a specific communicator. A collective component may return an arbitrary number of collective modules during the query. A collective module may have one or more (opaque) collective functions to perform the collective operation available. Additionally, each module defines an evaluation function which returns a collective function pointer and an estimated time for each MPI argument set.

We divide the architecture into three main parts. The software architecture defines the nesting of software entities. The usage and interaction of the software entities during the program run is defined in the runtime architecture. The decision architecture, which can be omitted with the "fast path", defines the decision logic used during function invocation and possible optimizations.

Software Architecture

The software architecture is explained by example in Fig. 1. This example shows only a subset of all available collectives. However, a basic implementation of all collectives is provided with the framework, therefore at least one collective function is available at any time. The example shows two available collective components, called "Component A" and "Component B". Both components are loaded by the framework during start-up and maintained on

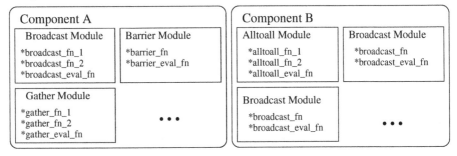

Figure 1.   Software Architecture

a list of active components. The initialization of the framework during start-up (MPI_INIT), where all available components are loaded and initialized, is shown in Fig. 2. The user can select specific components via framework pa-

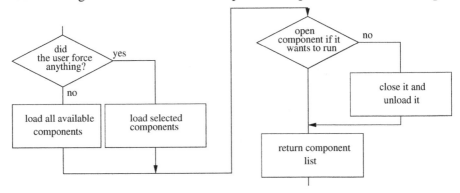

Figure 2.   Actions during MPI_INIT

rameters. Each loaded component may disable itself during start-up if not all requirements (e.g., special hardware) are met. Fig. 1 shows that implementations for MPI_BCAST, MPI_BARRIER, MPI_GATHER, and MPI_ALLTOALL are available to the framework. All available components are queried with each communicator during its construction, including the default communicators MPI_COMM_WORLD and MPI_COMM_SELF. This procedure is shown in Fig. 3. Each component returns an array of available modules to the frame-

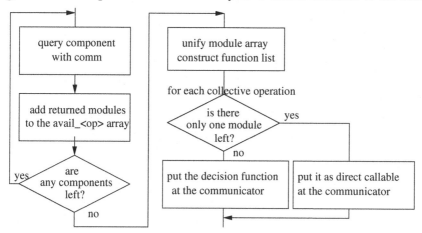

Figure 3. Actions during Communicator Construction

work which adds the modules to a list of runnable modules (avail_<op>) on each communicator. A unification, typically represented by a global operation, of this list ensures that all selectable modules are available on all nodes of this communicator (some of them may not have the right hardware requirements). Finally, the runtime architecture of this communicator is initialized by the framework. This architecture is described in detail in the next section.

Runtime Architecture

Each instantiated module offers an evaluation function to the framework. This evaluation function returns the function pointer to the fastest internal implementation. This means that more than one implementation may exist inside a single module. Our example in Fig. 1 depicts a single MPI_BCAST implementation and two opaque MPI_BCAST functions implemented in "Component A". This shows that the module is allowed to implement opaque functions and to select between them independently of the framework. This offers the possibility to implement a more sophisticated selection inside a single module if the module implementer is able to simplify the decision. This reduces the number of modules, the memory footprint, and the decision costs which are discussed later. However, the component is free to return any number of collective modules for a single collective operation. So does "Component B" and offers two distinct MPI_BCAST implementations which can be turned into two MPI_BCAST modules.

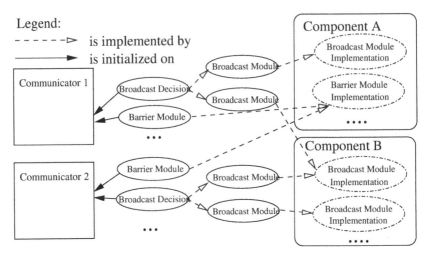

Figure 4. Runtime Architecture

Fig. 4 shows the runtime architecture for two communicators, "Communicator 1" and "Communicator 2". All modules returned by queried components are attached to communicator which was used to query the component. The framework maintains a communicator-specific list of available modules per collective operation. Each module implements a single collective operation which meets the fine grained selection criterion in goal 1. The dashed arrows in Fig. 4 point to the collective implementation in the "Component A" or "Component B" component which acts as a code-base for the collective module. This shows that each component can create multiple modules which can be attached to different communicators. Each communicator can manage an arbitrary number of collective modules to perform a collective operation. The module to process a specific collective call is selected depending on the actual MPI arguments during invocation. However, the collective function is called directly if there is only a single module available, or a single module is enforced by the user (cf. Fig. 3). This direct invocation is called "fast path" as it does not introduce any additional overhead.

4.   Selection Logic

The example in Fig. 4 shows that there is only a single MPI_BARRIER and MPI_GATHER module available for "Communicator 1". As a result, both operations are called directly using the "fast path" without any selection overhead. However, there are two MPI_BCAST implementations available for this communicator which means that there has to be some intermediate layer to select one of those depending on the arguments. This layer is called selection logic and is implemented in a set of MPI operation specific decision functions. The "fast path" enforces that the function arguments of these decision functions are identical to the actual arguments of the collective functions because the upper layer is not aware of the selection logic. This means that the call to the decision function is completely transparent to the upper layer. The selection logic with the MPI_BCAST decision function is shown in Fig. 4 and the actions performed during the invocation of a collective operation are shown in Fig. 5. The first

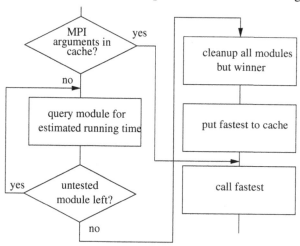

Figure 5. Actions during a collective function call

action is to check if these arguments have already been issued and if the decision result is in the cache. If this is true, the whole decision functionality and the related overhead can be skipped and the fastest function is called directly via its cached function pointer. However, if the arguments have not been called before (or have been evicted from the cache to free memory), the selection needs to be performed for the particular argument set. This means that all runnable modules (modules in the `avail_<op>` array at the communicator) are queried for their estimated running time. The module that returns the lowest running time is added to the cache for future calls and invoked to perform the collective operation.

The decision function performs the MPI argument specific selection of collective modules based on querying the evaluation function of each module. The module's evaluation function returns an estimated time in microseconds and a function pointer to its fastest function. Absolute time was chosen as an evaluation criterion because it denotes the least common denominator for our case. This enables the component author to predict or benchmark the running time of all possible collective implementations no matter if it is performed hardware supported or simply on top of point-to-point messages. It is obvious that querying all available modules each time a collective call occurs is extremely costly and can have a catastrophic impact at the application performance. The decision function implements an MPI-argument specific cache which stores the collective function pointer to speed up the critical path to reduce the number of the costly queries. The fastest collective function pointer is added to the cache and called after each evaluation. This introduces two questions: How much overhead does the evaluation add to the collective latency and how cache friendly will an application really be. The overhead of the evaluation and the cache friendliness of three MPI applications are analyzed in Section 5

For example, a direct call occurs to Component A's Barrier Module if the application calls `MPI_Barrier(Communicator 1)`. This shows the "fast path" which is enabled for the barrier call on Communicator 1. The next MPI call of the application is `MPI_Bcast(sbuf, 1, MPI_INT, 0, Communicator 1)` which uses the decision function. This arguments are not yet in the cache (i.e., have not been called before). The decision function queries both Broadcast Modules of Component A and Component B for their fastest function (-pointer) and its estimated running time. The function pointer of the fastest function is inserted into the cache and it is called to perform the collective. If another call to `MPI_Bcast(sbuf, 1, MPI_INT, 0, Communicator 1)` occurs, we already know the fastest function (in the cache) and call it without evaluating all modules. However, if a call to `MPI_Bcast(sbuf, 2, MPI_INT, 0, Communicator 1)` occurs, we have to reevaluate all modules again.

Decision Overhead

The argument cache can be implemented as a collision-free hash-table which has an ideal complexity of $O(1)$. The costly part is if a cache miss occurs (i.e., the called argument set is not in the cache, has not been called before). This results in a serial query to the evaluation functions of all available modules. There are many different ways to implement this evaluation function, we will discuss the costs of two approaches on detail.

Benchmark Based Implementation. The evaluation function could return a time that is based on an actual benchmark which has previously been run on the system. We assume that the benchmark data has a small memory demand and was loaded during startup. The cost will be approximately a indirect function call and several cache misses. The indirect function call costs has been evaluated in [Barrett, B. et. al., 2005] and turns out to be between $2ns$ and $10ns$. We implemented a simple x86 RDTSC based micro benchmark to measure cache miss penalty which was between $0.5\mu s$ and $1.5\mu s$ on all evaluated architectures (Opteron 2.0 GHz, Xeon 2.4 GHz, Athlon MP 1.4 GHz). This shows that each evaluation function call may take some microseconds for a benchmark based implementation.

Model Based Implementation. The time to return could also be calculated using a model function like LogP or LogGP. We can assume that the small set of necessary model parameters are already in the cache. Our micro-benchmark measures access times between $10ns$ and $50ns$ for cached items and a calculation time of $200ns$ up to $500ns$ for the evaluation of a 4th grade polynomial (model function). The overall evaluation should take less than $1\mu s$ for this case.

This shows that well implemented evaluation functions may need up to $5\mu s$ to return the result. This should not hurt the application performance to much, because the expected benefits are higher (previous studies show differences in the millisecond scale for several collective implementations). However, the cache may even speed thing up for repeated arguments. The next section analyzes the cache-friendliness of a small set of applications.

Analyzing the Cache Friendliness

The usage of the cache (i.e., hit and miss rates) are not easily predictable because they depend entirely on the application. We measured two different applications to measure their cache friendliness. The first is ABINIT (http://www.-abinit.org) which offers two distinct parallelization schemes, band parallelization and CG+FFT parallelization. The second application is CPMD (http://www.cpmd.org/) which is used in its standard configuration. Both applications have been run with a real-world input file and a special library which logs collective calls using the MPI profiling interface. ABINIT issues 295 collective operation calls with 16 different parameter sets (hit rate: 94.6%) for band parallelization. The CG+FFT parallelization uses 53887 collective operations with 75 different argument sets (hit rate: 99.9%). CPMD issues 15428 collective operations with 85 different argument sets (hit rate: 99.4%). Both applications utilize the cache very efficiently.

5. Conclusion and Future Work

We have shown that our new design to select collective implementations during runtime is able to support all kinds of possible collective function implementations. We have also shown that the idea of the MPI argument cache to store the optimal selection will work well with at least some real world application. It is possible to disable the whole selection logic and call every operation via the "fast path". The selection logic enables scientists to add new collective functionality easily and to use it also in productive environments. Next steps will include the implementation and testing of the proposed approach and the analysis of more real applications for their argument cache friendliness.

Acknowledgments

This work was supported by a grant from the Lilly Endowment and National Science Foundation grant EIA-0202048.

References

Alexandrov, A. et. al. (1995). LogGP: Incorporating Long Messages into the LogP Model. *Journal of Parallel and Distributed Computing*, 44(1):71–79.

Barrett, B. et. al. (2005). Analysis of the Component Architecture Overhead in Open MPI. In *Proc., 12th European PVM/MPI Users' Group Meeting*.

Burns, G. et. al. (1994). LAM: An Open Cluster Environment for MPI. In *Proc. of Supercomputing Symposium*, pages 379–386.

Chan, E.W. et. al. (2004). On optimizing of collective communication. In *Proc. of IEEE International Conference on Cluster Computing*, pages 145–155.

Culler, D. et. al. (1993). LogP: towards a realistic model of parallel computation. In *Principles Practice of Parallel Programming*, pages 1–12.

Fagg, G.E. et. al. (2004). Extending the MPI specification for process fault tolerance on high performance computing systems. In *Proceedings of the International Supercomputer Conference (ICS) 2004*. Primeur.

Gabriel, Edgar and et al. (2004). Open MPI: Goals, Concept, and Design of a Next Generation MPI Implementation. In *Proceedings, 11th European PVM/MPI Users' Group Meeting*, Budapest, Hungary.

Gropp, W. et. al. (1996). A high-performance, portable implementation of the MPI message passing interface standard. *Parallel Computing*, 22(6):789–828.

Hartmann, O. et. al. (2006). A decomposition approach for optimizing the performance of MPI libraries. In *Proc., 20th International Parallel and Distributed Processing Symposium IPDPS*.

Hoefler, T. et. al. (2005). A practical Approach to the Rating of Barrier Algorithms using the LogP Model and Open MPI. In *Proc. of the 2005 International Conference on Parallel Processing Workshops (ICPP'05)*, pages 562–569.

Huse, Lars Paul (1999). Collective communication on dedicated clusters of workstations. In *Proc. of the 6th European PVM/MPI Users' Group Meeting on Recent Advances in PVM and MPI*, pages 469–476.

Mitra, Prasenjit, Payne, David, Shuler, Lance, van de Geijn, Robert, and Watts, Jerrell (1995). Fast collective communication libraries, please. Technical report, Austin, TX, USA.

MPICH2 Developers (2006). http://www.mcs.anl.gov/mpi/mpich2/.

Pjesivac-Grbovic, J. et. al. (2005). Performance Analysis of MPI Collective Operations. In *Proc. of the 19th International Parallel and Distributed Processing Symposium*.

Rabenseifner, R. (1999). Automatic MPI counter profiling of all users: First results on a CRAY T3E 900-512. In *Proc. of the Message Passing Interface Developer's and User's Conference*, pages 77–85.

Squyres, J. M. et. al. (2004). The component architecture of Open MPI: Enabling third-party collective algorithms. In *Proc. 18th ACM International Conference on Supercomputing, Workshop on Component Models and Systems for Grid Applications*, pages 167–185.

Vadhiyar, S.S. et. al. (2000). Automatically tuned collective communications. In *Proc. of the ACM/IEEE conference on Supercomputing (CDROM)*, page 3.

SUPPORTING MPI APPLICATIONS IN P-GRADE PORTAL* †

Zoltán Farkas
MTA SZTAKI Computer and Automation Research Institute
H-1518 Budapest, P.O. Box 63, Hungary
zfarkas@sztaki.hu

Zoltán Balaton
MTA SZTAKI Computer and Automation Research Institute
H-1518 Budapest, P.O. Box 63, Hungary
balaton@sztaki.hu

Péter Kacsuk
MTA SZTAKI Computer and Automation Research Institute
H-1518 Budapest, P.O. Box 63, Hungary
kacsuk@sztaki.hu

Abstract   P-GRADE portal is a multi-grid portal that can support GT2, LCG and gLite based Grid systems. In order to enable MPI execution in a transparent way in any of these grids we have developed a generic MPI execution mechanism that can tolerate the lack of shared working directory and is able to work with local job managers unable to support MPI jobs. The solution can support both direct job submission to selected grid sites as well as broker-based job submission. In case of using the EGEE broker the developed method enables the access of remote files stored in storage elements even if the executable code can access only local files.

Keywords: MPI, Grid, Portal, EGEE, Broker

---

*This research work is carried out under the FP6 Network of Excellence CoreGRID funded by the European Commission (Contract IST-2002-004265).
†SEE-GRID-2 South-Eastern European GRid-enabled eInfrastructure Development 2, Contract Number 031775

1.   Introduction

MPI became more and more important for EGEE, so there have been serious efforts to make EGEE Grid resources capable of running MPI jobs. This article is about the achievements of this work implemented directly in P-GRADE Portal[1], that allows users to use grid resources without detailed knowledge about the Grid. It supports running both sequential and parallel applications through a graphical user environment.

EGEE does not support MPI applications officially yet, however, there are some sites, that make this service available, to satisfy user requirements.

In the EGEE Grid users can connect to a resource broker (RB) that accepts a file written in the Job Description Language (JDL[3]). The purpose of this file is to describe the job itself and various requirements set up by the user represented as attribute-value pairs. The possible attributes include for example the executable name, the input files used by the executable, or the number of nodes required by the job. By using the values defined in this file and the information present in the information system the resource broker can decide about the destination resource of the job.

Besides the brokered method, Grid users have the possibility to access the resources directly. In this case no broker is used to find a matching resource: it is the user's responsibility to send the job to a correct resource. Direct usage can be achieved through standard GT-2 calls: GRAM[4] and GridFTP.

P-GRADE Portal makes it possible for the user to use EGEE resources in any of the above described ways, through a common graphical user interface.

During the development of EGEE Grid support in P-GRADE Portal, we have faced the following differences in EGEE infrastructure and previously used Grid infrastructures: first, many jobmanagers create a new working directory for each GRAM call. As a consequence, the job should be started using only one GRAM call.

Second, there are resources, that do not share the working directory among worker nodes. This means, that input files need to be copied to all of the worker nodes, because in case of MPI applications, all of the processes may access the input files. However, it is possible to detect the presence of shared working directories, in this case optimizations should be considered.

Third, the jobmanager used may not be able to handle MPI jobs. In order to make MPI jobs runnable on such resources, P-GRADE Portal has to start the MPI application.

Finally, there are some new services in EGEE: files may reside on Storage Elements, which can not be used by legacy applications, the user has to add support for them in his/her application. This is a serious problem, if the user does not have the possibility to modify the application. Another important service is the EGEE broker.

The execution layer of P-GRADE Portal has to be able to handle both traditional GT-2 Grid resources, and EGEE Grid resources, which may differ from traditional resources in the ways described above.

There are HOWTOs describing the way MPI applications can be started on EGEE resources. One of this HOWTOs is the INFN-GRID mini-howto[2]. This HOWTO describes running MPI jobs on INFN-GRID using pbs jobmanagers.

Section 2 will describe how direct MPI job submission is solved in the P-GRADE portal. Section 3 addresses the main problem of the broker-based MPI job submission of EGEE Grids and shows how to solve this problem by the P-GRADE portal MPI execution mechanism. Section 4 describes the experiments we have gained with the described generic MPI Grid execution mechanism.

2. Direct MPI job submission

In case of direct job submission, the specialties mentioned in the previous section have to be kept in mind during implementation.

It is important to write some words about the P-GRADE Portal execution layer. As a workflow scheduler Condor DAGMan is used, which can run scripts before and after the job is executed. These scripts are called pre and post scripts. The task of the pre script is to prepare the job execution (for example copy input files used by the job to the requested resource). The post script is responsible for after-job tasks (for example downloading output files from the resource). The actual job, which is executing between the two scripts, is either a Globus universe job or another script run in the Scheduler universe, depending on the method used for job execution (brokered or direct). The scripts will be described in detail, where required.

In order to make the execution layer work for both traditional and EGEE-like resources, the following points must be considered.
As jobmanagers may not support MPI jobs, the job type should be specified as 'single', and not 'mpi', but the required number of nodes must be specified for MPI jobs. This enables to start the application even if the jobmanager does not support MPI applications, but the resource is configured to do so.

When the working directories are not shared, it is impossible to copy input files to the worker nodes using GridFTP. Thus, files must be copied to a temporary working directory instead on the frontend machine. A GRAM call can be used to create this temporary working directory. The requested jobmanager might be unusable for this, as the directory is created on one of the worker nodes, and cannot be accessed using GridFTP. So the 'fork' jobmanager must be used to create this working directory, which runs the jobs on the frontend machine. In this case the job to be run is a simple 'create directory' command. After the directory is created, it is possible to copy input files to this directory using GridFTP. P-GRADE Portal must not specify the working directory, where the job is to be run, as it may be different for each GRAM call.

The jobmanager knows nothing about the input files used by the job (there is no way to specify them), so moving the input files from the frontend to the worker nodes has to be done by the job. As P-GRADE Portal offers the possibility to submit grid un-aware jobs which do not know anything about the infrastructure used, this task has to be done by the execution layer. Not on the Portal machine, but on the resource, after the job has been submitted, and before the job is started. The trivial solution for this situation is to copy the executable to the frontend machine just like an input file, and specify a wrapper script as the executable in the Condor-G submit file. The wrapper script is described below. The wrapper script can do all the necessary tasks which can not be done before the job is submitted, or is not handled by the real executable.

With all the above in view, the execution layer of P-GRADE Portal is described on figure 1. The steps in detail are:

1 The pre script queries the HOME directory on the frontend node using the fork jobmanager. Next, a temporary working directory is created in the HOME directory also using the fork jobmanager. The final step of the preparation is copying the input files and the executable to this working directory.

2 The wrapper script is submitted to the requested jobmanager (pbs on figure 1) using the Condor-G submit file. In case of MPI applications, the job is submitted as a 'single' job type, for which the requested number of nodes to be allocated is also specified. This step means setting the 'jobType' RSL[5] attribute to 'single', and the 'count' and 'hostCount' attributes to the requested number of nodes. The wrapper script requires the following parameters: the fully qualified domain name (FQDN) of the frontend node, the path of the temporary working directory on that machine, the

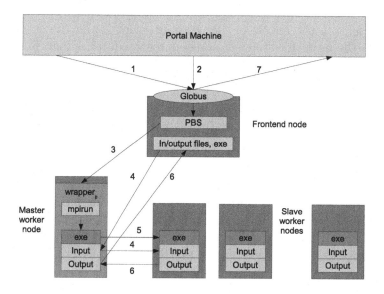

Figure 1. Direct MPI job submission using P-GRADE Portal

job name, and the real executable name. All these variables are specified as environment variables in the wrapper script. These variables are updated by the pre script.

3 In this step, the jobmanager script running on the frontend node creates a submit file for the local resource management system (LRMS, pbs on figure 1), and submits it to the LRMS. The LRMS allocates the number of nodes requested, and starts the wrapper script on one of the allocated nodes. We will refer to the node where the wrapper is started as the master node.

4 After the wrapper script is started, it checks if the temporary working directory created by the pre script is present. If yes, the selected resource uses shared working directories. Otherwise the executable and input files are copied from the frontend node using the command scp or rcp. If the job type is sequential, the executable is simply started at this point. If it is an MPI job, 'mpirun' is being searched for: first GLOBUS_LOCATION/libexec/globus-sh-tools.sh file is read, and if the GLOBUS_SH_MPIRUN environment variable is defined, its value is used, otherwise 'mpirun' is used assuming it is in the PATH. The number of nodes is queried from the job description file. If the PBS_NODEFILE environment variable is defined, its value is used as the machinefile for mpirun. In case

PSB_NODEFILE is defined and no shared working directories are present on the resource, the wrapper script copies the executable, and the input files to each node enumerated in the file. The target directory is the current working directory, as MPI starts processes in that directory. So the executable, and input files are distributed.

5 Next, the real executable is started using the found 'mpirun', the specified process count, and the possibly found machinefile.

6 After the real executable has been run, and the PBS_NODEFILE environment variable is defined and no shared working directories are present on the resource, the output files found in the job input/output file description file are copied from the worker nodes enumerated in the file referenced by PBS_NODEFILE to the master worker node using scp or rcp. If a file is not present, the error is simply ignored. After this, output files are copied from the master worker node to the frontend machine temporary working directory. Finally the wrapper script exists with the return value of the real executable.

7 After the Condor-G job has successfully finished, the post script copies the output files from the temporary working directory on the frontend to the the Portal machine using GridFTP.

Using the above method makes it possible for users to run both sequential and MPI applications, irrespective of the resource environment: both shared and unshared HOME directories are supported. Moreover, the jobmanager may create a separate context (working directory) for each GRAM call.

In case of a non-pbs jobmanager, it is impossible to determine the slave worker node hostnames. So input files can not be copied to the worker nodes before the executable is started. MPI applications sent to non-pbs jobmanagers should open input and output files in the master process.

3.   MPI job submission using the LCG broker

In the introduction we have mentioned, that in case of submitting a job through the EGEE broker, users do not have the possibility to make the broker copy their remote input files residing on a storage element to the worker node where the job is run. It is possible to specify the remote input files, but this is only a hint for the broker: it can place the job close to a storage element, which has the requested files. It is the job's responsibility to download the remote input files from the storage element as requested.

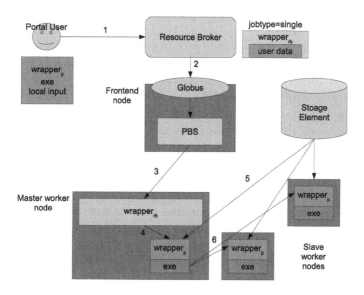

Figure 2. Brokered MPI job submission using P-GRADE Portal

P-GRADE Portal offers the possibility to users to run their legacy applications using remote input files, even if the application does not support using storage elements. In order to achieve this, on the user interface the input file type has to be set to Remote, and the file must be specified using a Logical File Name (lfn) or a GUID.

The P-GRADE Portal brokered job submission is described on figure 2. The steps in detail are:

1 The Portal submits the job to the resource broker. A portal wrapper script ($wrapper_p$), the real executable, and local input files are sent with the job. $wrapper_p$ is used, as the executable to run.

2 The resource broker creates a submit file for the GRAM jobmanager requested. The job type is specified as single, and a new script, the broker wrapper script ($wrapper_{rb}$) is specified as the executable to be run. $wrapper_p$, the real executable and local input files are sent as job input.

3 This step is the same as step 3 in case of direct MPI job submission.

4 $wrapper_{rb}$ starts $wrapper_p$ on the allocated nodes using 'mpirun'. The first instance of $wrapper_p$ starts on the master worker node.

5 $wrapper_p$ check if the requested remote input files are present. If not, they are downloaded from the storage element. Next, the real

executable is started. This step triggers the MPI_Init function in the MPI library.

6 MPI_Init starts $wrapper_p$ on the other worker nodes. $wrapper_p$ and not the real executable, because $wrapper_p$ has been specified as the executable to 'mpirun'.
$wrapper_p$ running on slave worker nodes behaves just like on the master worker node: checks if the remote input files are present. If yes (probably because working directories are shared), the real executable is simply started. If not, remote input files are downloaded from the storage element.

This method copies remote input files only in case of they are really needed: for shared working directories only once, for unshared working directories only if they are not present. The created portal wrapper script is universal: works for both sequential and MPI applications.

As it can be seen, the main difference between direct and brokered job submission implementation is, that in case of brokered submit the implementation does not need to take care of running 'mpirun', as it is done by the broker wrapper script. In case of direct job submission, the portal wrapper script behaves just like the broker wrapper script mentioned in this section.

4.   Experimental results

In order to test the developed solutions, we have taken an EGEE VO, and checked which resources are prepared to start MPI applications. During the tests we have used the slightly modified 'cpi' example application. The only modification is, that the executable tries to open an input file. The started application used 2 processes.

The selected VO is SEEGRID [6]. We have checked the resources, and created a list about the resources which successfully ran the modified application. For determining the list, for each resource a JDL file has been created, in which the resource to use has been specified as a requirement:

```
Requirements = other.GlueCEInfoHostname=="..."
```

where ... must be replaced with the fully qualified domain name of the resource to run the job.

The computing elements capable of running the job are:

- ce.ulakbim.gov.tr:2119/jobmanager-lcgpbs-seegrid

- grid01.rcub.bg.ac.yu:2119/jobmanager-pbs-seegrid

- seegrid2.fie.upt.al:2119/jobmanager-pbs-seegrid.

Using the P-GRADE Portal with the broker, jobs which finished successfully ran exactly on the same computing elements, as without the P-GRADE Portal.

Submitting the executable directly to the resources, job finished successfully on the same computing elements, as in the brokered case, and on one more resource: grid2.cs.bilkent.edu.tr:2119/jobmanager-lcgpbs-seegrid. On this resource HOME directories are not shared among the nodes. This is because in case of direct resource usage the P-GRADE Portal wrapper script copies the executable and input files to the requested nodes.

5. Conclusion

P-GRADE portal is already used for several types of Grids as production service: UK NGS, VOCE, SEE-GRID, GILDA, EGRID, etc. The UK NGS is a GT2 Grid, VOCE is an LCG Grid and GILDA has a gLite version. In all these Grids we had to support the MPI job submission both directly and through the broker. In order to achieve this we have developed a generic MPI Grid execution mechanism. The advantage of this new mechanism is that it does not require either shared working directory of the MPI Grid sites or local job managers that can support MPI execution.

The direct MPI job submission mechanism can be used in Grids without brokers (e.g. UK NGS) but also useful in Grids where brokers available like in EGEE type Grids. Our experiments showed that in EGEE Grids the direct MPI job submission could be very advantageous because more sites can be used for MPI job execution by the direct job submission than by the broker. Furthermore, our solution improves the usability of EGEE sites in case of MPI jobs by enabling their use for MPI jobs that require the access of remote files without the capability of handling Grid files.

References

[1] P. Kacsuk et al: P-GRADE: a Grid Programming Environment
     Journal of Grid Computing, Vol. 1, No. 2, pp.

[2] G. Andronico, R. Barbera, G. Donvito. G. La Rocca, S. Dalla Fina: Running MPI
     jobs on INFN-GRID mini-howto
     http://grid-it.cnaf.infn.it/index.php?mpihowto&type=1

[3] F. Pacini: JDL Attributes
     http://server11.infn.it/workload-grid/docs/DataGrid-01-TEN-0142-0_2.pdf

[4] K. Czajkowski, I. Foster, N. Karonis, C. Kesselman, S. Martin, W. Smith, S. Tuecke: A Resource Management Architecture for Metacomputing Systems The 4th Workshop on Job Scheduling Strategies for Parallel Processing Springer-Verlag LNCS 1459, pages 62–82

[5] The Globus Resource Specification Language RSL v1.0 http://www-fp.globus.org/gram/rsl_spec1.html

[6] South Eastern European GRid-enabled eInfrastructure Development http://www.see-grid.org/

TUNED: AN OPEN MPI COLLECTIVE COMMUNICATIONS COMPONENT

Graham E. Fagg, George Bosilca, Jelena Pješivac-Grbović,
Thara Angskun and Jack J. Dongarra
Dept. of Computer Science, 1122 Volunteer Blvd., Suite 413, The University of Tennessee, Knoxville, TN 37996-3450, USA

fagg,bosilca,pjesa,angskun,dongarra@cs.utk.edu

Abstract   Collective communications are invaluable to modern high performance applications, although most users of these communication patterns do not always want to know their inner most working. The implementation of the collectives are often left to the middle-ware developer such as those providing an MPI library. As many of these libraries are designed to be both generic and portable the MPI developers commonly offer internal tuning options suitable only for knowledgeable users that allow some level of customization. The work presented in this paper aims not only to provide a very efficient set of collective operations for use with the Open MPI implementation but also to make the control and tuning of them straightforward and flexible.

Keywords: Collective Communication, Communication Tuning, Runtime Selection

1.   Introduction

Collective (group) communications are of paramount importance to HPC users due to the extent on which developers rely on them for optimal performance[1]. In many cases obtaining optimal performance requires deep internal knowledge of the collective algorithms and the target architectures which many users may not either have access to or have no understanding of. The reasons for these gaps are many. The implementation of the collectives are often left to the middleware developers such as those providing an MPI library. As many of these libraries are designed to be both generic and portable the MPI developers are left in the difficuilt position of deciding just how to implement the basic operations in such a way that they meet the needs of all possible users without knowing just how they will be utilised.

Previous generations of collective implementations usually offered a number of possibly optimal low level implementations and some kind of a fixed decision on when to use one version or the other, in a hope that this would cover most usage cases. Although much previous work has focused on either measurement (instrumentation) or modelling to make these decisions (ACCT/ATCC[2], OCC[3], LogGP, MagPIe[4] etc) rather than on how to either incorporate them into a runtime system, or make them more accessible.

In many cases making the underlying decisions accessible either directly to knowledgable users, or via automated tools is enough to correct for any [performance] problems with the default decisions implemented by the MPI implementors.

This paper describes current work on the tuned collectives module developed by the University of Tennessee for distribution within the Open MPI 1.1 release. Some sections of the research shown here (i.e. dynamic rule bases) are still however experimental and may never be officially distributed with Open MPI. This paper is ordered as follows: Section 2 detailed related work in collective communications and control. Section 3 details the Open MPI MCA architecture and Section 4 describes the tuned collectives component design and performance, section 5 concludes the paper and lists future work.

2.   Related Work

All MPI implementations support MPI collective operations as defined in the MPI 1.2 specification [5]. Many of the portable implementations support a static choice mechanism such as LAM/MPI, MPICH [6], FT-MPI [7] and the basic collectives component [8] of Open MPI [9]. In many cases these implementations are tuned primarily for closely coupled systems and clusters and the decision functions are buried deep inside the implementations. System that are designed for Grid and wide-area use also have to differentiate between various collective algorithms but at a much higher level, such as when implementing hierarchical topologies to hide latency effects. Systems such a Magpie [4], PACX-MPI [10, 11] and MPICH-G2 all use various metrics to control which algorithms are used. Although these systems do not explicitly export control of these parameters to users, their code structure does allow these points to be more easily found than with closely coupled systems.

3.   Open MPI collective framework and basic components

The current Open MPI[9] architecture is a component based system, and is called the Modular Component Architecture (MCA). The MCA architecture was designed to allow for a customized (and optimized) MPI implementation that is built from a range of possible components at runtime, allowing for a well architect ed code base that is both easy to test across multiple configurations and easy to integrate into a new platform. The architectures design is a follow up to the SSI system [12] originally developed for the LAM7. The system consists of a MCA framework which loads components (shared objects) during MPI_Init. If any of these components can be utilized (they can disqualify themselves via a query function) they become modules (a component instance coupled with resources such as allocated memory). Many of the subsystems within Open MPI such as low level point-to-point messaging, collective communication, MPI-2 I/O, and topology support are all built as components that can be requested by the user at mpirun time.

The Open MPI 1.0 release supplied a number of MPI components for collective communication that each contained a complete set of MPI 1.2 collective operations. The components being: *basic, shm* and *self.*

The shm component contains collectives for use when Open MPI is running completely on a shared memory system. The self component is a special feature within MPI for use on the MPI_COMM_SELF communicator. The basic component is the default component used when not using either shared memory or self. The basic component contains at least one implementations per collective operation. For broadcast and reduce it offers two implementations, one linear and the other using a binary tree. Further details of the Open MPI collective framework can be found in [8].

4.   New tuned collectives and decision module

The tuned collectives module has a number of goals, and aims to support the following: 1: Multiple collective implementations, 2: Multiple logical topologies, 3: Wide range of fully tunable parameters, 4: Efficient default decisions, 5: Alternative user supplied compiled decision functions, 6: User supplied selective decision parameter configuration files, and 7: Provide a means to dynamically create/alter decision functions at runtime.

Items (1-3) are paramount for any collective implementation to be able to provide performance on an unknown system that the developer has no direct access to. Item (4) is required to allow users to just download and install Open MPI and get reasonable performance. Item (5) is for more knowledgeable users who wish to change the default decision and allow for the fastest use of that new decision without fully replacing the current default rules. If a comprehensive benchmarking of the Open MPI collectives module has been completed, then the output from this could be feed back into the MPI runtime (item 6) and used instead of the default rule base. The final item is quite unusual and allows for the entire (or part of) the rule base to be changed during runtime. This in effect allows for adaptive behavior of the decision functions, and has been applied to dynamically tuning the MPI_Alltoallv operation which is obmitted due to space.

4.1   Collective algorithms and parameters

Previous studies of MPI collectives have shown that no single algorithm or topology is optimal and that the variations in network topology, interconnection technology, system buffering and so on, all effect the performance of a collective operation [2]. Thus, the tuned module supports a wide number of algorithms for performing MPI collective operations. Some of these implementations rely on fixed communication topologies such as the Bruck and recursive doubling, others are general enough to handle almost any topology i.e. trees with varying fan-outs, pipelines etc. Another additional parameter implemented in the tuned collectives module is segmentation size. In an attempt to increase performance by utilizing as many communication links as possible we have modified most algorithms to segment the users data into smaller blocks (*segments*). This allows the algorithm to effectively pipeline all transfers. The segment size is however not a simple factor of network MTU, sender overhead gap etc, and usually has to be benchmarked fully to find optimal values.

4.2   Default tuned decision function

For the module to be named *tuned* implies that it is in fact tuned for some system somewhere. In fact it has been tuned for a cluster of AMD64 processors communicating across a Gigabit Ethernet interconnect located at UTK. The tuning was performed using an exhaustive benchmarking technique as part of the OCC[3] and Harness/FT-MPI [7] projects. (The module shares almost the same decision functions as FT-MPI although they both implement slightly different ranges of algorithms).

A comparison of the tuned component compared to the basic collectives module in Open MPI, MPICH2 and FT-MPI is shown in figures 1 a & b. The first figure shows absolute performances and the second is normalized to the optimal of the 4 systems (i.e. the Y-Axis shows how much slower the others are compared to the best for that message size and operation).

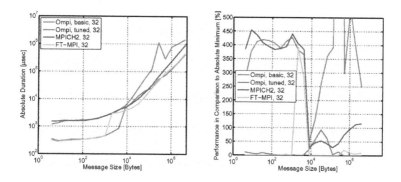

Figure 1.   Absolute and Relative (compared to best) performance of 4 collective implementations, Open MPI (basic,tuned), MPICH2 and FT-MPI

4.3   Architecture and calling sequence

The overall architecture of the tuned collectives component is governed by both the MCA framework and the structure of the communicator data structure. As the upper level MPI architecture calls the function pointer in the communicator directly, this forces the first level function in the component to have the same argument list as that of the MPI API, i.e. no extra arguments. As discussed above many of the backend implementations of the collectives require extra parameters, such as topology and segment size. We resolve this issue by using at a two level architecture. The first level takes normal MPI arguments, decides which algorithm/implementation to use, creates any additional parameters and then invokes it, passing any results or errors back to the MPI layer. I.e. the first level function is both a decision function and a dispatch function. The second or lower layer is the implementation layer, and contains the actual algorithm themselves. Adding this additional layer of redirection allows the component complete flexibility in how it handles requests, as all functions except the decision/dispatch are hidden from the above layers. The component additionally implements some support functions to create and manage virtual topologies. These topologies are cached on either the component, or on each instance of the module as configured by the user.

4.4   User overrides

One of the goals of the tuned module was to allow the user to completely control the collective algorithms used during runtime. From the architecture it is clear that the upper level MPI API does not offer any methods of informing the component of any changes (except through MPI attributes) as the decision/dispatch function has the same arguments as the collective calls. This issue is resolved by the MCA framework, which allows for the passing of key:value pairs from the environment into the runtime. These values can then be looked up by name.

To avoid incurring any kind of performance penalty during normal usage, these overrides are not checked for unless a special trigger value known as *mca_coll_tuned_use_dynamic_rules* is set. When this value is set, the default compiled in decision routines are replaced by alternative routines that check for all the possible collective control parameters. To further reduce overheads, these parameters are only looked up at the MCA level during communicator creation time, and their values are then cached on each communicators collective module private data segment.

Forcing choices.   The simplest choice that the user might want is the ability to completely override the collective component and choose a particular algorithm and its operating parameters (such as topology and segmentation sizes) directly. In the tuned component this is known as *forcing* a decision on the component, and it can be performed on as many or as few MPI collectives as required. The following example illustrates how the user can force the use of a binomial tree based Broadcast operation from the command line.

```
host% mpirun -np N -mca coll_tuned_use_dynamic_rules 1
        -mca coll_tuned_bcast_algorithm 6 myapp.bin
```

The range of possible algorithms available for any collective can be obtained from the system by running the Open MPI system utility *ompi_info* with the arguments *-mca coll_tuned_use_dynamic_rules 1 -param coll all*. The possible algorithm choices for MPI Broadcast is:

```
MCA coll: information "coll_tuned_bcast_algorithm_count"
        (value: "6") Number of bcast algorithms available
MCA coll: parameter "coll_tuned_bcast_algorithm"
        (current value: "0") Which bcast algorithm is used.
        Can be locked down to choice of:
        0 ignore, 1 basic linear, 2 chain, 3: pipeline,
        4: split binary tree, 5: binary tree, 6: BM tree.
```

It is important to note that the value *0* forces the component to default to the built in compiled decision rules. Further control parameters exist that control both topology and message transfers such as *coll_tuned_bcast_algorithm_segmentsize, _tree_fanout/_chain_fanout*. These parameter names are common to most collective operations.

Selective file driven decision functions.   Another alternative to forcing complete collective operations is to force only parts of the decision space in a semi-fixed manner. An example of such a usage scenario would be in the case of a user having tuned an MPI collective for a range of input parameters (message size, communicator size) either manually or via an automated tool [3]. The user could then tell the MPI collective component to use these values within a set range by supplying a file that contains as many data points as the user knows. To decrease both storage and evaluation time the file contents are stored using a run-length technique that effectively only stores the switching points for each algorithm. An example version for an MPI Alltoall operation is shown below:

```
1          # num of collectives
3          # ID = 3 Alltoall collective (ID in coll_tuned.h)
2          # number of com sizes
           # comm sizes (1-first-1) use defaults automatically
8          # comm size 8
2          # number of msg sizes
0 1 0 0 # message size 0, linear 1, no topo or segmentation
32768 2 0 0 # 32k, pairwise 2, no topo or segmentation
9          # comm size 9-(onwards)
1          # message sizes
0 0 0 0 # for datasize 0 onwards use default decisions
           # end of collective 1, ID 3
```

5.   Conclusions

The results presented in this paper show that the flexible control of the current Open MPI tuned collectives component do not effect communication performance, and that the component is still competitive with other MPI implementations such as LAM/MPI, FT-MPI and MPICH2. The component allows multiple varied and concurrent methods for the user or system administrator to control selectively the choice of backend collective algorithm and its parameters. We are hoping to extend this work in a number of ways. This includes adding more automated tools for file based rule generation (application targeted tuning) and using feedback from switch and network infrastructure to dynamically control algorithm choices during runtime.

References

[1] Rabenseifner, R.: Automatic MPI counter profiling of all users: First results on a CRAY T3E 900-512. In: Proceedings of the Message Passing Interface Developer's and User's Conference. (1999) 77–85

[2] Vadhiyar, S.S., Fagg, G.E., Dongarra, J.: Performance modeling for self adapting collective communications for mpi. In: Proceedings of the LACSI Symposium, Los Alamos, NM, Los Alamos Computer Institute (2001)

[3] Pješivac-Grbović, J., Angskun, T., Bosilca, G., Fagg, G.E., Gabriel, E., Dongarra, J.J.: Performance analysis of mpi collective operations. In: Proceedings of the 19th IEEE International Parallel and Distributed Processing Symposium (IPDPS'05) - Workshop 15, Washington, DC, USA, IEEE Computer Society (2005) 272.1

[4] Kielmann, T., Hofman, R.F.H., Bal, H.E., Plaat, A., Bhoedjang, R.A.F.: MagPIe: MPI's collective communication operations for clustered wide area systems. In: Proceedings of the seventh ACM SIGPLAN symposium on Principles and Practice of Parallel Programming, ACM Press (1999) 131–140

[5] Forum, M.P.I.: Mpi: A message passing interface standard. http://www.mpi-forum.org/ (1995)

[6] Gropp, W., Lusk, E., Doss, N., Skjellum, A.: A high-performance, portable implementation of the mpi message passing interface standard. Parallel Comput. **22**(6) (1996) 789–828

[7] Fagg, G.E., Bukovsky, A., Dongarra, J.J.: Harness and fault tolerant MPI. Parallel Comput. **27**(11) (2001) 1479–1495

[8] Squyres, J.M., Lumsdaine, A.: The component architecture of open MPI: Enabling third-party collective algorithms. In Getov, V., Kielmann, T., eds.: Proceedings, 18th ACM International Conference on Supercomputing, Workshop on Component Models and Systems for Grid Applications, St. Malo, France, Springer-Verlag (2004) 167–185

[9] Gabriel, E., Fagg, G.E., Bosilca, G., Angskun, T., Dongarra, J.J., Squyres, J.M., Sahay, V., Kambadur, P., Barrett, B., Lumsdaine, A., Castain, R.H., Daniel, D.J., Graham, R.L., Woodall, T.S.: Open MPI: Goals, concept, and design of a next generation MPI implementation. In: Proceedings, 11th European PVM/MPI Users' Group Meeting, Budapest, Hungary (2004) 97–104

[10] Keller, R., Gabriel, E., Krammer, B., Müller, M.S., Resch, M.M.: Towards efficient execution of MPI applications on the grid: Porting and optimization issues. Journal of Grid Computing **1**(2) (2003) 133–149

[11] Gabriel, E., Resch, M., Beisel, T., Keller, R.: Distributed computing in a heterogeneous computing environment. In: Proceedings of the 5th European PVM/MPI Users' Group Meeting on Recent Advances in Parallel Virtual Machine and Message Passing Interface, London, UK, Springer-Verlag (1998) 180–187

[12] Squyres, J.M., Lumsdaine, A.: A component architecture for LAM/MPI. In: Proceedings, European PVM/MPI Users' Group Meeting. (2003)

SELF-HEALING NETWORK FOR SCALABLE FAULT TOLERANT RUNTIME ENVIRONMENTS*

Thara Angskun, Graham E. Fagg, George Bosilca,
Jelena Pješivac–Grbović, and Jack J. Dongarra
Dept. of Computer Science, The University of Tennessee, Knoxville, USA
angskun,fagg,bosilca,pjesa,dongarra@cs.utk.edu

Abstract   Scalable and fault tolerant runtime environments are needed to support and adapt to the underlying libraries and hardware which require a high degree of scalability in dynamic large-scale environments.

This paper presents a self-healing network (SHN) for supporting scalable and fault-tolerant runtime environments. The SHN is designed to support transmission of messages across multiple nodes while also protecting against recursive node and process failures. It will automatically recover itself after a failure occurs. SHN is implemented on top of a scalable fault-tolerant protocol (SFTP). The experimental results show that both the latest multicast and broadcast routing algorithms used in SHN are faster than the original SFTP routing algorithms.

Keywords: Fault tolerance, Routing, Runtime Environment, Scalability, Self-healing.

1.   Introduction

Recently, several of high performance computing platforms have been installed with more than 10,000 CPUs, such as Blue-Gene/L at LLNL, BGW at IBM and Columbia at NASA [6]. However, as the number of components increases, so does the probability of failure. To satisfy the requirements of such a dynamic environment (where the available number of resources is fluctuating), a scalable and fault-tolerance framework is needed. Many large-scale applications are implemented on top of

*This material is based upon work supported by "Los Alamos Computer Science Institute (LACSI)", funded by Rice University Subcontract No. R7B127 under Regents of the University Subcontract No. 12783-001-05 49 and "Open MPI Derived Data Type Engine Enhance and Optimization", funded by the Regents of the University of California (LANL) Subcontract No. 13877-001-05 under DoE/NNSA Prime Contract No. W-7405-ENG-36

message passing systems for which the de-facto standard is the Message Passing Interface (MPI) [11]. MPI implementations require support of parallel runtime environments, which are extensions of the operating system services, and provide necessary functionalities (such as naming resolution services) for both the message passing libraries and applications. However, currently available parallel runtime environments are either not scalable or inefficient in dynamic environments. The lack of scalable fault-tolerance parallel runtime environments motivates us to design and implement such a system. A self-healing network (SHN) that can be used as a basis for constructing a higher level fault-tolerant parallel runtime environment is described in this paper. SHN was designed to support transferring messages across multiple nodes efficiently, while protecting against recursive node or process failures. It was built on top of a scalable and fault-tolerant protocol (SFTP) [1] and automatically recovered itself after a failure occurs.

The structure of this paper is as follows. The next section discusses previous and related work. Section 3 introduces the self-healing network and its recovery algorithm, while the section 4 presents the routing algorithm along with some experimental results, followed by conclusions and future work in the section 5.

2.   Previous and Related Work

Although there are several existing parallel runtime environments for different types of systems, they do not meet some of the major requirements for MPI implementations: scalability, portability and performance. Typically, distributed OS and single system image systems are not portable while the nature of Grid middle-wares has performance problems.

The MPICH implementation [9] uses a parallel runtime environment called Multi-Purposed Daemon (MPD) [4] to providing scalability and fault-tolerance through a ring topology for some operations and a tree topology for others. Runtime environments of other MPI implementations, such as Harness [2] of FT-MPI [7], Open RTE [5] of Open MPI [8] and LAM of LAM/MPI [3], do not currently provide both scalable and fault tolerance solutions for their internal communications.

The scalability and fault-tolerance issues have been addressed in several networking areas. However, those approaches could not be used or they are not efficient in the parallel runtime environments. Structured peer-to-peer networking based on distributed hash tables such as CAN [12], Chord [15], Pastry [14] and Tapestry [16] was designed for resource discovery. They are only optimized for unicast messages. Techniques used in sensor or large scale ad-hoc networking based on gossiping (or the epidemic algorithm) [10] [13] mainly focus on information aggregation.

The scalable and fault-tolerant protocol (SFTP) [1] was introduced to support parallel runtime environments. The protocol is based on a *k-ary* sibling tree. The *k-ary* sibling tree topology is a *k-ary* tree, where k is number of fan-out (k $\geq$ 2), and the nodes on the same level (same depth on the tree) are linked together using a ring topology. The tree is primarily designed to allow scalability for broadcast and multicast operations, while the ring is used to provide a well understood secondary path for transmission when the tree is damaged during failure conditions. The protocol could be used to build a self-healing network which automatically recovers itself to overcome the orphan situation, the situation where nodes are unreachable because the tree becomes a bisection.

3.   Self-Healing Network (SHN)

3.1   Overview

Although the self-healing network (SHN) is designed to support generic runtime environments of MPI implementations, the current work is in a progress to integrate it in a fault-tolerance implementation of message passing interface called FT-MPI as well as in the modular MPI implementation called Open MPI. The network is designed to support various operations needed by scalable and fault-tolerant MPI runtime environments. The example of those operations and the details of how SHN could be used for the operations are as follows.

Distributed Directory Service Directory service is a storage which maintains information used during running an MPI job such as contact information of each process, coordinator of recovery algorithm in FT-MPI etc. The SHN provides a possibility to use the network as a distributed directory service by mapping those information into the logical node ID. Scalable and fault-tolerant information management (update, query) could be done with unicast messages of SFTP routing (similar to resource discovery in the structured peer-to-peer networking).

Standard I/O Redirection Although MPI standard did not define how an input and an output could be treated, most of the MPI implementation redirect the standard output and the standard error to the user terminal (if not run under the batch scheduling). This operation could be done using the k-ary tree as a main route to forward the standard output/error and using the ring in case of failures.

Monitoring Framework A monitoring framework provides information such as processes, nodes, messages for tool and application de-

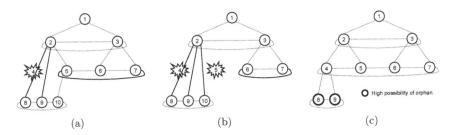

Figure 1.   (a) SHN after recovery [4 dies] (B) SHN after recovery [4,5 die]
(c) high possibility of orphan

velopment. Examples of those tools are parallel debuggers, runtime fault
detectors, runtime verification and load balancers etc. To build a scalable and fault-tolerant monitoring framework, all of the communication
underneath the framework can use multiple types of message transmis-
sions (unicast, multicast and broadcast) provided by the SHN.

In general, the SHN provides a capability to send unicast, multicast
and broadcast messages from any nodes while additionally protecting
against node and process failures, from effecting message delivery.

3.2   SHN Recovery

There are some situations where nodes do not die but become unreachable due to network bisectioning. This situation can be prevented
by self-recovery, when a node detects that its neighbor dies, it will send
a unicast message to establish the connection with the next neighbor in
the same direction of the dead node. If the next neighbor also dies, it
will continue trying to establish the connection with the next node and
so on until success or the next node in that direction is the node itself. If
two nodes try to establish a connection at the same time, the connection
which is initiated by higher ID will be dropped. Figure 1(a) illustrates
an example where logical node 4 dies. All neighbors of node 4 will begin
to recover the logical topology by reestablishing their connections in the
appropriate direction. If node 5 also dies, the same recovery procedure
will occur as shown in figure 1(b). However, there is an exception where
the number of node in the last level (highest depth) of the tree is less
than or equal to k, where k is fanout as shown in figure 1(c). In this case,
the grandparent of the last level needs to know the contact information
of the last level, because if the parent of the last level dies, those nodes
in the last level will become orphans before the self-recover procedure
can occur.

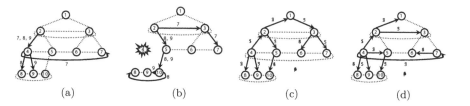

Figure 2. (a) mcast (b) mcast-failure (c) bcast-updown (d) bcast-spanning tree

4. Routing Algorithm in SHN

The SHN routing algorithm is based on the SFTP routing algorithm [1]. The initialize system protocol, unicast message protocol and broadcast from a specific root protocol are the same as the SFTP protocol. The new multicast and broadcast routing algorithms from any nodes in the network, which are an extension of the SFTP routing algorithm have been added. They can be used both before (including some node failures) and after recovery of the logical topology. The SHN routing algorithms can be described as follows.

Multicast messages in SHN

The multicast from any nodes in the SHN is a capability to send messages to several destinations (1 to m, where m < n). Unlike the IP multicast, multicast group management (group creation and termination) is not required. The multicast group members are embedded in the message header. Multicast messages in SFTP are delivered by a sender to the first destination in the destination lists. Then, the first destination will forward the message to the next destination and so on. If an intermediate node is one of the nodes in the destination list, it will remove itself from the list. The order of nodes in the destination list is a descending order sorted by number of hop from a sender to those destinations (i.e. the largest number of hop first). This routing algorithm works fine if the destination nodes are consecutive or they are located in the same area of the tree. The new multicast routing algorithm in SHN is an enhancement of the SFTP multicast routing algorithm. The multicast message can be splitted at an intermediate node, if the shortest paths to those destination nodes are not in the same direction from the intermediate node point of view. However, if there are more than one shortest path to a destination, the intermediate node will choose the next hop which can go along with other destinations. When a node receives a multicast message, it will first determine the header and choose the next hop for each multicast destination according to the shortest path to them. The node will recreate the header corresponding to the

direction of each next hop. Messages that contain the largest number
of hops will be forwarded first to increase network throughput by utilize
multiple links simultaneously. Figure 2(a) shows an example of node 2
sending a multicast message to nodes 7, 8 and 9 with the new routing
algorithm. In case of failure, if a node detects that the next hop for
the multicast messages has died, it automatically reroutes the multicast
messages using an alternate next hop as shown in Figure 2(b). Figure 3(a) depicts that the new multicast routing algorithm is faster than
the original algorithm used in the SFTP. The experiment results were
obtained from an average number of steps for sending multicast messages to 2 destinations with a dead node (fanout=2). The 2 destination
nodes (D) were obtained from combinations of all possible nodes (N) i.e.
$\binom{N}{D}$, where a source node $\notin$ D and the dead node was randomly selected.

Broadcast messages in SHN

Broadcast from any node routing protocol is an enhancement of broadcast routing in SFTP. In SFTP, the broadcast is done by sending messages to a root of the tree and it will forward the messages to the rest of
the tree. Only the tree portion of SFTP is used to prevent a broadcast
storm and duplicate messages. The ring is used only in the case of failure. The first obvious improvement of this routing protocol is to allow
a node between source and a root of the tree to send messages to their
children after they send the messages to their parent (called up-down) as
shown in 2(c) with node 4 as the root. The second improvement is using
a logical spanning tree from the source as shown in 2(d). When each
node receives broadcast messages, it will calculate the next hops using
spanning trees from the source node. There are two steps involving the
next hop calculation. The first step is to create a spanning tree using
a source node as the root node of the tree. The spanning tree creation
algorithm is based on a modified version of the breath first search with
a graph coloring algorithm. The second step is to calculate the next
hop. The next hop is chosen from children of each node according to
the spanning tree which has the highest cost among its children. The
cost is computed from the number of steps used to send a message to all
nodes in the children's subtrees. In case of failure, a broadcast message
is encapsulated into a multicast message, and then the message is sent
from parent of the failure node to its children in the spanning tree. Figure 3(b) indicates that the up-down algorithm is a marginally faster than
the original SFTP, while the new spanning tree broadcast routing algorithm is significant faster than the SFTP broadcast routing algorithm
due to increased parallelism. The experimental results were obtained
from an average number of steps for sending a broadcast message from
every node (fanout=2).

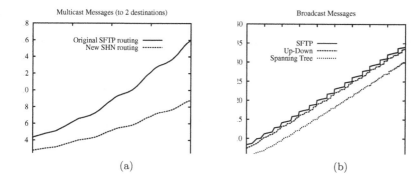

Figure 3. A comparison of routing protocols (a) multicast (b) broadcast

5. Conclusions and Future Work

The self-healing network (SHN) for parallel runtime environments was designed and developed to support runtime environments of MPI implementations. The SHN is implemented on top of a scalable fault-tolerant protocol (SFTP). Simulated performance results indicate that the new routing algorithms of SHN are faster than the original SFTP routing algorithms.

There are several improvements that we plan for the near future. Making the protocol aware of the underlying network topology (in both the LAN and WAN environments) will greatly improve the overall performance for both the broadcast and multicast message distribution. This is equivalent to adding a function cost on each possible path and integrating this function cost to the computation of the shortest path. In the longer term, we hope that the SHN will become the basic message distribution of the runtime environment within the FT-MPI and Open MPI runtime systems.

References

[1] T. Angskun, G. E. Fagg, G. Bosilca, J. Pjesivac-Grbovic, and J. Dongarra. Scalable fault tolerant protocol for parallel runtime environments. In *Proceedings of the 13th European PVM/MPI User's Group Meeting on Recent Advances in Parallel Virtual Machine and Message Passing Interface*, Bonn, Germany, September 2006. Springer-Verlag.

[2] M. Beck, J. J. Dongarra, G. E. Fagg, G. A. Geist, P. Gray, J. Kohl, M. Migliardi, K. Moore, T. Moore, P. Papadopoulous, S. L. Scott, and V. Sunderam. HARNESS: A next generation distributed virtual machine. *Future Generation Computer Systems*, 15(5–6):571–582, 1999.

[3] G. Burns, R. Daoud, and J. Vaigl. LAM: An Open Cluster Environment for MPI. In *Proceedings Supercomputing Symposium*, pages 379–386, 1994.

[4] R. Butler, W. Gropp, and E. L. Lusk. A scalable process-management environment for parallel program. In *Proceedings of the 7th European PVM/MPI User's Group Meeting on Recent Advances in Parallel Virtual Machine and Message Passing Interface*, pages 168–175, London, UK, 2000. Springer-Verlag.

[5] R. H. Castain, T. S. Woodall, D. J. Daniel, J. M. Squyres, B. Barrett, and G. E. Fagg. The open run-time environment (openrte): A transparent multi-cluster environment for high-performance computing. In *Proceedings 12th European PVM/MPI User's Group Meeting on Recent Advances in Parallel Virtual Machine and Message Passing Interface*, Sorrento(Naples), Italy, September 2005. Springer-Verlag.

[6] J. J. Dongarra, H. Meuer, and E. Strohmaier. TOP500 supercomputer sites. *Supercomputer*, 13(1):89–120, 1997.

[7] G. E. Fagg, E. Gabriel, G. Bosilca, T. Angskun, Z. Chen, J. Pjesivac-Grbovic, K. London, and J. Dongarra. Extending the mpi specification for process fault tolerance on high performance computing systems. In *Proceedings of the International Supercomputer Conference (ICS) 2004*, Heidelberg, Germany, June 2006. Primeur.

[8] E. Gabriel, G. E. Fagg, G. Bosilca, T. Angskun, J. J. Dongarra, J. M. Squyres, V. Sahay, P. Kambadur, B. Barrett, A. Lumsdaine, R. H. Castain, D. J. Daniel, R. L. Graham, and T. S. Woodall. Open MPI: Goals, concept, and design of a next generation MPI implementation. In *Proceedings 11th European PVM/MPI User's Group Meeting on Recent Advances in Parallel Virtual Machine and Message Passing Interface*, pages 97–104, Budapest, Hungary, September 2004. Springer-Verlag.

[9] W. Gropp, E. Lusk, N. Doss, and A. Skjellum. A high - performance, portable implementation of MPI message passing interface standard. *Parallel Computing*, 22(6):789–828, 1996.

[10] I. Gupta, R. van Renesse, and K. Birman. Scalable fault-tolerant aggregation in large process groups. In *Proceedings of The International Conference on Dependable Systems and Networks (DSN)*, pages 433–442, 2001.

[11] MPI Forum. MPI: A message-passing interface standard. Technical report, 1994.

[12] S. Ratnasamy, P. Francis, M. Handley, R. Karp, and S. Shenker. A scalable content addressable network. Technical Report TR-00-010, Berkeley, CA, 2000.

[13] R. V. Renesse, Y. Minsky, and M. Hayden. A gossip-style failure detection service. Technical Report TR98-1687, 28, 1998.

[14] A. Rowstron and P. Druschel. Pastry: Scalable, decentralized object location, and routing for large-scale peer-to-peer systems. *Lecture Notes in Computer Science*, 2218:329–350, 2001.

[15] I. Stoica, R. Morris, D. Karger, F. Kaashoek, and H. Balakrishnan. Chord: A scalable Peer-To-Peer lookup service for internet applications. In *Proceedings of the 2001 ACM SIGCOMM Conference*, pages 149–160, 2001.

[16] B. Y. Zhao, J. D. Kubiatowicz, and A. D. Joseph. Tapestry: An infrastructure for fault-tolerant wide-area location and routing. Technical Report UCB/CSD-01-1141, UC Berkeley, April 2001.

SUPPORTING SEAMLESS REMOTE I/O USING A PARALLEL NETCDF INTERFACE

Yuichi Tsujita
Department of Electronic Engineering and Computer Science,
Faculty of Engineering, Kinki University
1 Umenobe, Takaya, Higashi-Hiroshima, Hiroshima 739-2116, Japan
tsujita@hiro.kindai.ac.jp

Abstract   In scientific applications, netCDF was proposed for storing datasets created and used by them to provide portable I/O operations on a wide variety of platforms. Besides, its parallel I/O interface, parallel netCDF, was developed with the help of an MPI-I/O library. To realize the same operations among computers which have different MPI libraries, a remote I/O mechanism of a Stampi library, which is a flexible intermediate library to realize seamless MPI operations both inside a computer and among computers, has been introduced in some of parallel netCDF functions. This newly implemented mechanism has been evaluated on interconnected PC clusters, and sufficient performance has been achieved with huge amount of data.

Keywords: MPI, MPI-I/O, Stampi, MPI-I/O process, parallel netCDF

1.   Introduction

NetCDF [Rew et al., 2006, Rew and Davis, 1990] is a popular package for storing and retrieving data files in scientific computation application domains. It provides a view of data as a collection of self-describing, portable, and array-oriented objects that can be accessed through a simple interface on a wide variety of platforms. Atmospheric science applications, for example, use netCDF to store a variety of data types that encompass single-point observations, time series, regularly spaced grids, and satellite or radar images [Rew et al., 2006]. Its parallel I/O interface named parallel netCDF (hereafter PnetCDF) was developed with the help of an MPI-I/O library [Message Passing Interface Forum, 1997] such as ROMIO [Thakur et al., 1999], and the PnetCDF succeeded in scientific computation [Li et al., 2003]. Although it supports parallel I/O operations within the same MPI library, the same operations among computers which have different MPI libraries each other have not been available. To realize this mechanism, a remote MPI-I/O mechanism of a Stampi library [Tsujita

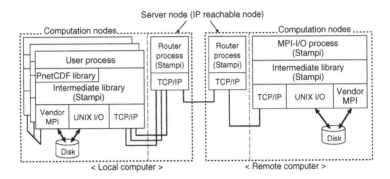

Figure 1.   Architecture of a seamless remote I/O system.

et al., 2005] has been implemented in a PnetCDF library as an underlying MPI-I/O layer.

The Stampi library was originally developed to support seamless MPI communications among different MPI libraries by deploying its wrapper interface library between a user program and an underlying communication library [Imamura et al., 2000]. It intermediates MPI communications among different MPI libraries and hides complexity and heterogeneity in communication mechanisms among different platforms. It also supports MPI-I/O operations not only inside a computer using an underlying MPI library but also among computers which have different MPI libraries [Tsujita et al., 2005]. MPI-I/O calls in a user program are switched to corresponding Stampi's MPI-I/O functions in the wrapper library, and it considers which I/O operation is appropriate, local or remote I/O operations, automatically. A PnetCDF library has been linked with the Stampi's MPI-I/O functions to support seamless remote I/O operations through a PnetCDF interface without paying attention to complexity and heterogeneity in underlying communication and I/O systems. In this paper, architecture and execution mechanism of it are discussed in Section 2. Preliminary performance results are reported in Section 3. Related work is discussed in Section 4, followed by conclusions in Section 5.

2.   Remote I/O with a PnetCDF Interface

In this section, details of architecture and execution mechanism of the remote I/O system are explained and discussed.

Architecture

Architecture of the I/O system is illustrated in Figure 1. A target computer name, file name, and so on are specified in an `info` object, and a Stampi library identifies which operation is requested, local or remote I/O operations,

Table 1.   Typical PnetCDF functions and used MPI functions.

PnetCDF function	Used MPI functions
ncmpi_create()	MPI_File_open(), MPI_File_delete(), etc.
ncmpi_open()	MPI_File_open(), MPI_File_delete(), etc.
ncmpi_put_var_int()	MPI_Comm_rank(), MPI_File_set_view(), MPI_Type_hvector(),
	MPI_Type_commit(), MPI_Type_free(), MPI_File_write(), etc.
ncmpi_close()	MPI_Allreduce(), MPI_File_close(), etc.

according to them in the info object. Typical PnetCDF functions and their associated MPI functions are listed in Table 1. ncmpi_create() creates a new netCDF data file, while ncmpi_open() opens an existing netCDF data file. Basically both functions use almost the same MPI functions as shown in the table. ncmpi_put_var_int() writes data to a netCDF data file with a derived data type in a non-collective manner. Therefore it uses MPI functions to make a derived data type and MPI-I/O functions. ncmpi_close() closes an opened netCDF file with the help of MPI_File_close(). To realize seamless remote I/O operations with a netCDF data format, Stampi's MPI functions are used as the MPI functions inside each PnetCDF function.

Inside a local computer, high performance MPI operations are realized using vendor's MPI library. When a PnetCDF function is called in a user program, the I/O call is translated into associated Stampi's MPI function calls. Later, parallel I/O operations are carried out by using vendor's MPI library through the Stampi's functions. If the vendor's one is not available, UNIX I/O functions are used instead of it.

On the other hand, an MPI-I/O process is invoked on a remote computer to realize remote MPI-I/O operations by using a remote shell command (rsh or ssh) when ncmpi_create() or ncmpi_open() is called, followed by a function call of MPI_File_open() inside them. Each I/O request from Stampi's MPI functions is transfered to the MPI-I/O process, and it plays requested I/O operations. The I/O operations are carried out on a target computer by using vendor's MPI-I/O library or UNIX I/O functions if the vendor's one is not available.

In the both operations, derived data types are created from primitive data types to support a PnetCDF API. Associated parameters for the derived ones such as an original data type and a stride length are stored in a linked list based table in both user and MPI-I/O processes. Prior to I/O operations, the parameters are retrieved from it to make the same derived data type and file view among a user process and an MPI-I/O process.

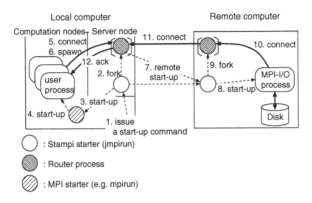

Figure 2. Execution mechanism of remote I/O operations.

Execution mechanism

Schematic diagram of an execution mechanism of the I/O system is depicted in Figure 2. Firstly, user issues Stampi's start-up command (Stampi starter; jmpirun), then it calls a native MPI start-up command (MPI starter) such as mpirun. The MPI starter invokes user processes. Besides, a router process is also created by it if computation nodes are not able to communicate outside directly. Once a function, ncmpi_create() or ncmpi_open(), is called, another Stampi starter is invoked on the remote computer by the Stampi starter or the router process on a local computer. The invoked Stampi starter kicks off an MPI-I/O process. In addition, a router process is invoked by the starter if computation nodes of the remote computer are not able to communicate outside directly. Finally, a communication path is established among the user processes and the MPI-I/O process.

After I/O operations, the MPI-I/O process closes the specified file, and it is terminated when ncmpi_close() is called. Finally, whole I/O operation finishes.

3.   Performance Evaluation

To evaluate the newly implemented remote I/O system, its performance was measured on two interconnected PC clusters. Specifications of the clusters are summarized in Table 2. Each cluster had one server node and four computation nodes. Interconnection between the clusters was made with 1 Gbps bandwidth via Gigabit Ethernet switches of both clusters.

In a PC cluster-I, MPICH [Gropp et al., 1996] version 1.2.6 was installed, and it was called from a Stampi library. In a PC cluster-II, an SCore cluster system [PC Cluster Consortium,] was installed. Although its built-in MPI library, MPICH-SCore, was available, it was not used in this test because an MPI-I/O

Table 2. Specifications of PC clusters which were used in performance evaluation, where **server** and **comp** in bold font denote server node and computation nodes, respectively

	PC cluster-I	PC cluster-II
server	DELL PowerEdge800 × 1	DELL PowerEdge1600SC × 1
comp	DELL PowerEdge800 × 4	DELL PowerEdge1600SC × 4
CPU	Intel Pentium-4 3.6 GHz × 1	Intel Xeon 2.4 GHz × 2
Chipset	Intel E7221	ServerWorks GC-SL
Memory	1 GByte DDR2 533 SDRAM	2 GByte DDR 266 SDRAM
Disk system	80 GByte (Serial ATA) × 1	73 GByte (Ultra320 SCSI) × 1 (**server**)
	(all nodes)	73 GByte (Ultra320 SCSI) × 2 (**comp**)
NIC	Broadcom BCM5721 (on-board)	Intel PRO/1000-XT (PCI-X card)
Switch	3Com SuperStack3 Switch 3812	3Com SuperStack3 Switch 4900
OS	Fedora Core 3	RedHat Linux 7.3
	kernel 2.6.11-1.14_FC3smp	kernel 2.4.20-29.7smp (**server**)
	(all nodes)	kernel 2.4.21-2SCOREsmp (**comp**)
NIC driver	Broadcom BCM5700 Linux	Intel e1000 version 5.5.4
	driver version 7.3.5	

process used UNIX I/O. In addition, PVFS [Carns et al., 2000] version 1.6.3 was available on its server node by collecting disk spaces (73 GByte each) of four computation nodes. Thus 292 GByte (4×73 GByte) was available for the file system. During this test, default stripe size (64 KByte) of it was selected.

A user process was executed on the PC cluster-I and an MPI-I/O process was invoked on the PC cluster-II. A router process was not invoked on both clusters because each computation node was able to communicate outside directly.

PnetCDF functions were evaluated using three-dimensional data. The data set with $16 \times 16 \times 16$ (16 KByte), $64 \times 64 \times 64$ (1 MByte), and $256 \times 256 \times 256$ (64 MByte) were prepared with an integer data type. Sequence of function calls in a test program is illustrated in Figure 3. In write operation which is shown in Fig. 3 (a), information which was associated with the I/O operations was set in an `info` object by `MPI_Info_set()` prior to I/O operations. `ncmpi_create()` created a new netCDF file according to the information. Besides, several kinds of parameters which were associated with the file were stored in a record header of it in define mode by using several PnetCDF functions. Independent I/O operation mode was set by `ncmpi_begin_indep()`. Real data were written to it by `ncmpi_put_var_int()` with an integer data type, and `ncmpi_end_indep_data()` finished the mode. Finally the file was closed by `ncmpi_close()`, and all the I/O operations finished. Read operation which is illustrated in Fig. 3 (b) was made in the same manner ex-

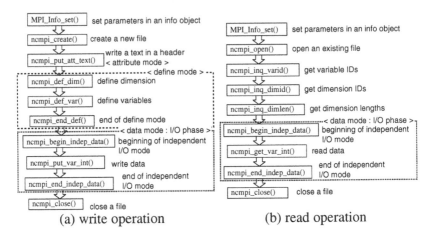

Figure 3. Sequence of function calls in a test program.

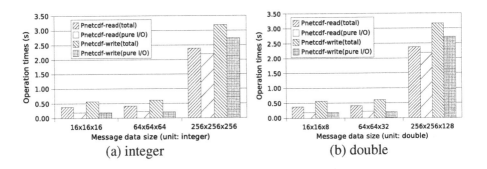

Figure 4. Total I/O times and pure I/O times for remote I/O operations using PnetCDF functions with (a) integer and (b) double data types.

cept that inquiry of parameters from record header of a PnetCDF file and reading data from it were done. Elapsed times from `ncmpi_create()` or `ncmpi_open()` to `ncmpi_close()` and times to issue `ncmpi_put_var_int()` or `ncmpi_get_var_int()` were measured using `MPI_Wtime()` in a test program.

Firstly, execution times for remote I/O operations using integer and double data types were measured. Figure 4 shows the times. In this figure, "Pnetcdf-read" and "Pnetcdf-write" denote read and write operations through PnetCDF functions, respectively. Besides, "total" in parentheses denotes times from opening to closing a netCDF file (total I/O times). While "pure I/O" in parentheses denotes times for real data I/O operations (pure I/O times). With $16 \times 16 \times 16$ and $64 \times 64 \times 64$ for message data size in the integer case, the pure I/O times were around a half of the total I/O times. The same results were observed in the double data type case with $16 \times 16 \times 8$ and $64 \times 64 \times 32$ in message data size. It is also noticed that there was not significant difference in the pure I/O times with those data sizes although message data size increased in both integer and double cases. On the other hand, the total and pure I/O times became long with $256 \times 256 \times 256$ for integer and $256 \times 256 \times 128$ for double. In these situation, times for real data I/O became dominant.

Times which had no relation with pure I/O operations (non-I/O times) were roughly estimated as total I/O times minus pure I/O times. For example, the times were about 0.2 s for $16 \times 16 \times 16$ and $64 \times 64 \times 64$ and 0.35 s for $256 \times 256 \times 256$ in the write operations. Thus the times were almost the same with respect to message data size although the times became slightly long with an increase in message data size in the write operations. As `MPI_File_open()` is called inside `ncmpi_create()` and `ncmpi_open()`, times to call the MPI function was measured. The times was about 0.2 s in this setup, and it is considered that the non-I/O times were almost the same with the times for `MPI_File_open()`. Inside the function, creation of an MPI-I/O process on a target remote computer and opening a target file were carried out. It is noticed that this is not significant problem because `ncmpi_create()` or `ncmpi_open()` are usually called once prior to I/O operations.

Secondly, the pure I/O times were compared with I/O times of Stampi's MPI-I/O functions in remote I/O operations to evaluate overhead introduced by implementation of PnetCDF functions. In this test, an integer data type was used for both functions. For the MPI-I/O functions, a primitive integer data type was used although the PnetCDF functions used a derived data type which was prepared from an integer data type. 16 KByte, 1 MByte, and 64 MByte were selected as data size for the MPI-I/O functions so as to be equal to message data size used in the PnetCDF I/O operations. Measured times are shown in Figure 5. In this figure, "MPI-I/O read (simple)" and "MPI-I/O write (simple)" denote I/O times for Stampi's `MPI_File_read()` and `MPI_File_write()`, respectively, while "Pnetcdf-read (pure I/O)" and "Pnetcdf-write (pure I/O)" denote pure I/O times for the previous PnetCDF's read and write functions, respectively. With small message data size, the MPI-I/O functions outperformed the PnetCDF functions, whereas times for the PnetCDF functions were comparable with those for the MPI-I/O functions with $256 \times 256 \times 256$ in message data size. In this case, they are 12 % and 0.8 % longer than those for the MPI-I/O functions in read and write operations, respectively. The differences in the times were due to calls of several MPI functions to make a derived data type in the PnetCDF case. It is noticed that data transfer among clusters in the functions was dominant in the

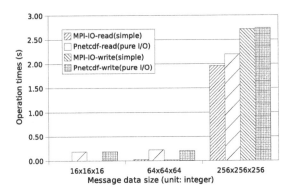

Figure 5.   Pure I/O times for PnetCDF functions and I/O times for Stampi's MPI-I/O functions in remote I/O operations.

whole operation time. It is considered that the PnetCDF functions are able to provide substantial performance with such huge amount of data.

4.   Related Work

Providing a common data format makes data I/O operations not only portable but also tolerate for application programmers. This kind of implementations such as netCDF [Rew et al., 2006] and HDF5 [The National Center for Super-computing Applications,] has been proposed.

NetCDF provides a common multi-dimensional data format which has a portability among different computer architectures. Users are able to access data via a netCDF API without paying attention to each computer architecture. Parallel I/O operations have been realized as parallel netCDF (PnetCDF), as an extension of the interface by introducing MPI-I/O functions as an underlying parallel I/O library [Li et al., 2003].

On the other hand, HDF5 provides hierarchical data format so as to access huge amount of data effectively. An HDF5 interface has two objects, one is "Dataset" and another is "Group". The Dataset manages multi-dimensional array data, while the Group provides relational mechanisms among objects. Parallel I/O operations are also available by introducing MPI-I/O functions as an underlying parallel I/O interface library [Ross et al., 2001].

An MPI-I/O interface was proposed in the MPI-2 standard [Message Passing Interface Forum, 1997] to realize parallel I/O operations in an MPI program. The MPI-I/O interface is available in several kinds of implementations such as ROMIO [Thakur et al., 1999]. Its MPI-I/O operations to many kinds of file systems are realized through an ADIO interface [Thakur et al., 1996]. The ADIO interface hides heterogeneity in architectures of each systems and provides a common interface to an upper MPI-I/O layer. Remote I/O operations using ROMIO are available with the help of RFS [Lee et al., 2004]. An RFS request handler on a remote computer receives I/O requests from client processes and calls an appropriate ADIO library. On the other hand, Stampi itself is not an MPI implementation, and it provides an intermediate library among different MPI libraries by using TCP socket communications for seamless MPI operations on heterogeneous environment. Stampi realizes MPI communications and MPI-I/O operations not only inside the same MPI library but also among different libraries without any attention to heterogeneity in underlying communication and I/O systems.

5. Summary

Remote I/O operations using a PnetCDF interface have been realized with the help of Stampi's remote I/O mechanism. Through performance measurement, the more message data size became long, the more times to open a PnetCDF file became negligible. With a huge amount of data, times for real data I/O operations using PnetCDF functions were comparable with times for I/O operations by using Stampi's MPI-I/O functions with a primitive data type. It is considered that the PnetCDF interface provides sufficient performance for such huge amount of data with seamless I/O accesses.

Although the primitive PnetCDF functions provided sufficient I/O performance, collective I/O operations have not been implemented yet. To expand its functionality in data-intensive parallel computation, it is required to implement collective functions as future plan. Besides, implementation in several kinds of applications is also planed to evaluate its performance in real applications.

Acknowledgments

The author would like to thank Genki Yagawa, director of Center for Computational Science and Engineering (CCSE), Japan Atomic Energy Agency (JAEA), for his continuous encouragement. The author would like to thank the staff at CCSE, JAEA for providing a Stampi library and giving useful information.

This research was partially supported by the Ministry of Education, Culture, Sports, Science and Technology (MEXT), Grant-in-Aid for Young Scientists (B), 18700074 and by the CASIO Science Promotion Foundation.

References

[Carns et al., 2000] Carns, P. H., Ligon III, W. B., Ross, R. B., and Thakur, R. (2000). PVFS: A parallel file system for Linux clusters. In *Proceedings of the 4th Annual Linux Showcase and Conference*, pages 317–327. USENIX Association.

[Gropp et al., 1996] Gropp, W., Lusk, E., Doss, N., and Skjellum, A. (1996). A high-performance, portable implementation of the MPI Message-Passing Interface standard. *Parallel Computing*, 22(6):789–828.

[Imamura et al., 2000] Imamura, T., Tsujita, Y., Koide, H., and Takemiya, H. (2000). An architecture of Stampi: MPI library on a cluster of parallel computers. In Dongarra, J., Kacsuk, P., and Podhorszki, N., editors, *Recent Advances in Parallel Virtual Machine and Message Passing Interface, 7th European PVM/MPI Users' Group Meeting, Balatonfüred, Hungary, September 2000, Proceedings*, volume 1908 of *Lecture Notes in Computer Science*, pages 200–207. Springer.

[Lee et al., 2004] Lee, J., Ma, X., Ross, R., Thakur, R., and Winslett, M. (2004). RFS: Efficient and flexible remote file access for MPI-IO. In *Proceedings of the 6th IEEE International Conference on Cluster Computing (CLUSTER 2004)*, pages 71–81. IEEE Computer Society.

[Li et al., 2003] Li, J., Liao, W.-K., Choudhary, A., Ross, R., Thakur, R., Gropp, W., Latham, R., Siegel, A., Gallagher, B., and Zingale, M. (2003). Parallel netCDF: A high-performance scientific I/O interface. In *SC '03: Proceedings of the 2003 ACM/IEEE Conference on Supercomputing*, page 39. IEEE Computer Society.

[Message Passing Interface Forum, 1997] Message Passing Interface Forum (1997). *MPI-2: Extensions to the Message-Passing Interface*.

[PC Cluster Consortium,] PC Cluster Consortium. http://www.pccluster.org/.

[Rew et al., 2006] Rew, R., Davis, G., Emmerson, S., Davies, H., and Hartnett, E. (2006). *NetCDF User's Guide*. Unidata Program Center. http://www.unidata.ucar.edu/software/netcdf/docs/netcdf/.

[Rew and Davis, 1990] Rew, R. K. and Davis, G. P. (1990). The unidata netCDF: Software for scientific data access. In *Sixth International Conference on Interactive Information and Processing Systems for Meteorology, Oceanography, and Hydrology*, pages 33–40. American Meteorology Society.

[Ross et al., 2001] Ross, R., Nurmi, D., Cheng, A., and Zingale, M. (2001). A case study in application I/O on Linux clusters. In *SC '01: Proceedings of the 2001 ACM/IEEE Conference on Supercomputing (CDROM)*, page 11. ACM Press.

[Thakur et al., 1996] Thakur, R., Gropp, W., and Lusk, E. (1996). An abstract-device interface for implementing portable parallel-I/O interfaces. In *Proceedings of the Sixth Symposium on the Frontiers of Massively Parallel Computation*, pages 180–187.

[Thakur et al., 1999] Thakur, R., Gropp, W., and Lusk, E. (1999). On implementing MPI-IO portably and with high performance. In *Proceedings of the Sixth Workshop on Input/Output in Parallel and Distributed Systems*, pages 23–32.

[The National Center for Supercomputing Applications,] The National Center for Supercomputing Applications. http://hdf.ncsa.uiuc.edu/HDF5/.

[Tsujita et al., 2005] Tsujita, Y., Imamura, T., Yamagishi, N., and Takemiya, H. (2005). Flexible message passing interface for a heterogeneous computing environment. In Guo, M. and Yang, L. T., editors, *New Horizons of Parallel and Distributed Computing*, chapter 1, pages 3–19. Springer.

III

GRID AND WEB SERVICES

GENERATING SEMANTIC DESCRIPTIONS OF WEB AND GRID SERVICES

Marian Babik,[1] Ladislav Hluchy,[1] Jacek Kitowski,[2] Bartosz Kryza,[3]
[1] *Institute of Informatics, Slovak Academy of Sciences, Slovakia*
[2] *Institute of Computer Science, AGH University of Science and Technology, Poland*
[3] *ACK Cyfronet AGH, Poland*

Abstract   Web Service Resource Framework (WSRF) is a recent effort of the grid community to facilitate modeling of the stateful services [11]. Design and development of the WSRF service based systems is quite common and there are several emerging WS initiatives, which tries to automate the process of discovery, composition and invocation of such services. The semantic web services are a typical example, showing the potential of how ontological modeling can improve the shortcomings of the service oriented computing. One of the major obstacles in the process is the development of the ontologies, which describe web and grid services. Although, there are numerous standards for modeling semantic services, there are very few frameworks and tools, which can help automate the process of generating the semantic descriptions of services. This article presents a tool, which can semi-automatically generate the OWL-S descriptions for both stateful and stateless services based on the Web Service Description Language (WSDL) and corresponding annotations. Such functionality is inevitable in the grid environment hosting a vast number of services, which have to be semantically described in order to enable automated discovery, composition and invocation.

Keywords: grid services, semantic grids, web services, wsrf, owl-s

1.   Introduction

Recently, Web service (WS) technologies are gaining importance in the implementation of distributed systems, especially grids. One such example is the Web Service Resource Framework (WSRF) [11], which extends the current WS technologies by modeling the stateful services. Design and development of the service oriented distributed system is quite common and there are several emerging WS initiatives, which tries to automate the process of discovery, composition and invocation of services. The semantic web services are a typical example, showing the potential of how ontological modeling can improve the shortcomings of service oriented computing.

In this paper we will introduce basic concepts of semantic web services (OWL-S) and web service resource framework (WSRF). Further, we will present the process of adding semantics to the stateful services and highlight the major issues, that we have faced during the development of the WSRF2OWL-S tool. We will also describe the corresponding architecture of the system and provide an illustrating use case of its functionality.

2.   Web Ontology of Services (OWL-S)

OWL-S is an ontology-based approach to the semantic web services [5]. The structure of the ontology consists of a service profile for advertising and discovering services, a process model which supports composition of services, and a service grounding, which associates profile and process concepts with underlying service interfaces (see Fig. 1). Service profile (OWL-S profile) has functional and non-functional properties. The functional properties describe the inputs, outputs, preconditions and effects (IOPE) of the service. The non-functional properties describe the semi-structured information intended for human users, e.g. service name, service description, and service parameter. Service parameter incorporates further requirements on the service capabilities, e.g. security, quality-of-service, geographical scope, etc. Service grounding (OWL-S grounding) enables the execution of the concrete Web service by binding the abstract concepts of the OWL-S profile and process to concrete messages. Although different message specifications can be supported by OWL-S, the widely accepted Web Service Description Language (WSDL) is preferred [9].

3.   Adding Semantics to the Stateful Services

Service annotation is the process of generating the semantic descriptions (i.e. OWL-S) of both stateless and stateful services from the web service descriptions (i.e. WSDLs). In K-Wf Grid it has become crucial in the process of providing application support and enabling semantics for semantically unaware grid application areas [14]. In the following we will present the issues that we have faced during the design of the ontologies for the stateful services and we will briefly describe the developed annotation tool called WSRF2OWL-S.

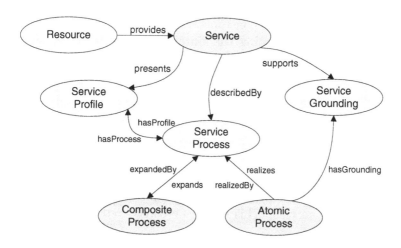

Figure 1. OWL-S concepts.

WS-Resource semantics

In OWL-S, the service capabilities are described by the corresponding IOPE (inputs, outputs, preconditions and effects). Such description can be partly annotated from the WSDL description of the service and is sufficient for the stateless service. Stateful services, i.e. WS-Resources, are, however, composed of a service and a stateful resource [11]. A stateful resource is defined by a single XML Global Element Declaration (GED) in a given namespace. Such GED defines the type of the stateful resource and is motivated by the modeling of complex objects for stateless services. For modeling semantics of the stateful resources this means there are no major differences between stateful and stateless services, i.e. the domain concepts can be derived from the complex types definitions in the service description. There are, however, few important issues, that should be noted.

Resource properties (RP), as defined in the WSRF specification, can be dynamic. This means that it is possible to create and destroy properties on the fly, i.e. if stateful service is providing access to the filesystem and resource properties are listing the file attributes, it is possible to add or remove a file attribute at any given time. In order to model such dynamic behavior by corresponding semantics, it is necessary to consider more advanced techniques for ontological mapping and concept definition. Since such procedures can become quite complicated, we have concentrated our work on the area of static resource properties, i.e. it is possible to change the values of the properties, but the set of properties for given resource remains constant over time.

In the process of designing the stateful services it is possible to use inheritance of the resource properties. Although explicit hierarchy of the resource properties can help in the generation of the semantics, there is no standard, which would describe in details how RP inheritance should be implemented. This can cause major difficulties in parsing of the services and it is necessary to introduce special parsers to extract the RP hierarchies. Furthermore, resource properties can often be used to model the actual inputs and outputs of the service, i.e. a service submitting specific jobs to the cluster can represent the inputs and outputs as properties of the job, thus hiding the inputs/outputs in the resource properties of the service. This has to be considered in the service composition.

Apart from the issues in the process of service discovery, there are also slight differences in the process of service invocation. The WS-Resource is composed of a service and a stateful resource, i.e. it is identified by the so called EPR (end point reference), which describes not only service address but also the identification of a resource. The service identification in the OWL-S Grounding has to be then extended to a more complex structure. For the grid services such extension can also consider the possibility of having multiple instances of the same service hosted by different servers. This can, however, be solved simply by introducing multiple OWL-S Groundings.

Generating OWL-S from web service descriptions

We have designed and developed a tool for generating the OWL-S description for stateful and stateless services from the corresponding web service descriptions (WSDLs) [9]. Such tool is inevitable in the grid environment hosting a vast number of services, which have to be semantically described in order to enable automated discovery, composition and invocation. In the initial stage of the K-Wf Grid project we have successfully used the tool to create semantic descriptions of the services for the flood forecasting domain.

The architecture of the so called WSRF2OWL-S tool is shown in Fig. 2. The main components of the architecture are WSRF2OWL-S engine, translator and GOMOWL-S API. GOMOWL-S API is an extension of the Mindswap's OWL-S API [5]; it defines additional vocabulary, converters and extensions needed by the WSRF (e.g. SimpleEffect, DataObjectInput, etc.). The translation procedure is quite complex and covers

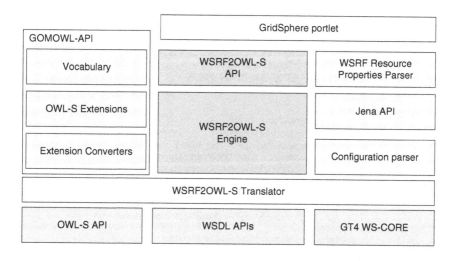

Figure 2. Architecture of the WSRF2OWL-S tool.

the areas already described in previous sections. The translation starts with a configuration and an URL of the WSDL document. The translator parses the WSDL document extracting the operations, port-types, inputs, outputs as well as resource properties. A combination of the WSDL4J [22], Axis WSDL [23] and Globus Toolkit WSDL utilities [12] are used in the process. The translator then generates for each WSDL operation a skeleton of the OWL-S document. Then it creates the inputs, outputs, preconditions and effects and maps the elements to the ontological concepts defined in the configuration. If needed, it will create an ontology, which models the resource properties of the given services. The GOMOWL-S API can be used to extend the OWL-S by the domain dependent constructs, e.g. FloodForecastingWSRFProfile, DataObject-Input, SimpleEffect, etc. The outcome of the process is OWL-S document describing the web service operations, which are then be composed into the workflow [19]. Additionally a GridSphere portlet was developed to provide a graphical user interface for the tool [17]. It supports browsing of the concepts for any given ontology, associating the concepts with the WSDL elements and generation of the OWL-S documents. An automated annotation procedure based on the case-based reasoning is also integrated.

WSDL description

```
<wsdl:portType name="MM5ServicePortType"
             wsrp:ResourceProperties="tns:MM5Properties">
  <wsdl:operation name="configureFromProperties">
   <wsdl:input message="tns:ConfigureInputMessage"/>
   <wsdl:output message="types:VoidOutputMessage"/>
  </wsdl:operation>

...
<wsdl:service name="MM5Service">
  <wsdl:port name="MM5ServicePortTypePort"
           binding="binding:MM5ServicePortTypeSOAPBinding">
   <soap:address location="http://localhost:8080/wsrf/services/"/>
  ...
```

Configuration

```
MM5Service.configureFromProperties.properties=
http://gom.kwfgrid.net/gom/ontology/DomainApplicationOntology/
FFSC#MM5Properties
MM5Service.configureFromProperties.voidResponse=
effect|http://gom.kwfgrid.net/gom/ontology/DomainServiceOntology/
FFSC#MM5isConfigured
```

OWL-S description

```
<service:Service rdf:ID="configureFromProperties_MM5Service">
  <service:presents>
   <profile:Profile rdf:ID="configureFromProperties_MM5Profile"/>
  </service:presents>
  <service:describedBy>
   <process:AtomicProcess
rdf:ID="configureFromProperties_MM5AtomicProcess"/>
  </service:describedBy>
  <service:supports>
   <grounding:WsdlGrounding
rdf:ID="configureFromProperties_MM5Grounding"/>
  </service:supports>
 </service:Service>
...
<profile:Profile rdf:about="#configureFromProperties_MM5Profile">
<profile:hasInput>
   <process:Input rdf:ID="properties">
    <process:parameterType>http://gom.kwfgrid.net/gom/
ontology/DomainApplicationOntology/FFSC#MM5Properties
   </process:parameterType>
   </process:Input>
  ...
```

Figure 3.   Sample translation of the MM5 configureFromProperties method

4.   Application Scenario

The flood forecasting application (FFSC) is based on a network of
loosely coupled, cooperating but independent services. It has been used
as a pilot application in the project K-WfGrid and CrossGrid [21, 13].
The application consists of three major components, namely, meteorol-

ogy, hydrology and hydraulics. Each component has several possible models of computation represented by the corresponding web or grid services, e.g., meteorological methods Aladin, MM5; hydrological methods HSPF, NLC, etc.

The translation of the WSDL description of a sample meteorological service MM5 is shown in Fig. 3. Since each service has multiple operations, the semantic descriptions are generated for each operation, thus enabling the possibility to create workflows of service operations [19]. In the example a sample operation configureFromProperties is shown. Apart from WSDL description the translation process also needs configuration, which describes the mapping of the WSDL inputs/outputs to the domain ontological concepts. These concepts can describe information about service (e.g. service name, provider), but also complex inputs and outputs of the service, such as geographical location, geographical information data, watershed, etc. Further they are used to identify the HTML forms, which are presented to the user if additional input is necessary.

Apart from flood forecasting simulations, WSRF2OWL-S was successfully used in generating the semantic description of services for the enterprise resource planning and coordinated traffic management applications [14]. In the future we would like to concentrate on improving the configuration capabilities and broader WSRF support.

5. Related work

One of the challenges of the loosely coupled distributed systems is the ability to dynamically discover and integrate the services needed by the applications. Interoperability among services is especially important in the distributed environments hosting a large number of services, i.e. grids. Semantic descriptions facilitates the process by expressing the characteristics of the service, which is one of the goals of the Semantic Grid initiative [1]. There are many projects, which are trying to develop an architecture for the Semantic Grid such as [2, 4, 3]. S-OGSA is trying to extend OGSA based architecture and provide a reference architecture with explicit handling of semantics as well as defining the associated knowledge services. Guided by the set of design principles it defines a model, the capabilities and mechanisms for the Semantic Grid [2]. InteliGrid aims at developing a grid architecture based on three layers, i.e. conceptual, software and basic resource [3]. Unlike our approach the mentioned projects are trying to address the Grid semantics by a top-down approach, creating reference architectures, which should cover a broad range of applications and requirements. In contrary,

WSRF2OWL-S can be seen as a bottom-up approach, which is trying to leverage as much as possible from the existing Semantic Web Service technologies. A similar approach can be seen in the ^{my}Grid, which is a pioneering Semantic Grid project, providing a set of tools and services to enable workflow composition in biological domain [4]. It is however more focused on the support for the OGSA and OGSA-DAI, while we aim at supporting WSRF and OWL-S, which have shown to be more suited for the domain of the K-Wf Grid applications.

The actual transformation process for the stateless services is provided by two WSDL2OWL-S tools [5, 7]. Both tools are based on the corresponding OWL-S API libraries and provide either web-based or graphical user interface. WSRF2OWL-S extends these tools with support for the WSRF service descriptions as well as possibility to use command line tool for batch processing multiple descriptions at once. In terms of service annotation, ASSAM is one of the existing automated semantic web service annotators with machine learning capabilities [8].

In the domain of Semantic Web Services, the Web Service Modeling Framework (WSMF)[15] is an industry scale framework for semantic web service discovery, execution and composition. It is a joint effort of the European research projects on the Semantic Web and Semantic Web Services. It has three development areas concerning conceptual model (WSMO), the representation language (WSML) and the execution framework (WSMX). Although WSMF approach is much more profound and shows many significant contributions to modeling semantic web services, the level of implementation and the development support at the time of evaluation was unacceptable for our purposes. However, since WSMF has gained an enormous momentum in the last year, it will be considered in our future work.

The Internet Reasoning Service (IRS-III) [18] is a Java framework for publishing, locating, composing and executing semantic web services. IRS-II is modeling service based on the tasks, that need to be fulfilled and the problem-solving-methods (PSM) that can be used to solve specific tasks. It utilizes a formal language called Operational Conceptual Modeling Language (OCML). It supports the specification and operationalization of functions, relations, classes, instances and rules. This appears to be more suitable for procedural knowledge representation than OWL. One of the disadvantages of the system is the process of assigning services the corresponding tasks, which has to be done manually, which introduces many possibilities for failure.

METEOR-S [16] attempts to add semantics to the basic stateless web service descriptions by adding semantics to current industry standards. It is an effort of the LSDIS Lab of the University of Georgia. The framework presents an interesting bottom-up approach to the semantic descriptions, the service annotation and WSDL-S, semantic extension of the WSDL.

Acknowledgments

Acknowledgments: The research reported in this paper has been partially financed by the EU within the project IST-2004-511385 K-WfGrid and Slovak national projects, APVT-51-024604; Tools for acquisition, organization and maintenance of knowledge in an environment of heterogeneous information resources, SPVV 1025/04 and VEGA No. 2/6103/6.

References

[1] Goble, C., De Roure, D., "The Semantic Grid: Myth Busting and Bridge Building", in Proceedings of the 16th European Conference on Artificial Intelligence (ECAI-2004), Valencia, Spain, 2004

[2] Alper, P., Corcho, O., Kotsiopoulos, I., Missier, P., Bechhofer, S., Goble, C., S-OGSA as a Reference Architecture for OntoGrid and for the Semantic Grid, GGF16 Semantic Grid Workshop. Athens, Greece. February 2006

[3] Turk, Z., Stankovski, V., Gehre, A., Katranuschkov, P., Kurowski, K., Balaton, E., Hyvarinen, J., Dolenc, M., Klinc, R., Kostanjsek, J. and Velkavrh J., "Semantic Grid Architecture," 2004

[4] C. Wroe, C. A. Goble, M. Greenwood, P. Lord, S. Miles, J. Papay, T. Payne, and L. Moreau, "Automating Experiments Using Semantic Data on a Bioinformatics Grid," IEEE Intelligent Systems, vol. 19, pp. 48-55, 2004

[5] A. Ankolekar et al, OWL-S: Semantic Markup for Web Service, 2003, http://www.daml.org/services/owl-s/1.1

[6] Mindswap OWL-S API, http://www.mindswap.org/2004/owl-s/api/

[7] CMU OWL-S API, http://www.daml.ri.cmu.edu/wsdl2owls

[8] A. He and E. Johnston and N. Kushmerick, ASSAM: A tool for semi-automatically annotating semantic web services, In proceedings of the 3rd International Semantic Web Conference, 2004, Springer

[9] E. Christensen, F. Cubera, G. Meredith, S. Weerawarana, Web Services Description Language (WSDL) 1.1, Technical report, WWW Consortium, 2001

[10] Resource Description Framework, http://www.w3.org/RDF/

[11] Web Service Resource Framework, http://www.globus.org/wsrf/

[12] Globus Toolkit, http://www-unix.globus.org/toolkit/

[13] CrossGrid consortium, CrossGrid Technical Annex, 2004, http://www.crossgrid.org

[14] The Knowledge-based Workflow System for Grid Applications FP6 IST project, http://www.kwfgrid.net

[15] Fensel D. and Bussler C., The Web Service Modeling Framework WSMF, Eletronic Commerce: Research and Applications, 1, 2002

[16] P. Rajasekaran and J. Miller and K. Verma and A. Sheth, Enhancing Web Services Description and Discovery to Facilitate Composition, International Workshop on Semantic Web Services and Web Process Composition, 2004

[17] GridSphere portal framework, http://www.gridsphere.org/gridsphere/gridsphere

[18] Motta E. and Domingue J. and Cabral L. and Gaspari M., IRS-II: A Framework and Infrastructure for Semantic Web Services, 2nd International Semantic Web Conference (ISWC2003), Sundial Resort, Sanibel Island, Florida, USA, 2003

[19] Gubala, T., Bubak, M., Malawski, M., Rycerz, K., Semantic-based Grid Workflow Composition, In: Proc. of 6-th Intl. Conf. on Parallel Processing and Applied Mathematics PPAM'2005, R.Wyrzykowski et al. eds., 2005, Springer-Verlag, Poznan, Poland

[20] Hoheisel, A., User Tools and Languages for Graph-based Grid Workflows. In: Special Issue of Concurrency and Computation: Practice and Experience, Wiley, 2005

[21] Hluchy, L., Tran, V.D., Habala, O., Simo, B., Gatial, E., Astalos, J., Dobrucky, M., Flood Forecasting in CrossGrid project. In: Grid Computing, 2nd European Across Grids Conference, Nicosia, Cyprus, January 28-30, 2004, LNCS 3165, Springer-Verlag, 2004, pp. 51-60, ISSN 0302-9743, ISBN 3-540-22888-8.

[22] IBM WSDL4J Project, http://oss.software.ibm.com/developerworks/projects/wsdl4j

[23] Apache WebServices - Axis Project, http://ws.apache.org/axis/

LEGACY CODE SUPPORT FOR SERVICE-ORIENTED PRODUCTION GRIDS

Thierry Delaitre[1], Tamas Kiss[1], GaborTerstyanszky[1], Stephen Winter[1], Peter Kacsuk[2]
[1] *Centre for Parallel Computing, Cavendish School of Computer Science, University of Westminster, London, United Kingdom*
[2] *MTA SZTAKI Lab. of Parallel and Distributed Systems, Budapest, Hungary*

Abstract: Current production Grid systems are just before a transition period when they are moving form resource-oriented to service-oriented Grid middleware. However, only changing the underlying Grid middleware and the basic services will prevent end-users to fully utilise the Grid. Users also require higher level services that make access the Grid easier. This paper presents how a higher level service like the GEMLCA legacy code solution can be connected to service-oriented production Grids. It identifies dynamic account management and automated resource testing as two main challenges to be solved and offers solutions for these challenges.

Key words: legacy code, production Grid, dynamic account pooling, resource & service monitoring, user support,

1. Introduction

There are several production Grid systems, like the TeraGrid [1] and the Open Science Grid [2] in the US, or the EGEE Grid [3] and the UK National Grid Service [4] in Europe, that already provide reliable production quality access to computational and data resources for the scientific community. Most of these Grid systems are just before a transition period. They were all set up as "traditional" resource-oriented grids based on Globus toolkit version 2 (GT2) [5], but all of them consider, in a shorter or longer term to move towards a service-oriented architecture. The TeraGrid is already running GT4-based services since December 2005, and plans to set up a full production GT4-based operation in early 2006. The EGEE Grid will also change its underlying infrastructure form the Globus based LCG [6] to gLite [7] in the first quarter of 2006, and other production Grids are also setting up different GT4-based services.

Porting legacy applications onto these production Grid systems is one of the most important tasks to be solved in order to support a more widespread scientific and industrial take-up of Grid computing. There is a vast legacy of applications solving scientific problems or supporting business critical functionalities. Institutions can ill-afford to throw such applications away for the sake of a new technology, and there is a clear business imperative for them to be migrated onto the Grid with the least possible effort and cost.

The Grid Execution Management for Legacy Code Architecture (GEMLCA) [8] enables legacy code programs written in any source language (Fortran, C, Java, etc.) to be easily deployed as a Grid Service without significant user effort. The current GEMLCA implementation is based on Globus Toolkit version 4 (GT4) but could also be ported to any service-oriented Grid middleware with reasonable effort. GEMLCA is also integrated with the P-GRADE Grid portal [9] providing a user friendly Web interface to publish legacy codes as Grid services and to create, execute and visualise the execution of complex Grid workflows from both legacy components and Grid services.

The integrated GEMLCA P-GRADE portal solution can interface with current GT2-based production Grids. It has already been running as a production level service [10] on the UK National Grid Service (NGS) since September 2005, and has also been successfully demonstrated on the EGEE Grid.

As GEMLCA is implemented as a GT4 Grid service it can be integrated with GT4-based production Grids. Moreover, through the P-GRADE portal, even current GT2-based Grids can be extended with GT4 GEMLCA resources bridging different Grid generations. This way GT4 GEMLCA services can be set up for current GT2-based production Grids assisting the transition of these Grid systems towards a service-oriented architecture, and providing useful experiment for both Grid operators and end users. However, before this extension two main problems have to be solved:

- Firstly, GEMLCA has to be extended with workspace management and dynamic account pooling support. In order to utilize GT4 GEMLCA services in a production environment Grid certificates need to be mapped into corresponding cluster accounts dynamically at run-time without manual interaction.
- Secondly, because of the transient nature of the Grid, and because GEMLCA relies on rather complex Grid middleware (like GT4) and local job manager (like Condor [11]) solutions, it is very important that both system administrators and end-users are aware of the failure of GEMLCA resources and could act accordingly. The GEMLCA P-GRADE portal environment has to be extended with a monitoring tool that reports automatically any failure to system administrators, and that also allows users to select only tested and working resources when mapping the execution of a newly created workflow, or when rescuing a failed workflow component.

This paper presents how GEMLCA can be extended with the above features. A unique solution is described for the integration of GEMLCA with the Workspace Management Service (WMS) [12] in order to support the dynamic mapping of user credentials to local accounts in a way that is totally transparent form the user's point of view. We also introduce the GEMLCA Monitoring Toolkit (GMT) [14] that supports the dynamic testing of legacy code resources on the Grid, and propose an architecture how the GMT can be extended and connected to existing Grid brokers to be used for resource availability prediction based on a historical database.

As production Grids are moving towards service-oriented Grid middleware solutions it will be extremely important to incorporate more and more user support services into these Grids. The problems and their solutions presented in this paper go far beyond the GEMLCA architecture and could be adapted to other GT4-based services offered for production Grid systems.

2.   GEMLCA and the P-GRADE portal

GEMLCA [8] represents a general architecture for deploying legacy applications as Grid services without re-engineering the code or even requiring access to the source files. The novelty of the GEMLCA concept, compared to solutions with similar aims like in [15], [16] and [17] is that it requires minimal effort from both Compute Server administrators and end-users of the Grid providing a high-level user-friendly environment to deploy and execute legacy codes on service-oriented Grids. The deployment of a new legacy code service with GEMLCA means to expose the functionalities of this legacy application as a Grid service that requires the description of the program's execution environment and input/output parameters in an XML-based Legacy Code Interface Description (LCID) file. This file is used by the GEMLCA Resource layer to handle the legacy application as a Grid service.

GEMLCA provides the capability to convert legacy codes into Grid services. However, an end-user without specialist computing skills still requires a user-friendly Web interface (portal) to access the GEMLCA functionalities: to deploy, execute and retrieve results from legacy applications. Instead of developing a new custom Grid portal, GEMLCA was integrated with the workflow-oriented P-GRADE Grid portal [9] extending its functionalities with new portlets. The P-GRADE portal enables the graphical development of workflows consisting of various types of executable components (sequential, MPI or PVM programs), execution of these workflows in Globus-based Grids relying on user credentials, and finally the analysis of the correctness and performance of applications by the built-in visualization facilities. The portal is based on the GridSphere [18] portal framework and the workflow manager subsystem is currently implemented on top of Condor DAGMan [19].

Following the integration of GEMLCA and the P-GRADE portal, end-users can easily construct workflow applications also including legacy code services running on different GEMLCA Grid resources. The workflow manager of the portal contacts the selected GEMLCA resources, passes them the actual parameter values of the legacy code, and then it is the task of the GEMLCA Resource to execute the legacy code with these actual parameter values. The other important task of the GEMLCA Resource is to deliver the results of the legacy code service back to the portal. For more detailed description of GEMLCA and the P-GRADE portal please refer to [8] and [9], respectively.

3.   Dynamic Account Management for Legacy Code Services

As GEMLCA uses local job managers, like Condor or PBS, to execute legacy code jobs through GT4 job submission, it requires a secure run-time environment. In order to achieve this Grid certificates have to be mapped to local user accounts. However, in case of a production Grid it is not scalable to create user accounts and do the mapping manually whenever a new user is added. In a production Grid environment user Grid credentials have to be mapped dynamically to local user accounts in a completely user-transparent way. Current GT2-based production Grids all tackles this problem. However, there are only limited solutions for GT4-based grids. This section describes a unique architecture how dynamic mapping can be integrated into GT4-based Grid services like GEMLCA, allowing the seamless integration of these services into GT4-based production Grids.

Overview of Dynamic Account Management in Current Grid Systems

To access a Grid resource, the user's global identity should be converted to a local identity. This conversion may be based on either a permanent one-to-one mapping or on temporary mapping. In Globus-based Grids the Globus gatekeeper maps Grid identities, based on X.509 certificates, to local Unix user accounts using the grid-mapfile, which allocates Grid identities to local accounts. The existing grid-mapfile based solutions are not scalable because they require frequent manual interaction to map identities. As a result, they are not suitable for production Grids with a large number of users. To have a scalable solution production Grids require a dynamic and flexible user management. As part of the user management, they need a dynamic and fine-grained authorisation mechanism to control users' access to resources. This authorisation mechanism could be implemented through dynamic account management and identity mapping.

There are several solutions, such as PRIMA [28], VOMS [26] and WMS [12] that implement dynamic and flexible user management based on account pooling and identity conversion used in GT2-based production Grids. All these solutions allocate accounts for Grid users on-demand from an account pool, i.e. they dynamically map global user identities to local accounts replacing the static mapping based on the grid-mapfile. Different GT2-based production Grids have different user management solutions.

The EGEE Grid uses VOMS with gridmapdir, LCMAPS and, LCAS. The Virtual Organisation Membership Service (VOMS) extended the Globus Gatekeeper with two new services to replace the grid-mapfile solution: the Local Credential Mapping Service (LCMAPS) [27] and the Local Centre Authorisation Service (LCAS) [28]. LCMAPS maps global identities to local ones using proxy certificates and job descriptions. It provides either pre-defined Unix accounts for permanent users or accounts from a pool of temporary accounts for temporary users using the gridmapdir mechanism. LCAS makes local authorisation by enforcing local security policies using VO membership, roles and capabilities. Similarly to the EGEE Grid, the UK NGS uses VOMS with gridmapdir, but it does not utilise LCMAPS and LCAS. However, both the EGEE Grid and the NGS extended the Globus Gatekeeper and Gridftp services with the gridmapdir patch. The patch maps Grid users automatically to a local Unix account from an account pool located on the compute node when Grid users issue requests for resources of this node.

The Open Science Grid uses VOMS with PRIMA. Authorisation in PRIMA (Privilege Management and Authorization in Grid Computing Environments) is built on privilege management using the minimum privilege access mechanism to give access to resources. This solution creates, configures and manages users' accounts on-demand. Users submit their privileges and PRIMA tries to find existing accounts that match these privileges and maps users to the corresponding accounts. If matching accounts are not found, it assigns a new account from the account pool.

EGEE, TeraGrid and Open Science Grid are all moving towards service-oriented Grids. The first one will use gLite, while the others GT4 as Grid middleware. The EGEE team has adapted VOMS with gridmapdir, LCMAPS and LCAS to G-lite. The TeraGrid is using the grid-mapfile based authorisation requiring manual intervention. The OpenScienceGrid set up a testbed to check the Edge Services Framework where services are deployed dynamically using WMS (Workspace Management Service). This service supports dynamic creation of workspaces and account pooling using gridmapdir and LCMAPS. Workspaces are currently implemented as Unix accounts on local nodes. They are represented by dynamic accounts, which are either generated on-demand or allocated from an account pool. Unfortunately, none of these solutions provide totally transparent and dynamic mapping required by GT4 services like GEMLCA.

Dynamic Account Management for GEMLCA

To provide a scalable user management GEMLCA was integrated with the Workspace Management Service using its identity mapping and dynamic account pooling features. The first feature maps Grid certificates into local accounts at run-time without manual intervention, while the second feature provides local accounts on demand. The previous GEMLCA security implementation [24] used the grid-mapfile to check authorization of Grid service requests. In the solution presented in this paper, authorisation of GEMLCA services, such as *GLCList, GLCProcess* and *GLCAdmin*, was adapted to the WMS Authorisation and Mapping Callout to make GEMLCA scalable. To get a workspace, *GLCProcess* issues a request on the user's behalf to the WMS to create and lease a workspace for the user. Leased workspaces allow Grid users to access GEMLCA resources and allow them to make subsequent service requests. The *GLCProcess* can extend the lease as required, for example until the service completes, during the execution of the legacy codes using a thread associated with the *GLCProcess* environment.

The GEMLCA lifecycle with WMS incorporates the following steps (Figure 1) (Please note that the original GEMLCA lifecycle and its detailed description are available in [8]. Here we only concentrate on changes required by dynamic account management):

1) The user signs its security certificates in order to create a Grid user proxy.
2) A Grid client creates a restricted Grid Legacy Code Process *(GLCProcess)* instance with no defined workspace, using the GEMLCA file structure.
3) The *GLCProcess* instance forwards the Grid user credential to the Workspace Management Service (WMS) that checks whether a workspace has been previously assigned to the user. If has not been, WMS converts global user identity to local one using the LCMAPS and selects a workspace from the workspace pool assigning it to the user with a lease before creating a *GLCProcess* environment. If the lease is about to expire *GLCProcess* contacts the WMS in order to extend it. As these steps are programmed within the *GLCProcess*, the dynamic creation and mapping of workspaces are totally transparent from the users' point of view.

4) Having a workspace allocated for the user, the Grid client sets and uploads the input parameters needed by the legacy code program exposed by the *GLCProcess*, deploys a *GLCJob* using the resource specification format of the Grid middleware (a Resource Specification Language (RSL) file in case of Globus), and creates a multi-user environment to handle input and output data.

5) The Grid user credential is delegated by the *GLCProcess* from the client to the underlying Grid Host Environment for the allocation of resources. For example, in case of a Globus-based implementation the resource allocation is the task of the Master Managed Job Factory Service (MMJFS). MMJFS validates global user identity mapped to a workspace.

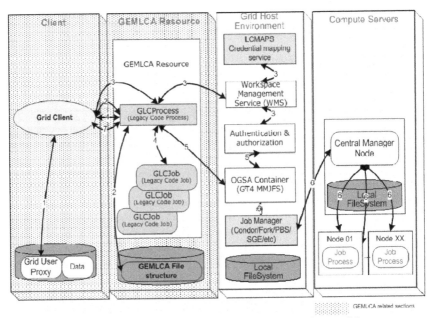

Figure 1. GEMLCA Lifecycle Management with Workspace Management Service

6) The Grid middleware contacts the appropriate job manager (Condor, Fork, PBS etc.) that allocates resources and executes the parallel or sequential legacy code on the Compute Servers.

7) As long as the client credential has not expired and the *GLCProcess* is alive, the client can contact GEMLCA for checking job status and retrieving partial or final results at any time.

4. Dynamic Testing of Legacy Code Services

In order to offer GEMLCA legacy code services for production Grid systems, automatic testing of these services is inevitable. Production Grids run thorough tests on their available resources on a regular basis to offer a high quality of service. The

UK NGS, for example, runs GITS (Grid Integration Test Script) tests to ensure the setup of Grid services on the infrastructure. Other, more advanced monitoring toolkits, like Inca [20], GRASP (Grid Assessment Probes) [21], or MonaLISA (Monitoring Agents in a Large Integrated Services Architecture) [22] are also available to test, monitor and verify the functionality of Grid resources by running a set of probes. However, none of these solutions are integrated with GT4 at the moment, and there are no probes that can directly test GT4-based services.

In order to overcome this problem the GEMLCA Monitoring Toolkit (GMT) was developed to provide monitoring information based on probes concerning the status of GEMLCA resources. Using the GMT, system administrators are automatically alarmed when a test fails and can also request the execution of any test on-demand. The GMT also assists P-GRADE portal users when mapping the execution of workflow components to resources by offering only verified Grid resources when creating a new workflow or when rescuing a failed one.

GMT tests GEMLCA resources in pre-defined regular intervals, and alarms and supports system administrators in identifying any problems with GEMLCA resources. It automates the validation of GEMLCA Grid services, and provide a user-friendly interface for this task by integrating it into the P-GRADE portal. GMT provides reliable and dependable environment for GEMLCA end-users by assuring them that the GEMLCA resources where the tasks are mapped working properly. It supports the further development of GEMLCA by collecting information regarding resource availability.

GMT performs the tests of the following types of resources:

- The basic network connectivity verifying that the remote sites are accessible.
- Services of the underlying Grid middleware. The current GEMLCA implementation is based on GT4 utilising the MyProxy, WS-GRAM and GridFtp services.
- Functionality of the local job manager. GEMLCA is submitting the legacy code as a batch job to a local job manager. Current GEMLCA implementation is capable to submit to the Fork and Condor schedulers.
- The three Grid services, GLCAdmin, GLCList and GLCProcess [8] providing the GEMLCA functionality.

Grid Monitoring Tool Implementation

The implementation of the GMT is based on MDS4 (Monitoring and Discovery System) [23] that is part of the Globus distribution. MDS4 is capable to collect, store and index information about resources, respond to queries concerning the stored information using the XPath language, and control the execution of testing and information retrieval tools built as part of the GEMLCA Monitoring Toolkit. It can be extended and tailored to obtain specific information by means of polling resources, subscription to obtain notifications regarding changes to the state of specific resources, and execution of test and information collection scripts (probes).

As part of the GMT, several probes were implemented that collect information concerning the state of basic Globus services, local job manager functionality, and GEMLCA services. The probes can immediately be used as standalone tools executed automatically from the MDS by implement these solutions and put them into production level operation on the UK National Grid Service.

Site administrators can configure the MDS4 service to run the various probes at pre-defined intervals. The results are collected by a portlet that is integrated into the P-GRADE portal. Administrators can also select a specific probe from a drop-down list displayed by a portlet and run it to verify the state of a specific service at a specific site on demand (Figure 2).

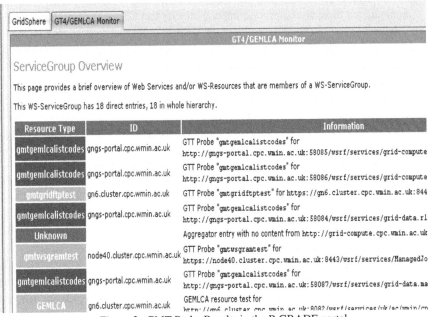

Figure 2. GMT Probe Results in the P-GRADE portal automatic execution mode

GMT probes can also be integrated into the workflow editor of the portal to assist end-users when mapping a new workflow execution onto available Grid resources, or when rescuing and re-mapping a failed workflow. In the latest P-GRADE portal release mapping of workflow components to underlying resources happens either manually by the end-user, or in case of LCG type Grids, by the LCG broker. The GMT aims to support manual mapping (when no LCG type broker is available) by dynamically querying the MDS4 during workflow creation time, and offering only those GEMLCA resources for mapping where the latest GMT test results were positive. Although, this does not guarantee that the resource will actually work when executing the workflow, but the probability of a successful execution will significantly be increased. Work is also undergoing to connect the GMT to the LCG resource broker, as illustrated on Figure 3. GMT, as shown on the figure, runs regular probes on the production Grid resources and, besides updating the MDS indexing service, also creates a historical database. When the portal submits a workflow, a classifier component runs data mining algorithms on this historical data and determines which resources are "very likely to be alive". This information can be passed to the production Grid broker, for example in case of an LCG broker within the JDL (Job Description Language) file. The broker then maps the execution to the appropriate resources taking now the GMT provided information into consideration too.

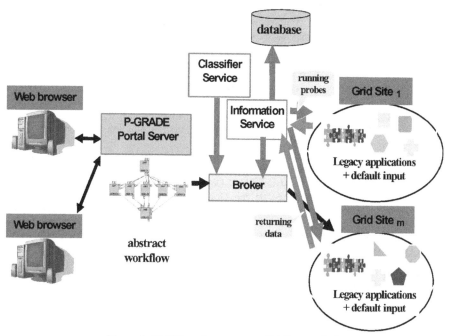

Figure 3. GMT-based resource availability prediction

5. Summary

Providing additional services that support the users of large production Grids is crucial for the more widespread take up of these Grid solutions. One example for these user support services is GEMLCA that presents legacy code applications as a Grid service with minimum user intervention. GEMLCA is already connected to resource-oriented GT2-based Grid systems. However, offering GEMLCA resources in service-oriented Grids requires dynamic account management and automated resource testing. This paper presented how these problems can be solved in GT4 services using GEMLCA as an example. Work is currently undergoing to fully implement these solutions and put them into production level operation on the UK National Grid Service.

References

[1] The TeraGrid Website, http://www.teragrid.org
[2] The Open Science Grid Website, http://www.opensciencegrid.org/
[3] The EGEE Website, http://public.eu-egee.org/
[4] The UK National Grid Service Website, http://www.ngs.ac.uk/
[5] The Globus Project Website, http://www.globus.org/
[6] The   LCG   project   Website,   Worldwide   LHC   Computing   Grid, http://lcg.web.cern.ch/LCG/
[7] EGEE gLite version 1.5 Documentation, http://glite.web.cern.ch/glite/documentation

[8] T. Delaittre, T. Kiss, A. Goyeneche, G. Terstyanszky, S. Winter, P. Kacsuk: GEMLCA: Running Legacy Code Applications as Grid Services, Journal of Grid Computing Vol. 3. No. 1-2. June 2005, Springer Science+Business Media B.V., ISSN: 1570-7873, pp 75-90

[9] P. Kacsuk G. Sipos: Multi-Grid, Multi-User Workflows in the P-GRADE Grid Portal, Journal of Grid Computing, , Springer Science + Business Media B.V., 25 January 2006,

[10] The P-GRADE NGS GEMLCA Portal Website, http://www.cpc.wmin.ac.uk/ngsportal/

[11] Condor Team, University of Wisconsin-Madison: Condor Version 6.4.7 Manual, http://www.cs.wisc.edu/condor/manual/v6.4/

[12] K. Keahey, M. Ripeanu, K. Doering: Dynamic Creation and Management of Runtime Environment in the Grid, Workshop on Designing and Building Web Services, GGF9, Chicago, October 2003

[13] Martijn Steenbakkers, LCMAPS - A Local Credential Mapping Service, http://www.dutchgrid.nl/DataGrid/wp4/lcmaps/

[14] L. Bitonti, T. Kiss, G. Terstyanszky, T. Delaitre, S. Winter, P. Kacsuk, Dynamic Testing of Legacy Code Resources on the Grid, To appear in Conf. proc. of the ACM International Conference on Computing Frontiers, Ischia, Italy, May 2-5, 2006.

[15] Y. Huang, I. Taylor, D. W. Walker, "Wrapping Legacy Codes for Grid-Based Applications", Proceedings of the 17th International Parallel and Distributed Processing Symposium, workshop on Java for HPC), 22-26 April 2003, Nice, France.

[16] B. Balis, M. Bubak, M. Wegiel. A Solution for Adapting Legacy Code as Web Services. In Proceedings of Workshop on Component Models and Systems for Grid Applications. 18th Annual ACM International Conference on Supercomputing, Saint-Malo, July 2004

[17] D. Gannon, S. Krishnan, A. Slominski, G. Kandaswamy, L. Fang, "Building Applications from a Web Service based Component Architecture, in "Component Models and Systems for Grid Applications" edited by V. Getov and T. Kiellmann, Springer, 2005, pp 3-17, ISBN 0-387-23351-2.

[18] J. Novotny, M. Russell, O. Wehrens: GridSphere, "An Advanced Portal Framework", Conf. Proc. of the 30th EUROMICRO Conference, August 31st - September 3rd 2004, Rennes, France.

[19] James Frey, Condor DAGMan: Handling Inter-Job Dependencies, http://www.bo.infn.it/calcolo/condor/dagman/

[20] Shava Smallen, Catherine Olschanowsky, Kate Ericson,, Pete Beckman, Jennifer M. Schopf, The Inca Test Harness and Reporting Framework, Conf. proc of the Supercomputing 2004 Conference, Pittsburgh, November 6-12, 2005.

[21] Greg Chun, Holly Daily, Henri Casanova, Allan Snavely, Benchmark Probes for Grid Assessment, http://grail.sdsc.edu/projects/grasp/probes/grasp.pdf

[22] I.C. Legrand, H.B. Newman, R. Voicu, C. Cirstoiu, C. Grigoras, M. Toarta, C. Dobre, MonaLISA: An Agent based, Dynamic Service System to Monitor, Control and Optimize Grid Applications, CHEP 2004, Interlaken, Switzerland, September 2004,

[23] Globus Team, Globus Toolkit 4.0 Release Manuals, http://www.globus.org/toolkit/docs/4.0/

[24] G. Terstyansky, T. Delaitre, A. Goyeneche, T. Kiss, K. Sajadah, S.C. Winter, P. Kacsuk, Security Mechanisms for Legacy Code Applications in GT3 Environment, Conf. Proc. of the 13th Euromicro Conference, Lugano, Switzerland, February 9-11, 2005

[25] XACML project, Microsoft, 2004, http://sunxamcl.sourceforge.net

[26] R. Alfieri et. al: Managing Dynamic User Communities in a Grid of Autonomous Resources, CHEP 2003, La Jolla, San Diego, March 24-28, 2003

[27] M. Steenbakkers: Guide to LCMAPS, 2003

[28] M. Lorch, D. Adams, D. Kafura. M. Koneni, A. Rathi, S. Shah: The PRIMA System for Privilege Management, Authorisation and Enforcement in grid Environments

CLIENT-SIDE TASK SUPPORT IN MATLAB FOR CONCURRENT DISTRIBUTED EXECUTION

Christian Hoge[1], Dan Keith[1], Allen D. Malony[1,2]
Neuroinformatics Center[1]
Department of Computer and Information Science[2]
University of Oregon
{hoge,dkeith,malony}@cs.uoregon.edu

Abstract   Matlab is a popular interactive computing environment that gives scientists a powerful and easy to use set of analysis and visualization tools. However, Matlab has been criticized for performance limitations on computationally and memory intensive applications. In addition, because of Matlab's single-threaded processing model, long-running processes prevent a user from performing other tasks while computation occurs. We discuss a framework for remote, concurrent execution of tasks in the Matlab environment that address these shortcomings by asynchronously distributing tasks to dedicated high-performance compute servers. We employ a client-server model based on web-standards and Matlab's built in scripting and Java environment.

Keywords: Matlab, distributed, concurrent, context, high-performance

Introduction

Matlab is an integrated computational environment for scientists and engineers with support for interactive analysis and visualization. The popularity of Matlab comes from its integrated functionality and workstation platform ubiquity, but it has been criticized for performance limitations on computationally and memory intensive applications. In this respect, there has been significant work on enhancing the Matlab environment with support for parallel and distributed execution [Kepner and Travinin, 2003].

One approach for parallel execution extends Matlab for message passing, for instance, with an MPI interface [Kepner, 2001, MultiMatlab, 1995] . Other projects allow Matlab to operate in a distributed system [Matlab DCET, 2005] or computational grids [Matlab*G, 2003, A. Reuther, 2004]. In all of the above cited cases, the entities inter-operating are Matlab processes only. Geodise [Geodise, 2005] implements a grid computing toolbox for Matlab making it possible to use Matlab for scripting grid work flows for engineering design optimization. Non-Matlab processes may be executed in Geodise work flows, but all host machines must be grid-enabled for this purpose.

In addition to allowing execution on multiple processes, these toolkits attempt to seamlessly integrate with the Matlab programming model. The above projects do this by providing the same "look and feel" of Matlab procedure calls to access message passing or grid computing functions. In contrast, the pMatlab [Kepner and Travinin, 2003], Matlab*G [Matlab*G, 2003], and StarP [StarP, 2006] systems apply syntax and function overloading to provide implicit data and task parallelism. While effective at abstracting away low-level parallel programming details, these approaches work only at the Matlab level, making it harder to parallelize non-Matlab routines.

Our objective is to support concurrent task processing in a distributed client-server environment where Matlab operates as a task generating client The tasks represent procedures (services) that the servers provide. The servers publish the procedure interfaces so that the Matlab client knows the calling parameters and can automatically generate an object-oriented interface to the remote service. In this manner, the operation between the Matlab client and the server is similar to a remote procedure call (RPC) model. However, the RPC model normally blocks the caller (the client), restricting the ability to have multiple tasks operating concurrently. In addition to remote procedure invocation, we want the execution of the tasks to be asynchronous to Matlab execution. Once this requirement is specified, the problem becomes one of introducing task semantics in the Matlab programming environment because it is reasonable to expect Matlab users to want to generate multiple remote, possibly long-running, tasks to take advantage of available computing resources. Our application is EEG data processing where the ability to process multiple data sets simultaneously on parallel servers is important.

Unfortunately, none of the methods above provide the necessary support needed with Matlab. The following sections describe our solution approach: the general model, the client design and implementation, and application to EEG signal analysis. The result is a new toolkit for Matlab, called MC, that task-based parallelism that we will distribute and extend in the future.

1.   Model

Our concurrent distributed system is based on a standard client-server model as shown in Figure 1. The client resides in MATLAB and generates multiple tasks to execute on remote servers. The servers provide computational procedures that can be invoked by the clients. From the client's perspective, it creates tasks that are to be executed in a concurrent manner. This abstraction is implemented in a library that interfaces with Matlab and its underlying Java

Virtual Machine (JVM) and utilizes distributed system mechanisms to execute the tasks on the servers.

Figure 1.   Client-Server Model

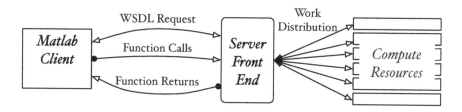

We assume that the server provides a Simple Object Access Protocol (SOAP) interface to its computational services with the interface published as a Web Services Description Language (WSDL) file. In addition to computational services, the server also provides methods for uploading files, requesting the status of processes, and requesting the results of processes.

On the client side, our library requests a WSDL from available servers and automatically generates a programatic interface to each service provided. When a remote task execution is requested by the user, our system performs these operations: it uploads large data sets to the server, makes a process request, receives a task id, stores the Matlab context of the process call as an object, and associates the task id with the context. We define a *context* to be a set of inputs, environment state variables and outputs associated with a remote function call.

Control is then handed back to the user, and a background thread periodically checks the state of the remote task. When the client receives notification that the remote task is complete it notifies the user. At that point the user can request that the results of the computation be fetched from the server, and that the workspace context be restored. Figure 2 illustrates the interaction between the client and sever components.

While a remote task is running other work can be done. Because we store the context of the remote call, the user can continue to work in the Matlab workspace without fear of overwriting data associated with the remote call. The context can even be saved to disk or transmitted to a different machine, and then restored at a later time at the convenience of the user.

Because the server implementation is independent of the client it is possible to achieve several layers of parallelism. Obviously, the first is task parallelism, where many client tasks can be run simultaneously on different severs. The second is intra-task parallelism, handled on the server by interfaces such as MPI, OpenMP, or pthreads. That is, remote tasks themselves can be parallelized, and can be implemented in any programming language desired. Even remote

Figure 2.   Matlab-Task Manager-Server Interaction Diagram

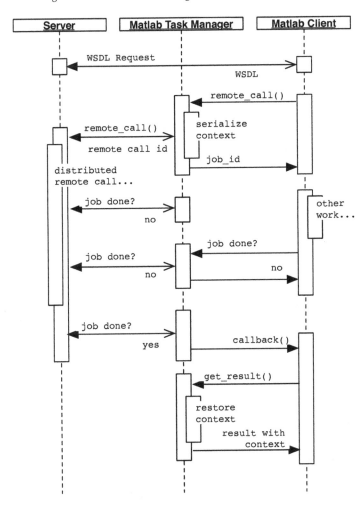

Matlab tasks are possible, as long as the task interface registration and invocation methods are followed.

The rest of the paper will focus on the implementation of the Matlab client. The server can be viewed as a black box within the framework as long as it provides the interface required by the client.

2. Client Design

There are two major components to the client design: the user interface to the toolkit and the software to manage the remote tasks. Our goal in designing the user interface was to provide an intuitive library of calls for executing and managing remote tasks, while providing a useful library to integrate with other Matlab-based applications. For task management we needed a lightweight yet extensible system that could keep track of asynchronous tasks and manage contexts, all without blocking the Matlab workbench.

The user interface layer is built upon existing Matlab functions and Java classes available through Matlab's JVM. Maintaining responsiveness and transparency in the user environment is key. When a remote call is made, instead of blocking and waiting for an answer to be computed, the function call returns a *Remote Task ID* (RTID) that acts as a reference to the complete state of the remote execution, much like a Matlab file id can be used as a pointer to a file. In general all function calls will give immediate responses.

While the interface is intuitive enough for general interactive use, it also provides an API for integration with applications that run inside of Matlab. For example, one could build a graphic user interface where the state of the GUI is associated with the context of the remote call. The application could then restore the state of the work at a later time, freeing the user to shut down the application to perform other work. We discuss this more below.

The responsiveness of the library is made possible by the *Task Manager* layer, which runs as a background process. The Task Manager maintains contexts and manages remote calls. It provides an interface to the Matlab environment for user interaction. By applying interval timers and callbacks the Task Manager can automatically perform scripted tasks such as checking the status of remote tasks, freeing the user or applications from having to perform these tasks manually.

3. Client Implementation

To meet the goals of the client design we used two different approaches for the user API and the task manager. The interface is largely implemented using Matlab's *m-script* language. Since the task manager must run concurrently with the Matlab workspace, we took advantage of the JVM that comes bundled with

Table 1. User Functions Available in Matlab

Matlab function	input	output
makeServiceFromWsdl	url	service id (SID)
serviceHelp	SID	list of available methods
serviceHelp	SID, function	input and output for function
callFunction	SID, inputs, context, call-back	RTID
functionStatus	RTID	status of call
retreiveOutput	RTID	context with function output
saveContext	RTID, filename	success or failure
restoreContext	filename	RTID

Matlab and run the Task Manager as a Java thread. It can be called directly from the Matlab workspace, and supports timed actions and scripting.

The implementation of the user interface models existing Matlab functions. For example, Matlab provides a function for interfacing with web-services called makeClassFromWsdl. In our implementation we wrap around this built-in method with a function called makeServiceFromWsdl. This function will automatically generate the interface necessary for running remote services asynchronously, and returns a *Service ID* (SID) that is used as an identifier of the remote service. Table 1 lists some of the functions available in the interface.

The Task Manager is implemented as a single background thread running in the JVM, with the user interface specified in Table 2. It uses the *Singleton Pattern* to ensure that only one Task Manager thread is running. The Task Manager coordinates several components. File transfer is handled by the *Ganymed* SSH2 implementation for Java [Alonso and Plattner, 2005], and interaction with Matlab is through the MatlabControl class [Whitehouse, 2002]. Scripting is handled with *Jython*, which not only provides dynamic access to objects in the JVM, but also allows scripting with Matlab m-script by interfacing with the MatlabControl class. When executing Matlab code the Task Manager will wait until the Matlab workbench has free cycles available for the task to occur, reducing the likelihood of the user and the Task Manager contending for resources. The Task Manager thread has a run loop that responds to user or timer events. To ensure that no messages are lost due to race conditions or synchronization problems, events are added to a queue that is maintained by the Task Manager, which will execute every task in the queue once woken.

The Task Manager also keeps a list of tasks that it has launched. Each task is associated with a state: *running*, *stopped*, and *stopped-notified*. The Task Manager uses these states to query the server for job status, notifying the user when a job is completed, and executing call-back functions attached to a remote process. The task objects include the RTID, the SID, the context of the task, and call-back functions.

Table 2. Task Manager interface

Task Manager function	input	output
runPython	python code	string
runMatlab	Matlab code	string
startTimer	period in milliseconds	
stopTimer		
instance		the Task Manager object
matlabControl		the MatlabControl object

4. Example 1:APECS and the HiPerSAT Server

As an example application, we consider analysis of electroencephalography (EEG) data in the context of APECS [Frank and Frishkoff, 2006], an interactive environment for evaluating the ability of independent component analysis (ICA) algorithms to extract artifacts from EEG data. Ideally, ICA algorithms separate EEG data into streams of independent activity (components), some of which may capture unwanted artifacts (e.g., eye blinks or EKG [Frank et al., 2006]) and brain activity. These components, along with their respective spatial topographies, can be used to understand brain function. APECS, by using prior knowledge of time and spatial properties, evaluates the ability of different ICA methods to extract that activity based upon the performance of each algorithm's component separation.

Normally ICA is a time intensive process, with some algorithms growing in time complexity as $O(n^2)$ in the number of channels, and $O(n)$ in the number of time samples. We are working with data sets up to 256 sensor channels and hundreds of seconds of recording at 1 msec time intervals. ICA algorithms in the EEGLAB [Delorme and Makeig, 2004] Matlab toolkit have performed poorly with large EEG data because of single threaded execution and Matlab memory management. We have implemented optimized and parallelized C++ implementations of ICA and other EEG signal analysis algorithms in a library call HiPerSAT [D. Keith, 2006]. Clearly, there is an advantage in being able to run ICA tasks in APECS (for different algorithms and data sets) externally on a HiPerSAT server and concurrently with other APECS operations.

Using our framework the user can set up an experiment in APECS, start several remote HiPerSAT jobs simultaneously, then checkpoint the experiment using the context serialization feature of our framework. If the user chooses to leave APECS running, the application can notify the user when every remote job is complete. The user can also serialize the state of the experiment, shut the APECS and Matlab environment down, and restore the application context at a later time after the computation has been completed.

We have demonstrated APECS with 20 simultaneous HiPerSAT servers running parallel ICA tasks. Compared to sequential ICA processing of 20 one-GB EEG files in EEGLAB we see a 5x speedup for C++ optimization plus 2-way parallel execution and 10x speedup from running 20 HiPerSAT tasks. We have also demonstrated multiple APECS clients running on different workstations and accessing the HiPerSAT servers. An high utilization of the servers was obtained in one test case, but in general the overall throughput will be determined by server configuration and network bandwidth.

5.   Example 2:Dense Array EEG and Signal Discrimination

As a second example application, we again consider the analysis of EEG data, this time in the context of building a functional discriminator to distinguish between target brain-wave activity and non-target brain-wave activity. Experimental EEG data is collected by having a subject watch a sequence of images, shown in rapid succession, with the subject instructed to distinguish between images with a target feature and images without.

This data is used to build a model to differentiate between brain activity when a target image is shown and brain activity when a non-target image is shown. To improve robustness of the model and prevent over-training, we use various permutations of the training data set to build a multitude of models. This set of operations constitutes an embarrassingly parallel computation, which we implemented using our system.

With a cluster running 83 heterogeneous computational nodes running Octave (a free software Matlab clone), we observed almost a 10x speedup over the same serial computation in Matlab alone (Figure 3).

6.   Conclusions and Future Work

Matlab is one of the most popular interactive computing environments, giving scientists a powerful and easy to use set of analysis and visualization tools. Our parallel execution framework compliments and enhances the environment by providing support for asynchronous parallel computation. The Matlab user is free to perform other actions while long running and computationally intensive processes happen remotely. We leverage the strengths of Matlab's interactive environment, along with it's integrated JVM, to access SOAP web-services. By using open, widely available, and standard tools, we provide an easy to use interface that can be easily integrated into existing projects and extended to meet user's needs.

We anticipate integrating the Matlab client software with the GEMINI software being developed at the Neuroinformatics Center [GEMINI, 2006]. GEMINI (Grid Environment and Methods for Integrated Neuroimaging) is a middleware system that implements a distributed storage and work-flow environment.

Figure 3.   Speedup of Signal Discrimination Model Generation

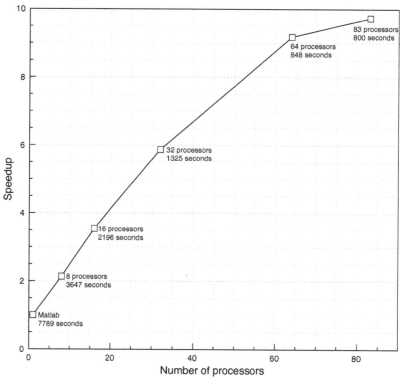

This middle-ware will integrate with existing problem-solving environments and will support the development of powerful neuroimaging applications for both research and clinical purposes. GEMINI is being built upon the Globus Toolkit 4.0 [GLOBUS, 2006].

References

[A. Reuther, 2004] A. Reuther, et al. (2004). Llgrid: Enabling on-demand grid computing with gridmatlab and pmatlab. In *High Performance Embedded Computing*.

[Alonso and Plattner, 2005] Alonso, G. and Plattner, C. (2005). Ganymed ssh2 library for java. urlhttp://www.ganymed.ethz.ch/.

[D. Keith, 2006] D. Keith, et al. (2006). Parallel ica methods for eeg neuroimaging. In *IEEE International Parallel and Distributed Processing Symposium*.

[Delorme and Makeig, 2004] Delorme, A. and Makeig, S. (2004). Eeglab: an open source toolbox for analysis of single-trial eeg dynamics including independent component analysis. *Journal of Neuroscience Methods*, pages 9–21.

[Frank and Frishkoff, 2006] Frank, R. and Frishkoff, G. (2006). Automated protocol for evaluation of electromagnetic component separation (apecs). *Clinical Neurophysiology*. To appear.

[Frank et al., 2006] Frank, R., Frishkoff, G., M.Brown, Tucker, D., and Holmes, M. (2006). Evaluation of two methods for separation of ekg artifacts from eeg recordings in patients with interictal spiking activity. In *Human Brain Mapping*.

[GEMINI, 2006] GEMINI (2006). Gemini. http://www.nic.uoregon.edu/gemini/index.php.

[Geodise, 2005] Geodise (2005). Geodise. http://www.geodise.org/.

[GLOBUS, 2006] GLOBUS (2006). Globus toolkit. http://www.globus.org/toolkit/.

[Kepner, 2001] Kepner, J. (2001). Parallel programming with matlabmpi. In *High Performance Embedded Computing (HPEC) Workshop*.

[Kepner and Travinin, 2003] Kepner, J. and Travinin, N. (2003). Parallel matlab: The next generation. In *High Performance Embedded Computing (HPEC) Workshop*.

[Matlab DCET, 2005] Matlab DCET (2005). Matlab distributed computing engine and toolbox. http://www.mathworks.com/products/distriben/.

[Matlab*G, 2003] Matlab*G (2003). Matlab*g. http://ntu-cg.ntu.edu.sg/Grid_competition/report/grid-9.pdf.

[MultiMatlab, 1995] MultiMatlab (1995). Multimatlab: Matlab on multiple processors. urlhttp://www.cs.cornell.edu/Info/People/lnt/multimatlab.html.

[StarP, 2006] StarP (2006). Starp. urlhttp://www.interactivesupercomputing.com.

[Whitehouse, 2002] Whitehouse,   K.   (2002).   Matlab   control.   url-http://www.cs.berkeley.edu/ kamin/matlab/JavaMatlab.html.

MESSAGE LEVEL SECURITY FOR GRID SERVICES USING S/MIME

Daniel Kouřil, Ondřej Krajíček, Martin Kuba, Michal Procházka
Masaryk University, Botanická 68a, 602 00 Brno, Czech Republic
{kouril,krajicek,makub,michalp}@ics.muni.cz

Abstract   Message level security is essential in knowledge grids, where digital signing of messages is a natural requirement. XML-Signature based digital signatures were reported to be very slow. We present an alternative, based on long-established standard for signing e-mails, together with performance measurements.

Keywords: grid, S/MIME, SOAP, web services

1.   Introduction

The ability to digitally sign SOAP messages flowing among grid services is essential in some types of grids. Some grid applications need to be able to prove who has sent a message and thus who is responsible for the provided data, even long time after the communication is finished.

We have found this ability to be a basic requirement in knowledge grids for biomedicine, where the shared resource is medical knowledge [1] and non-repudiation is an essential feature.

So far, reports of performance of web service security based on XML-Signature and XML-Encryption, as detailed in [2, 4], found it to be very slow when compared to SSL, mainly due to very expensive canonicalization of XML. However SSL has other shortcomings, namely it cannot provide digital signatures and non-repudiation.

Message-level security (MLS) is very important, since it provides the necessary granularity for access control in systems, where the messages are routed in "networks" with complex topologies, i.e. where more sophisticated model than simple point-to-point (client/server) message exchange is used. We propose solutions which implements message-level security. It is based on the observation that much of the MLS-related overhead comes from the XML nature of the digital signatures and encryption.

However, there is a long-established and widely used solution for signing Internet e-mails, called S/MIME (Secure/Multipurpose Internet Mail Extensions). The HTTP (Hyper Text Transfer Protocol) protocol, used by web services for transferring messages, is based on MIME (Multipurpose Internet Mail Extensions) and thus is very similar in structure to e-mails. So we got the idea of using S/MIME over HTTP for transferring signed SOAP messages.

We implemented the S/MIME-over-HTTP solution twice as plugins for two popular web service toolkits: gSOAP (C/C++) and Axis (Java). This article presents speed measurements and experience gathered during the implementation.

2. Message Level Security

Web service security can be dealt with on two levels, on the transport level, or on the message level. The transport level security is usually done using SSL/TLS (Secure Socket Layer/Transport Layer Security), by encrypting all data using a temporary symmetric encryption key. One or both ends of the communication can be authenticated using X509 certificates. The SSL/TLS security is relatively fast, however it has two principal disadvantages. First, it is two-point only, so a SOAP message sent through intermediaries cannot be secured. Second, it does not support signatures, so while one end of the communication knows who is the other end, it cannot prove later that the data were really sent by the communicating partner.

Message level security, on the other hand, can use an unsecured transport, as it performs encryption and/or signatures on the message itself. It has several advantages. A signed message can go from a sender to a recipient through intermediaries that cannot change the message. The messages can also be stored and used later for non-repudiation if some disagreement arises.

The message level security is usually handled using signatures and/or encryption in the XML content of SOAP messages, using W3C standards XML-Encryption and XML-Signature. However implementations of such XML-based message level security were reported as very slow when compared to SSL [2]. So we decided to try an alternative solution, which does not involve manipulation of XML.

3. S/MIME

S/MIME (Secure/Multipurpose Internet Mail Extensions) is an established and standard way for digitally signing and/or encrypting Internet emails. S/MIME is implemented by many e-mail programs, including

Mozilla Suite, Mozilla Thunderbird, Microsoft Outlook, Microsoft Outlook Express and others.

According to [9], S/MIME was originally developed by RSA Data Security Inc. The current work on S/MIME is being done in the IETF's (Internet Engineering Task Force) S/MIME Working Group. S/MIME v3 was made a standard in July, 1999, and is described by a group of RFC (Request For Comments) documents, which are listed in [10].

S/MIME is layered on top of MIME, which defines structure for e-mails containing other media than plain text, like images, video, audio or arbitrary file attachments. Each MIME-compliant message contains headers and a body, separated by an empty line. One of the headers is `Content-type:`, which specifies the so called MIME type of the body content. It can be `text/plain` for plain text, or `image/gif` for a GIF image, but it can also describe more structured content using `multipart/*`, where * can be `mixed` when the second and later parts are attachments to the first part, or some other values.

S/MIME uses MIME type `multipart/signed` for signed content and `application/pkcs7-mime` for encrypted content. For details see [8]. When an e-mail is signed using S/MIME, the signed content is in the first part, followed by a binary attachment containing the signature and information about the signer.

4. S/MIME and HTTP

The HTTP protocol used on web and also for web services shares many constructs with MIME. A HTTP request or response also consists of headers and a separating empty line, and (if the method is POST) also a body content. One of the headers is `Content-type:` specifying a MIME type of the body content. HTTP even uses multipart types, like `multipart/form-data` for uploading files from HTML forms (see [5],[6] section 19.4,[7]).

So it feels natural to use HTTP for transferring content with MIME type `multipart/signed`, i.e. an S/MIME signed content.

The MIME type may be unusual for HTTP clients, but there is a standard mechanism for dealing with it - each HTTP client should send `Accept:` header ([6] section 14.1) indicating which MIME types it can accept. So web service clients should use this `Accept:` header to indicate whether they can accept `multipart/signed` responses. There is no similar mechanism for indicating which MIME types a HTTP server can accept in POST requests. WSDL description of a web service seems to be the proper place for such indication, however there is no standard binding defined for such description as of now.

Public Key Distribution Problem for Message Level Encryption

There is one principal problem with encryption and message level security. The sender must first have the public key of the recipient, before the encryption can take place. But it means that some preliminary communication must be done before the encrypted message can be sent. In SSL, this happens behind the scenes on the transport level, when the SSL channel is established. In message level security, it means some special mechanism for key distribution must be established.

However encrypted communication between two parties is inherently two-point only, and is better solved on the transport level. Message level encryption may be useful when a message is encrypted and sent for more than one recipient. Either the whole message may be readable by all recipients, or possibly only some parts may be readable for some recipients. This scheme was used for example in the SET (Secure Electronic Transactions) payment protocol, where one message had two parts readable only by the merchant and only by the bank respectively.

5.   Implementation of S/MIME based Message Level Security

We created two proof-of-concept implementations of S/MIME-over-HTTP message level security, one in C language for gSOAP toolkit, and the other in Java language for Apache Axis toolkit. They are fully interoperable, so a gSOAP client can be used with an Axis server and vice versa.

Both implementations have separate client and server sides. Both sides wrap outgoing SOAP message into an S/MIME structure, and unwrap a SOAP message from incoming S/MIME structure. For incoming signed messages, the signature is verified (whether the content was not changed), and the signer's certificate is verified against a list of accepted Certificate Authorities, stored in **/etc/grid-security/certificates** folder by default.

Axis implementation

The Java implementation was created for Apache Axis version 1.4. For S/MIME implementation, we used BouncyCastle 1.33 crypto provider and S/MIME library. JavaMail 1.4 and Java Activation Framework 1.1 were used for MIME implementation.

On the client side, a new implementation of HTTP transport had to be created, as the two implementations of HTTP transport provided with

Axis (one Commons HttpClient based and second Axis's own) could not be reused. It is using the standard java.net.HttpURLConnection class. On the server side, a servlet Filter was created which intercepts requests to the AxisServlet.

gSOAP implementation

The C implementation is a plugin for gSOAP 2.7.1. For S/MIME implementation we used OpenSSL 0.9.7.

6.   Evaluation

To evaluate the implementations, we created a benchmark web service, with one operation called **roundtrip**, which gets and returns an array of 10-character strings. We evaluated the role of SOAP message size by using sizes of 1, 10, 100 and 1000 strings.

We measured the number of calls per second, it means two SOAP messages for each call. The measurements were done on a machine with dual core AMD Opteron 280 (2.4GHz) CPU, 512MB memory, running 64-bit SUSE Linux 10.0 operating system with kernel version 2.6.16. For the Java implementation, SUN 64-bit server JVM was used, and the server side was deployed in Tomcat 5.5.12 servlet container. For the C implementation, GCC 4.0.2 compiler was used. Both client and server were running on the same machine to minimize communication latencies.

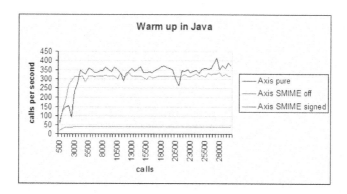

Figure 1.   Gradual increase in speed due to HotSpot Java Virtual Machine dynamic optimizations.

There is a small problem with measuring performance of Java applications. The modern HotSpot virtual machine starts interpreting byte codes, and then performs gradual compilation and dynamic optimizations of the most frequently used parts of code. So application perfor-

mance is increasing over time, before it reaches a stable level, as can
be seen on figure 6. Also garbage collection is done in unpredictable
moments, which account for oscillations of the performance. A JVM
option `-XX:CompileThreshold=1500` was used to suggest early compilation of byte codes. And the performance was measured after each 500
calls, then average was computed from values after the stable level was
reached. The gSOAP implementation in C, on the other hand, has stable
performance over time.

calls per second	string array length			
	1	10	100	1000
Axis pure AxisHttp	350	320	90	13
Axis pure CommonsHttp	210	190	84	13
Axis SMIME off	316	260	90	13
Axis SMIME signed	40	38	30	8
Axis WSS4J signed	33	32	23	5
gSOAP pure	5319	4717	2304	360
gSOAP SMIME signed	300	300	257	78

Table 1. Processing speed of the same web service roundtripping an array of 10-
character strings.

The results are summarized in table 1. The columns show number
of average calls per second for various message sizes. The rows show
various configurations.

The first three cases were measured to get comparison with configurations with no security at all. They are represent Axis with three different
implementations of HTTP transport on the client side, the Axis's own,
the one based on Commons HttpClient 3.0.1, and our S/MIME transport
with signing switched off.

The *Axis SMIME signed* line shows the results of our S/MIME transport with signing enabled. It means that both SOAP messages for each
call were signed using S/MIME and the signature and signer were verified.

For comparison with XML-based security, the *Axis WSS4J signed* line
shows results for Axis with WSS4J plugin, which is an implementation
of OASIS WS-Security. The results are for signed messages with in-
cluded X509 certificate, so they are functionally adequate to S/MIME
signatures. WS-Security allows other modes of operation, by default
WSS4J does not include certificates, just DN of their signing CA and
serial number.

Lines titled *gSOAP pure* and *gSOAP SMIME signed* show results
for gSOAP without any plugin and with S/MIME plugin creating sig-

natures and verifying signatures and signers as described for the Java implementation.

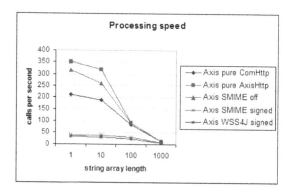

Figure 2. Processing speed of Axis with SMIME signatures, WSS4J signatures, and without any signatures with various HTTP implementations.

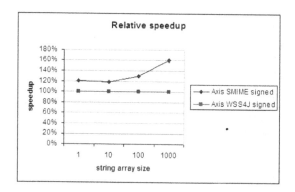

Figure 3. Relative processing speed of Axis with SMIME signatures compared to Axis with WSS4J signatures.

Discussion

Clearly, gSOAP is much faster than Axis. How much this can be attributed to the difference between C and Java is an open question. But according to [3], gSOAP is optimized for maximum performance using clever tricks like schema-specific recursive-descent XML parsers, while Axis uses general-purpose XML parser. We were surprised that the WS-Security implementation of WSS4J was not two orders of magnitude slower, as was reported in [2] for Globus Toolkit 3.2 implementation of XML-Signature. It is about ten times slower than the same service without any security overhead. The S/MIME implementation provides slightly better results, as is shown in figure 2, and the difference is increasing with message size. The S/MIME implementation was not optimized for performance though, so there is some room for improvement.

7.   Conclusion

We presented an alternative to XML-based web service message level security. The alternative is based on S/MIME standard, which is used for securing Internet e-mails, but due to similarities between HTTP and MIME, it can be used for HTTP transfers without modifications. The S/MIME-over-HTTP solution was implemented for gSOAP and Axis toolkits.

8.   Acknowledgments

This research is supported by a research intent "Optical Network of National Research and Its New Applications" (MSM6383917201) and research project "MediGrid – methods and tools for GRID application in biomedicine" (Czech Academy of Sciences, grant T202090537)

References

[1] Kuba M., Krajíček O., Lesný P., Vejvalka J. and Holeček Tomáš. "Grid Empowered Sharing of Medical Expertise", Proceedings of HealthGrid 2006, IOS Press, Amsterdam, NL, 2006. ISBN: 1-58603-617-3

[2] Shirasuna S. et al., "Performance Comparison of Security Mechanisms for Grid Services," grid, pp. 360-364, Fifth IEEE/ACM International Workshop on Grid Computing (associated with Supercomputing 2004), Pittsburgh, PA, 2004. ISBN: 0-7695-2256-4. ISSN: 1550-5510. http://doi.ieeecomputersociety.org/10.1109/GRID.2004.50

[3] Head M. et al., "A Benchmark Suite for SOAP-based Communication in Grid Web Services", Proceedings of ACM/IEEE SC 2005 Conference (SC'05), p. 19, 2005.
http://doi.ieeecomputersociety.org/10.1109/SC.2005.2

[4] Liu H., Pallickara S.,Fox G., "Performance of Web Services Security", Proceedings of the 13th Annual Mardi Gras Conference, February 2005, Baton Rouge, Louisiana
http://grids.ucs.indiana.edu/ptliupages/publications/WSSPerf.pdf

[5] RFC 2388: Returning Values from Forms: multipart/form-data
http://www.ietf.org/rfc/rfc2388.txt

[6] RFC 2616: Hypertext Transfer Protocol – HTTP/1.1
http://www.ietf.org/rfc/rfc2616.txt

[7] http://www.w3.org/Protocols/HTTP/Object_Headers.html#z16

[8] RFC 3851: Secure/Multipurpose Internet Mail Extensions (S/MIME) Version 3.1 Message Specification `http://www.ietf.org/rfc/rfc3851.txt`

[9] S/MIME and OpenPGP page on Internet Mail Consortium website `http://www.imc.org/smime-pgpmime.html`

[10] IETF's S/MIME Working Group charter `http://www.ietf.org/html.charters/smime-charter.html`

IV

GRID INFRASTRUCTURE

FAULT TOLERANT GRID REGISTRY

Marek Kasztelnik[2], Marian Bubak[1,2], Cezary Górka, Maciej Malawski[1,2] and Tomasz Gubała[2]

[1]*Institute of Computer Science, AGH, al. Mickiewicza 30, 30-059, Kraków, Poland*

[2]*Academic Computer Center CYFRONET, ul. Nawojki 11, 30-950 Kraków, Poland*
m.kasztelnik@cyfronet.pl, bubak@agh.edu.pl,
czgorka@o2.pl, malawski@agh.edu.pl, gubala@scienc e.uva.nl

Abstract   Development of tools that assist efficient computing in a distributed environment is a challenging problem in modern and future Grid systems. A registry that aids searching for information about existing components of distributed applications belongs to this class of tools. This work presents the Grid Registry, which is a distributed, scalable and fault-tolerant facility that stores information about structure and semantics of Grid/Web services. A set of performance tests that present the behavior of the registry are also described.

Keywords: Distributed registry, Grid service, fault-tolerance, data synchronization, load balancing.

1.   Introduction

Building applications using Web or Grid services is becoming more and more popular. The appropriate usage of the service-oriented computing paradigm [1] enables us to connect various resources into a workflow that performs the required computation. One of the most important functionalities for service-oriented software development is the ability to find suitable services published in the Grid and it may be accomplished by a registry which stores necessary information about services. If the registry operates in a Grid environment it has to be scalable and resilient to failures and overloads. The Grid Registry [2, 4] is a distributed system used to maintain information concerning semantic, syntactic and human-readable descriptions of Web or Grid services.

The paper is organized as follows. First, an overview of existing registries is presented. Next, the description of the structure of the registry is given. The third section of the paper is focused on one of the most important aspects of functionality in the registry - fault tolerance. Subsequently, descriptions of algorithms that realize failure resiliency are presented. The fourth section includes some performance tests that present the behavior of the registry. The last section describes the conclusions and the possible future work.

2.   Overview of existing solutions

Searching Web or Grid services has become important problem. Information about services should be available in one place so that the user can easily query it. This issue is undertaken by Universal Description, Discovery and Integration (UDDI) protocol [5]. A disadvantage of this solution, however, is that it does not contain any information about service input and output semantics. Grimoires Registry [6] address this issue. This registry adds metadata that give information about existing entities. It is a considerable improvement but other disadvantages still remain. If all data is stored on many places, this kind of solution is not very scalable, and when the number of locations grows, keeping all information copies up to date is very difficult. On the other hand, when the volume of information about a service grows, every location presents more and more demands (e.g. computer power). A solution to this problem is a registry that is distributed across several hosts on the Internet. The Eco Grid Registry is this kind of a system [7]. It is a distributed registry that contains information about logical service names, URL of WSDL, type and service classification. Despite many advantages, this system does not guarantee nontrivial quality of service and thus another solution has to be proposed.

3.   Overview of the Grid Registry

The Grid Registry is a distributed, scalable, fault-tolerant, semantic-based, Grid-enabled registry storing information about Web or Grid services. There are two kinds of registry users. An administrator is a actor responsible for configuring the registry and managing information about the stored services while a user can search for information about services using semantic, syntactic or human-readable descriptions.

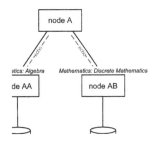

The fundamental element of the registry is a single node. It is a computer

Figure 1.   Simple Grid Registry structure

system that acts as a provider and makes all functionalities of the registry available for the user. The registry is built using these basic elements. It has a hierarchical structure and it is based on the ancestor-descendant relation. A simple configuration of the registry is shown in Figure 1. The "Mathematics" node is a root of the registry and it has two children (descendants) "Algebra" and "Discrete Mathematics". What is more, "Mathematics" is the ancestor of nodes "Algebra" and "Discrete Mathematics" - of course these domains can have sub-domains too. The information stored in the Grid Registry is conceptually divided into domains and it is distributed throughout the nodes of the registry topology. All nodes have a routing table that contains information about all its ancestors and descendants. Therefore, a user can ask a selected branch of the registry about a service that fulfils the specified conditions, and there is no difference which node is used by the user to connect to the registry.

4.   Fault-Tolerance and Data Synchronization

Introduction

Non fault-tolerance version of the Grid Registry [2, 3] allowed only for service searching and it did not guarantee nontrivial quality of service. Every node was a single point of failure and some of them could be overloaded. When a domain node crashed, all the information stored there and in all its sub-domains was inaccessible to the user. Still worse, when many queries were sent to a specific domain node, this node may have become overloaded. These disadvantages were the reason behind adding a fault-tolerance mechanisms to the registry [4]. The implementation of a fault-tolerant registry has to provide the following functionalities:

- **Fault-Tolerance.** This mechanism ensures that the system can be used by the user even when something goes wrong in one or more elements in the software and hardware configuration. To fulfill this functionality, all single points of failure have to be eliminated. Moreover, the mechanism responsible for checking if a task is processed correctly has to be made available. In case of a failure, the task has to be redirected to a backup system.

- **Data Synchronization.** Each fault-tolerant system must remain operational even if a part of it has crashed. To ensure high availability for such a system, all information has to be backed up. A data synchronization process ensures that all these backups are up to date even in case of a failure of the system.

- **Load Balance.** It is a technique to spread work between many computers or other resources to get optimal resource utilization.

Concept

The main purpose of the Grid Registry fault tolerance mechanisms is to meet all the presented requirements. All data in the registry can be duplicated and stored in geographically distributed locations. In case of an error with delivering the message, the query is redirected to a backup system where computation can be performed. When the system crashes and afterwards comes back online, there is a mechanism responsible for data resynchronization. Another element of functionality is a load balancing mechanism which checks if there are no overloaded nodes. All these functionality elements are based on the "echo" mechanism, as explained in the following subsection.

Fault-Tolerance scenarios

This part presents an expanded example of using the registry, both by an administrator and by a user. All cases from this example were implemented and tested, so it proves that the Grid Registry fulfills the requirements for a fault-tolerant system.

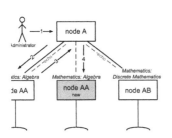

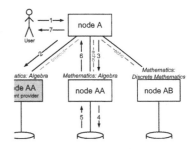

Figure 2. An example of adding a new node when all nodes work

Figure 3. A sample user query; the message can not be delivered to a broken node and it is redirected to a backup node

Assume that we have following initial registry structure (see Figure 1): one root node **A** (domain "Mathematics"), which has two children: **AA** (domain "Mathematics : Algebra") and **AB** (domain "Mathematics : Discrete Mathematics"). This structure was configured by an administrator when starting the system. Such a topology does not guarantee correct processing if a node fails. To improve fault tolerance, the administrator of such a system should add some backups. In Figure 2 an example of adding a new node **AA** is presented. In this case an administrator, who is connected to the node **A**, sends request that adds a new empty node to the registry.

New added node is not synchronized with other one and need to be updated. It sends echo message to node **A**, which, after receiving all echo messages, compares their time stamps. Node **A** observes that one of its children is not updated, so it begins the synchronization process. During this operation the new node **AA** receives all documents from most up-to-date **AA** node and stores them in its own local database. When the operations of adding a node and synchronizing the data are completed, the fault tolerance of the whole system is improved. Even if one of the nodes **AA** fails, the registry still works correctly. To prove this, the next example is presented.

In the example in Figure 3 the user wants to find some service located in the domain "Algebra". He or she sends a query to the node **A** which redirects it to the current provider **AA**. When this node does not respond, the node **A** sends the same query to the second node **AA**. In this case, the operation is successful so the user receives a response. Furthermore, the current provider of the domain "Algebra" is internally changed because only the second node **AA** has sent an echo message to its parent.

Implementation

Fault Tolerance. Thanks to the fault tolerance mechanism the registry with some broken domains looks to a user like a fully functional system. To provide that functionality, the domains are duplicated and there is a mechanism designed to check if the connection between nodes is broken. When such a problem is discovered, the system checks which messages have been sent to the broken nodes (and are still waiting for an answer) so that alternative nodes can respond. When the next message is sent, it avoids the broken node and is delivered to a place where it can be processed. Another possible scenario occurs when a message is sent to a node and it causes an error message with a code describing the problem of delivering the query to the destination host (e.g. there are connection problems or some technical issues with the machine where one of the registry nodes is installed). In this situation, an alternative node where the query should be sent is found.

Knowledge about node status can be reached by using a static link between registry elements. This solution is very difficult in a dynamically changing environment [10]. Another possibility is an "echo" mechanism. All nodes send echo messages containing information about themselves to their ancestors. When an ancestor receives this information, it sends back the response with the required information. Through this mechanism, the registry obtains knowledge about ancestors and descendants and in case of any error the Grid Registry can properly react to it.

Data Synchronization. In the Grid Registry, even if one of its nodes breaks, the whole system can continue to work correctly. However, this broken node cannot respond to any kind of messages, such as adding or removing nodes or services. When it returns to life, its database and routing table may not be up to date. Therefore the data synchronization between nodes in the same domain is added.

Each node in the registry stores information about the time of the last update (global node time stamp). This time stamp is put into each "echo" message and is periodically sent to the ancestor. Therefore, each node knows the time stamps of its children, so it can notice that some of them are out of date and begin the synchronization process. In such a case, the most up to date node inside one domain sends data to this unsynchronized node. The advantage is that not the entire database and routing table data is transmitted but only the needed documents and entries. This is possible because each document in the database and each entry in the local routing table inside a node store their own time stamp fields.

Load Balancing.   A domain in a registry can occupy several nodes. If more than one node exists in a domain ("Algebra" is such domain in Figure 3), the current provider is specified. All queries are routed through the current provider, whereas remaining nodes in that domain store backup information. In order to provide load balancing in the registry the roles of nodes inside one domain must change. Therefore, each node that has recently sent an echo message is chosen as the current provider and, consequently, the numbr of overloaded nodes are reduced.

5.   Performance evaluation

All tests were performed on the local network, using hosts that had similar hardware and software configurations (Athlon XP 2000+, 512M RAM, 100Mb LAN). Grid Registry Services (with and without fault tolerance mechanisms) were deployed in a GT3 (Globus Toolkit 3.x) [11] containers and the Xindice [12] database – in Tomcat 5.0 [13] Application Server. The main goal of these tests was to show the behavior of the registry and the comparison between user's query response time in two cases: with and without the fault tolerance mechanisms. The tests also show some specific behavior of the Grid Registry when some nodes are broken.

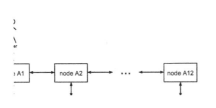

Figure 4.   Performance test configuration of the Grid Registry.

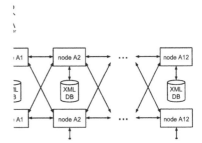

Figure 5.   Performance test configuration of the fault-tolerance version of the Grid Registry.

The first test was conducted in order to measure the performance of the query routing and processing messages by the query handlers. The configuration of the registry that does not have any fault-tolerance mechanisms is shown in Figure 4, and the fault-tolerant registry is presented in Figure 5. These configurations were similar from the user's point of view. In both cases the user was connected to the first node in the hierarchy (**A1** – the root node). Every query to the domain **A12** database had to pass all eleven nodes before it reached its destination. The client program sends "ping" and "find service" queries to all domains in the registry configuration and the time of the response is measured. The result can be seen in Figure 6.

The system scales well with the length of query route and the communication overhead is relatively large in simple queries such as "ping", where the handling mechanism only answers the message and does not perform any other computations. In the case of messages like "find service", where an XML database has to be queried, the time spent on communication is shorter than the time required to answer specific queries.

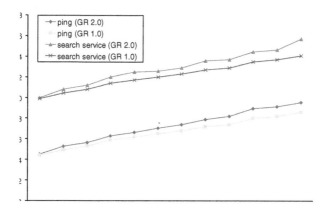

Figure 6. Result of sending "ping" and "findSerivce" queries in both versions of the Grid Registry.

One more characteristic can be observed in the registry with fault tolerance mechanisms – every time a message arrives to a specific node necessary information has to be stored in case of any error. This is why there are differences in times between answering the queries in both version of the registry. A further factor that influences the result of the test is that specific information providing the fault tolerant behavior of the registry has to be sent periodically. What is more, when a crashed node "returns to life", specific synchronization messages are sent.

The second test was conducted with the same configuration as the previous one (see Figure 5). This test presents the behavior of the system when some nodes are out of order. The user was connected to node **A1** and sent queries to node **A12**. The crash of the node was simulated by shutting down the OGSI container where it was installed. In the configuration of the registry, the time of sending an "echo" message was set for ten seconds and queries were sent after this period, when a node was unavailable. All the queries were sent after the registry received all information about nodes, so the broken node was not taken into account when the next hop of the message was chosen. If every node from the domain was installed on one physical computer system, significant differences in times of query response to "ping" and "find service" messages in both cases were not observed (0.95s for "ping" queries and 1.59s for "findService" queries).

Figure 7. Configuration of the fault-tolerance version of the Grid Registry used in the third test.

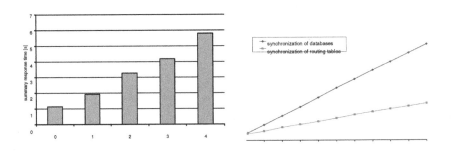

Figure 8. Result of the query redirected to a backup node test.

Figure 9. Result of database and routing table synchronization tests

The next test presents the behavior of the registry when it receives an error return message. The structure of the registry was similar to the previous one but there were only six domains (see Figure 7) and, in configuration of the registry, a long period of time between sending "echo" messages was set. The user was connected to node **A1** and sent "ping" messages all the time to node **A6**. As a result, the time between the error and sending information was relatively short. Without any knowledge about broken node, the message was sent to that node and generated an error message. Consequently, the initial query had to be redirected to a backup node. The result of this test is shown in Figure 8. It presents the time of response to the "ping" queries in a situation where one, two, etc. errors were returned and the initial message had to be redirected to a backup node.

As can be seen in the graph with the result of the test, there are marks-up connected with received error responses, which redirect the initial message to another working node. This test also shows another characteristic of the registry: only one message can be sent to a broken node because after receiving an error response all subsequent queries are sent to backup nodes. This is achieved by setting proper information about the status of the node in the local routing table. That is why the response times of the second and further queries are the same as in the situation where all nodes work. In this way the knowledge about broken nodes is propagated in the registry topology.

Finally, two tests concerning synchronization performance were conducted. Figure 9 presents results of these tests with the same simple configuration: there was one node **A**, which had two children **B**, and one of these children was not updated. The first test shows times of database synchronization and the second one presents routing table synchronization performance. As can be seen, time was linearly increasing according to the number of items (database or routing table entries) which needed synchronization. In the first case, synchronization was longer because the size of the database entry was larger than the size of routing table entry, so the document, which was sent from the first node **B** to the second one, was also bigger. Nevertheless, as can be seen, even if one hundred items required synchronization, the time needed for this process was acceptable. However, this also depends on network quality – in the case of a network with low-bandwidth connections the process may take much longer.

6. Summary and Future work

This work presents the design and implementation of a Grid Registry with fault tolerance mechanisms such as load balancing, system backup and data synchronization. The performance tests have shown that the overhead introduced by implementing these features is low and acceptable. Future work will include migration to the newest versions of Grid technologies, such as WSRF [14] or component technologies, as well as a support for multiple standards for semantic service descriptions. Fault-tolerance mechanisms should be separated from normal communication between user and nodes. The mechanisms of echo sending and data synchronization should be developed as separate components that can be plugged into the registry.

Aknowledgements This reserach was partially funded by the EU IST Project ViroLab and SPUB-M. The authors are very grateful to Mr. Piotr Nowakowski for his remarks.

References

[1] M.P. Singh, M.N. Huhns, *Service-Oriented Computing: Semantics, Processes, Agents*, Wiley, 2005

[2] M. Kapałka, M. Bubak (Supervisor). *Distributed, Semantics-Based Workflow Composition on a Grid*. Master of Science Thesis, AGH University of Science and Technology, Faculty of Electrical Engineering, Automatics, Computer Science and Electronics, Institute of Computer Science, Kraków, Poland, June 2004.

[3] M. Bubak, T. Gubała, M. Kapałka, M. Malawski, K. Rycerz *Grid Service Registry for Workflow Composition Framework*. Computational Science - ICCS 2004. 4th International Conference, Kraków, Poland June 2004 34-41

[4] M. Kasztelnik, C Górka, M. Bubak (Supervisor). *Tools for development of workflow-based grid applications*. Master of Science Thesis, AGH University of Science and Technology, Faculty of Electrical Engineering, Automatics, Computer Science and Electronics, Institute of Computer Science, Kraków, Poland, August 2005.

[5] Universal Description, Discovery and Integration protocol. http://www.uddi.org.

[6] Grimoires: Grid Registry with Metadata Oriented Interface: Robustness, Efficiency, Security http://www.ecs.soton.ac.uk/research/projects/grimoires

[7] S. Bowers, K. Lin, and B. Ludäscher *On integrating scientific resources through semantic registration*. Proceedings of the 16th International Conference on Scientific and Statistical Database Management (SSDBM), IEEE Computer Society (2004).

[8] M. Bubak, T. Gubała, M. Kapałka, M. Malawski, K. Rycerz: textitWorkflow composer and service registry for grid applications. Future Generation Computer Systems **21**(1) (2005) 79–86

[9] Knowledge-based Workflow System for Grid Application. http://www.kwfgrid.net.

[10] Incorporating Fault Tolerance into an Autonomic-Computing Environment http://csdl2.computer.org/comp/mags/ds/2004/02/o2003.pdf

[11] The Globus Toolkit™ Project. http://www.globus.org/toolkit.

[12] Apache Xindice, The Apache XML Project, http://xml.apache.org/xindice.

[13] The Apache Jakarta Project: Apache Tomcat. http://jakarta.apache.org/tomcat.

[14] Web Services Resource Framework (WSRF). http://www.globus.org/wsrf/.

SECURE APPLICATION DEPLOYMENT IN THE HIERARCHICAL LOCAL DESKTOP GRID

Attila Csaba Marosi, Gábor Gombás and Zoltán Balaton
MTA SZTAKI
Laboratory of Parallel and Distributed Systems
atisu@sztaki.hu, gombasg@sztaki.hu, balaton@sztaki.hu

Abstract   The Desktop Grid model harvests the unused CPU cycles of any computer connected. In this paper we present a concept how the separated Desktop Grids can be used as building blocks for larger scale grids by organizing them in a hierarchical tree. We present a prototype implementation and show the challenges and security considerations we discovered. We describe methods and give solutions how security can be enhanced to satisfy the requirements for real-world deployment.

Keywords: Public Resource Computing, Volunteer Computing, BOINC, Hierarchy, Local Desktop Grid

1.   Introduction

Contrary to traditional grid[11] systems where the maintainers of the grid infrastructure provide resources where users of the infrastructure can run their applications, desktop grids provide the applications and the users of the desktop grid provide the resources. Thus, a major advantage of desktop grids is that they are able to utilize a huge amount of resources that were not available for traditional grid computing previously.

Users of scientific applications usually are concerned only about the amount of computing power they can get and not about the details how a grid system delivers this computing power. Therefore, they want to develop a single application that in turn can run on any infrastructure that provides the most appropriate resources at a given time. Unfortunately existing applications have to be modified in order to run on desktop grid systems and this makes desktop grids less attractive for application developers than traditional grid systems.

2.   Desktop Grids

The common architecture of desktop grids consists of one or more central servers and a large number of clients. The central server provides the applications and their input data. Clients join the desktop grid voluntarily, offering to download and run an application with a set of input data. When the application has finished, the client uploads the results to the server. Based on the environment where the desktop grid is deployed we must distinguish between two different concepts.

Global Desktop Grids

Global Desktop Grids (also known as Public Desktop Grids) consist of a publicly accessible server providing projects and the attached clients. There are several unique aspects of this computing model compared to traditional grid systems. First, clients may come and go at any time, and there is no guarantee that a client that started a computation will indeed finish it. Furthermore, the clients cannot be trusted to be free of either hardware or software defects, meaning the server can never be sure that an uploaded result is in fact correct. Therefore, redundancy is often used by giving the same piece of work to multiple clients and comparing the results to filter out corrupt ones.

Local Desktop Grids

To fill the gap between the traditional grids and the desktop grids SZTAKI introduced the concept of Local Desktop Grids. Local Desktop Grids are intended for institutional or industrial use. Especially for businesses it is often not acceptable to send out application code and data to untrusted third parties (sometimes this is even forbidden by law). The project and clients are shielded from the world by firewalls or any other means. This environment gives more flexibility by allowing the clients to access local resources securely and since the resources are not voluntarily offered the performance is more predictable.

SZTAKI Local Desktop Grid

As we can see there is a huge difference between traditional grids and desktop grids. We also have to make a distinction between the publicly used Global Desktop Grids and the Local Desktop Grid concept. The SZTAKI Local Desktop Grid[4] (or SZTAKI LDG) implements the latter. It is based on BOINC[1] technology and extends it according to the needs of institutional and business users. BOINC is originating from the SETI@Home[3] project to provide an open infrastructure for utilizing the computers of people interested in the outcome of a project.

We faced several possibilities when designing SZTAKI LDG: to develop our own solution[15], to use other desktop grid systems and approaches like Distributed.net[9], Legion[13], JXTA[8] or Entropia[10]. We decided to build on BOINC, because it has a large user base, it's open source, cross-platform and has a clean design[2] and implementation making it the best target for (third party) enhancements[5].

SZTAKI Desktop Grid has a Public Desktop Grid version[6] running currently with more than 12000 registered users.

3. Hierarchy

One of the enhancements of the SZTAKI Local Desktop Grid hierarchy. Hierarchy allows the use of desktop grid projects as building blocks for larger grids, for example divisions of a company or departments of a university can form a company or faculty wide desktop grid. Every project has a classical parent-child relationship with the others. They may request work from a project above (*consumer*) or may provide work for a project below (*producer*). The project server can enter a hierarchical mode, when one of it's consumers require more work than it has for disposal. It will then contact one of it's producer nodes and request more work.

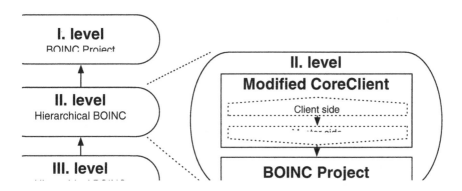

Figure 1.   The split architecture of the Hierarchy prototype. Inside the *CoreClient* the *Client side* is acting as a consumer by requesting work and the *Master side* as a producer by providing work for the project.

It is allowed for a project to have more consumers and producers. We use the simple layout in *Figure 1* for presenting the enhancements of the architecture only. The architecture consists of a modified BOINC CoreClient and a project. The CoreClient is required normally for the clients to participate in any project, but now the CoreClient is running on the machine hosting the consumer project. Originally it's task is also to dynamically download the application of the project which is doing the actual computation for the project.

BOINC terminology uses the *platform* expression for the specific combinations of architectures and operating systems. We modified the CoreClient such that we may specify what platform it should pretend to be using. This allows us to query all the predefined platforms for applications however, the deployment of the application on the lower levels is not handled by the CoreClient, it is the task of the project administrator. When the number of unsent workunits runs below a specified threshold the CoreClient will contact a producer for work. A project may have more producers configured each with a priority assigned. First the producer with the highest priority will be contacted for work, if it fails to provide work then the next one is queried and so on. The modified CoreClient has a split architecture, first it consumes work from a producer (*Client side*), second it injects the requested work in the local consumer project, thus acts as a provider (*Master side*).

To test our prototype we deployed a seven-level hierarchical environment with clients attached to the lowest level. Six of the servers were running on Debian Linux 3.1/Intel, one was using Mac OS/X 10.4/PowerPC. Six clients were attached, three using Debian Linux 3.1/Intel, two Windows XP and one Mac OS/X 10.4/PowerPC. We also created a simple application for all *platforms*, with the only purpose to produce high load and run exactly for the time given in the *workunit*. Our goal with this diverse environment was not to measure performance, simply to test the environment for possible problems and bottlenecks. Using the prototype we were able to provide basic hierarchical functionality without modifying existing projects. Only a modified CoreClient was needed for work request and distribution. However, this method does not solve issues with the automatic deployment of applications coming form a higher level of the hierarchy, the exponentially growing number of workunits caused by redundancy or any security considerations.

4.   Challenges and solutions

We discovered various problems which the prototype described in the previous section could not solve. In order to be able to provide a model which is mature enough for industrial or institutional deployment the following issues need to be addressed.

Redundancy and deadline

Redundancy ensures every workunit will have a correct result by simply sending the same piece of work to multiple clients and comparing the results to filter out corrupt ones. *Figure 2* shows a three level layout with the redundancy

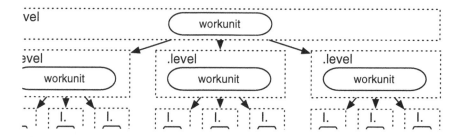

Figure 2. Growing number of redundant workunits in the hierarchy demonstrated with a simple three level layout.

of three on each level. In this case each producer on each level creates three copies of any workunit received. By the third level there will be nine redundant ones. This means that nine clients will compute the same workunit instead of the supposed three (which was the requested redundancy on the first level). If more levels are added to the hierarchy this number will exponentially grow. It can be solved easily by forcing redundancy to be disabled on all but the first level. This way exactly the requested number of redundant workunits will be distributed.

Deadline is to prohibit workunit-hijacking by clients. Set when the workunit is downloaded, after it passes the workunit is considered invalid and resent to another client. Since each level of hierarchy is recreating the workunits from its producers for distribution, the deadline of the original workunit at the top level is not propagated. The problem is requesting too many or too few workunits in the hierarchy. In the first case the clients, may be normal or hierarchical, won't be able to upload them before the deadline passes, in the latter some of the clients are left without work. Predicting the performance is not the subject of this paper, but we needed a simple way to do it. We created a monitoring and statistics tool, which monitors the performance, number of users, hosts, sent and unsent workunits and many more. Since our main focus is on the *Local Desktop Grid* environment, where the performance should be less fluctuating, this enables us to have a good enough guess on the number of workunits to be requested based on the recent events.

Trust

BOINC uses an asymmetric key pair for code and workunit signing. When multiple clients interact with a single project the key pair is sufficient for authentication and authorization. In case where multiple projects interact with each other additional information is required. We think it is also important to identify the origin of the application the project is currently using, since it may be from anywhere. This and the problems we describe in the following two sections can be easy solved by introducing *certificates* and defining various *administrative units*. We were considering GnuPG[16] and X.509[17]. GnuPG has a good infrastructure for key-distribution, but since X.509 is widely used and de facto standard for authentication and authorization[12, 14] we think it will provide a better solution for us.

Currently BOINC has one administrative unit, the *project* itself with it's key pairs. It's the task of the *project* to sign any application deployed and to sign the workunits sent to clients (using another key pair).

We want to distinguish between the *Application Developer*, the *Project*, the *Server* and the *Client*, each with a certificate assigned. The *Application Developer* is an individual or group of individuals who develop and sign their applications but she is often not involved in the management of the BOINC project. We think the application itself should not be a separate administrative unit, it can be identified among others with the signature of it's developer. The *Server* is the node hosting one or more *Project*. The *Client* is the *BOINC Local Client* or *CoreClient* whose task is to run the application of the *Project* with the given set of input data (*Workunit*).

Application representation

BOINC currently identifies the applications with a *name* and a *version*. This does not provide information about the developer or the origin of the application. We want to distribute them in the hierarchy, this requires a unique identifier for each version of each application. We want to extend the definition of the application by bundling the new signature and for the validation required certificates with it. This allows us to uniquely distinguish any application with the combination of the *name*, *version* and it's *Application Developer*'s signature.

Application registration

With the introduction of certificates and *Application Developer*s the application signing by the projects is not needed anymore. Instead, the project now publishes the list of trusted *Application Developers*. Thus applications can be distributed automatically in the hierarchy, but with security considerations.

Figure 3 shows the flow of the registration. Communication is always performed via the HTTP over TLS protocol (HTTPS)[7]. First the *Hierarchical Client* running on the *consumer* will contact the *producer* with the highest priority identifying itself with one of the defined *platforms*. Since both Projects have a *certificate* assigned they will authenticate mutually, they also have a list of the certificates of trusted *Projects* and *Application Developers*. This allows

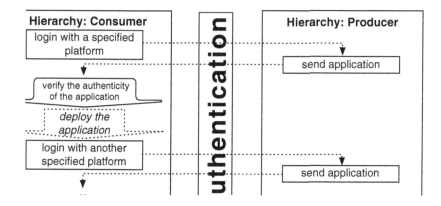

Figure 3. Application registration

to perform authorization on both sides. After a successful authentication and authorization the consumer will request the latest version of the application of the producer. The producer sends the executable, the signature and any certificates needed to verify the signature. The consumer verifies the authenticity of the application and check if its developer is authorized to deploy applications to the consumer Project. If authorized then the normal BOINC application deployment follows: copying the files to an HTTPS accessible directory and registering the metadata in the backend database. Updating and signing the list of trusted certificates is the responsibility of the project administrator.

The *Hierarchical Client* repeats this procedure for each platform defined. After querying all platforms, since no new application version is available it will start to request workunits.

The steps involved in the application registration process are presented in *Figure 4*. All communication between projects and clients is via the HTTP over TLS protocol. First step is for the *Application Developer* to sign her *Application*, producing a signature (*Sig*). Second step is to *Install* the application to *Project 2*. This initial installation is the task of the project administrator and is done manually. The project administrator adds the certificates required to verify the signature to the projects list of certificates (*Cert List P2*), runs the BOINC application registration procedure by copying the signature and executable(s) to the desired place and registers the metadata in the backend database. The project may sign the application, thus certifying its origin. When a *consumer* (*Project 1*) runs out of work the *Hierarchical Client* belonging to the project contacts a *producer* (Project 2). After mutual authentication the consumer downloads

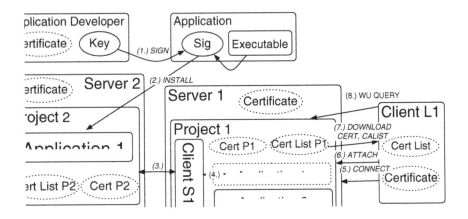

Figure 4.   Application registration and work distribution

Application 1, verifies the signature, authorizes the developer and *register*s the application (*3.* and *4. step*). When the registration succeeds, the *Hierarchical Client* will start requesting workunits from the producer and injecting them in the consumer project. A *Local Client* contacts *Project 2* by connecting to the server first (*5. step*). After mutual authentication the client is authorized either by a certificate belonging to the *Client* or by a BOINC account key (*6. step*). In the first case the project's list of certificates (*Cert List P1*) should contain the client's certificate, this is another task which is performed manually by the project administrator. The client downloads the application, and adds all certificates from the project to its list (*Cert List, 7. step*) and verifies the application. The last step for the client is the downloading of workunits (*8.*). After computing the result of a workunit, it is uploaded to *Project 1* where the *Hierarchical Client* notices it and uploads it to the producer of the project and reports it as finished.

5.   Conclusion and future work

SZTAKI Local Desktop Grid is based on BOINC, its main enhancement is allowing hierarchical setups. Hierarchy allows to build larger desktop grids by using existing projects as building elements. We have shown that it is possible to have basic functionality for work distribution without modifying already deployed projects. Our prototype implementation was tried in a test environment revealing issues we need to address. We think security is crucial for real-world deployment, and this increased security can be achieved by using already proven technologies, like X.509 certificates. With the introduction of certificates, issues like application representation, distribution and registration can be solved. In the future we will work on solving the remaining issues and refining the security enhancements discussed. We want to work on estimating the number of required workunits to be transfered between different levels of the hierarchy. We also need to implement a better certificate distribution solution. Currently we don't have any certificate revocation implementation, so we want to address this problem in the future too.

6.   Acknowledgement

The work presented in this paper has been partially supported by the Development and Meteorological Application of New Generation Grid Technologies in the Environmental Protection and Building Energy Management Project (NKFP2-00007/2005) and the CoreGRID (FP6-004265) Project.

References

[1] Berkeley Open Infrastructure For Network Computing. http://boinc.berkeley.edu

[2] D. P. Anderson: BOINC: A System for Public-Resource Computing and Storage. 5th IEEE/ACM International Workshop on Grid Computing, November 8, 2004, Pittsburgh, USA.

[3] SETI@home: Search for Extraterrestrial Intelligence at Home. http://setiathome.berkeley.edu

[4] Peter Kacsuk, Norbert Podhorszki and Tamas Kiss. Scalable Desktop Grid System. Technical report, TR-0006, Institute on System Architecture, CoreGRID - Network of Excellence, May 2005.

[5] Jakob Gregor Pedersen & Christian Ulrik Sottrup. *Developing Distributed Computing Solutions Combining Grid Computing and Public Computing*. Master's thesis from University of Copenhagen, 2005.

[6] SZTAKI Desktop Grid. http://szdg.lpds.sztaki.hu/szdg.

[7] HTTP Over TLS. http://www.ietf.org/rfc/rfc2818.txt

[8] Sun Microsystems, JXTA. http://www.jxta.org.

[9] Distributed.net, The fastest computer on earth. http://www.distributed.net.

[10] Entropia, Inc. http://www.entropia.com.

[11] I. Foster, The Grid: Blueprint For a New Computing Infrastructure, Morgan Kaufmann, Los Altos, CA, 1998.

[12] I. Foster, C. Kesselman, S. Tuecke, The anatomy of the grid: Enabling scalable virtual organizations, Internat. J. Supercomput. Appl. 15 (3) (2001) 200-222.

[13] A. Grimshaw, W. Wulf, The legion vision of a worldwide virtual computer, Comm. ACM 40, 1997, 39-45.

[14] Foster, I., Kesselman, C., Tsudik, G. and Tuecke, S. A Security Architecture for Computational Grids. In ACM Conference on Computers and Security, 83-91.

[15] Myers, D.S., and M. P. Cummings. Necessity is the mother of invention: a simple grid computing system using commodity tools. Journal of Parallel and Distributed Computing, Volume 63, Issue 5, May 2003, pp. 578-589.

[16] The GNU Privacy Guard. http://www.gnupg.org

[17] Internet X.509 Public Key Infrastructure Certificate and CRL Profile. http://www.ietf.org/rfc/ rfc2459.txt

DESIGNING A DISTRIBUTED MEDIATOR COMPONENT FOR THE C-GMA MONITORING ARCHITECTURE

Ondřej Krajíček[2], Andrea Ceccanti[1], Aleš Křenek[2],
Luděk Matyska[2], Miroslav Ruda[2]

[1] *INFN-CNAF, Bologna, Italy*
[2] *Institute of Computer Science, Masaryk University, Brno, Czech Republic*

Abstract   Grid Infrastructure Monitoring is distinguished as important technique for diagnosing, addressing and preventing problems which may occur in the grids. It is also source of valuable information suitable for scheduling, load balancing and other applications. Currently, infrastructure monitoring is done using specialised toolkits which provide complete solution for single infrastructure and middleware. In large-scale grids, where it is necessary to comprise resources from multiple virtual organisations, it may be necessary to integrate various platforms into single ubiquitous monitored fabric. C-GMA provides tools for such integrations. In this paper, we address the scalability of the C-GMA by proposing a distributed design of C-GMA mediator component. In particular, we examine the properties of Publish/Subscribe systems for this purpose.

Keywords: grid monitoring, C-GMA, content-based publish/subscribe systems

1.   Introduction

Capability-based Grid Monitoring Architecture [3, 7] is an extension to the original GGF-standardised Grid Monitoring Architecture [1]. The C-GMA extends the GMA model to provide monitoring framework for true interoperability of various grid monitoring toolkits and infrastructures. One of the notable extension to the original GMA model is introduction of additional component, which encapsulates the GMA directory called the *mediator*. The purpose of the mediator component is to proactively monitor component registrations and notify producers and consumers of interesting and potentially compatible counterparts. This paper focuses on designing the mediator component as a distributed system, based on the concept of Content-Based Networking, to ensure scalability even in large-scale environment.

After a brief review of related work in the following section, we introduce the main ideas of the C-GMA in Sect. 2 and Content-based Publish/Subscribe

Systems in Sect. 4. Sect. 3 presents the core design of the distributed mediator service.

2.   The C-GMA Architecture and Components

The GMA provides a general view of a monitoring system, which is based on a model consisting of three components: *producer, consumer*, and *directory service*. The monitoring data are transferred from producer to consumer in the form of events. GMA does not specify any implementation details (such as data presentation mechanisms or communication protocols) but states general implementation requirements (such as scalability of all system components).

Currently, several different Grid monitoring infrastructure implementations exist, e. g. Mercury [9] or R-GMA, Relational Grid Monitoring Architecture [8], Ganglia, SCALEA-G and others. We briefly mention basic properties of two of them. The Mercury system describes data types in terms of *metrics*. GMA directory is not present at all—producers and consumers communicate with each other only directly. R-GMA is based on the relational data model, using a subset of the SQL language to describe both data and queries. Scalability is addressed by R-GMA to some extent as well since The R-GMA Registry (the specific incarnation of the GMA directory service) is replicated in the recent releases.

Inherently, the generality of the GMA specification allows multiple GMA-compliant but not interoperable implementations. The C-GMA is designed to extend GMA with a framework that, besides GMA compliance, provides another level of interoperability. The goal of the C-GMA is a framework for *co-existence* and *collaboration* of components coming from diverse GMA implementations rather then proposing a universal architecture. We base our effort on the hypothesis that designing such a universal system is either not possible or it would be too restrictive.

The component model of the C-GMA is illustrated in Fig. 1. It defines four basic components:

Producer produces the monitoring data in the form of events.

Consumer consumes the monitoring data. Individual consumers are connected directly to the appropriate producers.

Registry (Directory Service) is an information service which stores information about available producers and consumers and also the data type schema.

Mediator is used by consumers and producers to discover potential partners (producers and consumers, resp.). The actual discovery process is described later.

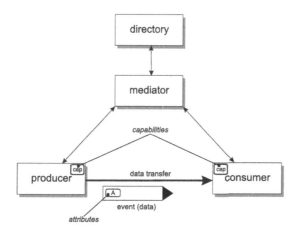

Figure 1. The C-GMA Component Model

Distinction between mediator and registry is important, since it presents separation of concepts of active discovery and storage of component registrations. This allows for grater flexibility in implementations.

Besides the component model of C-GMA, another model is necessary for the C-GMA to work. We denote this model as *metadata model*. The metadata model defines two *metadata layers*:

- **the capability and attribute layer**: describes properties, working conditions and requirements of components and data they exchange; metadata on this layer are further refined with scope, which specifies the range of metadata application (e.g. whether the metadata apply to whole class of components or just a single one, etc.);

- **the data definition layer**: typically adopted from an existing GMA implementations. In this layer, the metadata describe data types (e. g. table names, metrics, etc.) of published and requested data, as well as further data specifications (WHERE clause in R-GMA). This leads to multi-criteria matching of producers with consumers;

A notable extension to the GMA model is the addition of the mediator component. Mediator separates the concepts of producer/consumer discovery and matching from the registration of producer/consumer components. The registration and storage of producer/consumer information is handled by the registry, as in GMA. However, the discovery of producers and consumers is the responsibility of the mediator component.

Capabilities and Attributes

Each particular GMA implementation represents a *world*, with its own data schema. These worlds are often incompatible, the capabilities and attributes describe the properties of components and data, respectively. With explicit access to such description, "gates" between worlds can be created—components with interfaces "speaking" languages (i. e. understanding the capabilities and attributes) of two worlds.

Using *capabilities*, components declare any features that may affect either the communication with other components or the ability to handle any particular data. For instance, capabilities may define security mechanism, quality of service offered, level of persistence, etc. Similar mechanism is used with data, *attributes* describe the requirements that must be fulfilled by components to process particular piece of data.

Neither data attributes nor component capabilities are related with event data types. The data schema is managed according to the GMA, at the C-GMA data-definition layer. Capabilities and attributes are properties orthogonal to data types.

A *capability language* [4] is used to define capabilities and attributes. The common language reflects the necessity to treat component capabilities and data attributes in a symmetric way. This allows to express requirements on capabilities via attribute description and vice versa. The capability language must satisfy certain minimal requirements but no fixed language is prescribed. Particularly, two operations must be supported by the capability language: capability matching and attribute matching. Both are essentially compatibility checks on the sets of capabilities/attributes of two or more components.

Currently, we are evaluating two different capability languages. One is XML-based, using XPath expressions to refer from attributes to capabilities and vice versa. The other uses the Classified Advertisements (ClassAds) language [5].

Mediator—Producer/Consumer Discovery

The mediator is responsible for discovery of appropriate producer or consumer partner. It normally operates actively, by monitoring registrations in the registry and continually evaluating them for potential possible matches between producers and consumers.

As mentioned above, the matching is done along two axis—metadata must match at both capability and data layers. Every time a potential matching pair of component/producer is found, active mediator generates a *proposal* and sends it to both potential parties. The main purpose of mediator component is thus to aid the discovery process.

The active mode is complemented with the *passive* mode, in whichthe mediator can serve requests to discover potential parties based on provided characteristics, i. e. to discover all suitable producers for a particular consumer.

Component Interaction

In the C-GMA compliant monitoring systems, the following component interactions occur (naming is adopted from Condor Matchmaking [6]):

Advertising – registration of producers and consumers. Besides general information like component identification and address the registration record contains component capabilities and data attributes (if they are uniform for all data) at the capability metadata layer, as well as data description at the data-definition layer. Registration is soft-state, components must renew registration before expiration.

Matching – based on registered metadata, mediator is looking for matching pairs. When new pair is found, both parties are informed about the potential pairing.

Claiming – direct communication between producer and consumer (occurs when a component is notified about the potentially pairing component). Mutual compatibility between components must be verified in this phase by the components themselves.

Data transfer – data (events) are send directly between producer and consumer. Starting from this phase, communication occurs only between producer and consumer C-GMA architecture makes no assumptions regarding the involved communication strategy and protocol.

3. The Distributed Mediator

The C-GMA specification defines the mediator as a logically centralised component. However, a central service implementation is a serious performance bottleneck and a potential single point of failure. To provide a scalable solution, a distributed implementation is necessary. The obvious objective of our effort is to obtain a reliable, scalable and robust design for the mediator that is free from the drawbacks of a centralised solution.

As introduced in previous sections, the C-GMA capabilities describe what components can do, while attributes provide hints to the C-GMA components on how the data itself should be handled. This information together with metadata of the data-definition layer is kept in a specific document—the C-GMA *registration*. The C-GMA registrations are used to advertise components' capabilities and attributes and provide the basis for the mediator matchmaking process.

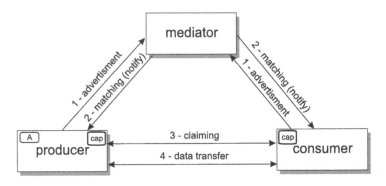

Figure 2.   Interaction of C-GMA Components

A simple distributed implementation of the mediator can be based on the replication of all the registrations on all the brokers. In this rather "naive" approach each broker manages the matchmaking for local clients and broadcasts each C-GMA registration to all other brokers for further matchmaking. The main advantage of this replication strategy is that it is simple to implement and it provides good fault tolerance (in case of failures, little work has to be done to ensure consistency between the replicas and to redirect orphaned C-GMA components to other active brokers). However, this approach may have significant scalability problems since it considerably wastes network and storage resources by replicating information where it is not needed for the matchmaking process. A more efficient approach can be built over the Content-base Publish/Subscribe system.

The order of component interactions is shown in Fig. 2.

4.   Content-based Publish/Subscribe Systems

Recently, the Publish/Subscribe (P/S) communication paradigm is receiving increasing attention due to its asynchronous, loosely-coupled and flexible style of communication [14]. Applications that leverage this communication paradigm exchange information asynchronously in the form of event notifications produced by *publisher* components that are dispatched to interested *subscriber* components by the P/S middleware. The P/S middleware responsibility is thus to match consumers' subscriptions with published notifications in order to convey messages only where it is explicitly requested.

Content-based P/S (CBPS) [2] systems extend the well known P/S interaction scheme supporting fine-grained subscription languages that enable subscribers to select very precisely the notification of their interests according to their content.

Scalable CBPS systems (e. g. Siena [13]) are typically constructed out of a network of brokers that cooperate in forwarding event notifications to remote interested parties. In such distributed design, each broker acts as an access point for the whole CBPS service, collecting subscriptions and dispatching notification for local clients, that may be producers or consumers of information. From an implementation point of view, each broker manages a forwarding table that maps received subscriptions to outgoing interfaces (i.e., network connections towards other brokers or local clients); at forwarding time, notifications are sent only towards local clients or remote destinations that match received subscriptions. This scheme requires that received subscriptions at each broker are broadcasted to all the other brokers in order to consistently establish the routes that are to be followed by published events.

Two generic requirements drive the CBPS routing strategies: *downstream replication* of event notifications and *upstream evaluation* of filters[13]. Downstream replication means that a notification should be routed in one copy as far as possible and duplicated only as close as possible along the paths leading to interested subscribers. Upstream evaluation implies that subscription filters are applied on events as close as possible to publishers. The design goal underlying these requirements is to minimise the usage of network resources when routing events to large numbers of distributed subscribers.

The CBPS system seems to be an ideal candidate for design of a distributed mediator component, alleviating this potential C-GMA bottleneck.

5. P/S Based Distributed Mediator

The mediator service can be built as an overlay network of distributed brokers that implement a content-based P/S system. In particular, we leverage CBPS so that each mediator broker receives information *only* regarding remote consumer components that are compatible (i. e. whose capabilities and component attributes match) with locally managed producer components. To do so, each broker has a forwarding table built according to the registered C-GMA registration and executes a routing strategy that satisfies the CBPS downstream replication and upstream evaluation principles introduced in Sect. 4.

In the proposed scheme (see Figure 3), producers drive the interaction (a consumer driven scenario is also possible). When a producer registers with a mediator broker, two actions are performed:

1 locally managed matching consumers are notified of the producer existence,

2 the producer registration is broadcasted to the other brokers. This last step is necessary to ensure consistency across all brokers and correctly establish the routes that C-GMA consumers' registration will follow in the CBPS overlay network. More specifically, whenever a mediator broker

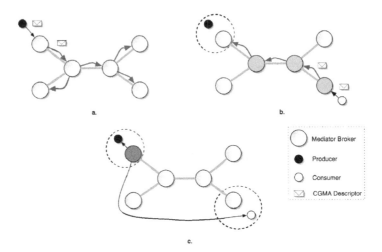

Figure 3. The distributed mediator content-based replication strategy. Figure a) shows the broadcasting of a producer C-GMA registration. In figure b), a C-GMA consumer registration is forwarded by each broker towards the matching producer. Finally, in figure c), the last mile broker performs the final matchmaking between component capabilities and data attributes and types and sends a matching proposal to interested C-GMA components.

receives a producer's registration from a neighbour, it updates its forwarding table adding the received registration to the set of registrations associated with that specific neighbour.

Consumer C-GMA registrations are treated differently. Whenever a consumer component registers itself, the local mediator broker starts a matchmaking process comparing its registration with:

- locally managed producer registration, so that matching producers are immediately notified of the newly arrived consumer;

- producers registration appearing in the forwarding table. If a matching registration is found, the received consumer registration is forwarded towards the matching neighbours for further matchmaking by remote brokers.

The main advantage of the CBPS replication strategy is that it limits the spreading of consumer registration only where these are really needed for the matchmaking process, allowing for better scalability. The immediate consequence is a gain in scalability and performance of the infrastructure, since the amount of administrative traffic introduced in the overlay is limited and the distributed matchmaking function is ran only when strictly necessary (i. e. on all the brokers appearing on the shortest path that connects the producer edge broker with the consumer edge broker). In contrast, the naive replication approach states that all C-GMA registrations are broadcasted to all the brokers so that the matchmaking process is executed on each broker even on registrations that will not match locally managed C-GMA components.

The C-GMA matchmaking performed by the brokers may happen at different levels. We assume here that only capabilities and attributes associated with the components are taken into consideration, leaving the check of compatibility between data attributes and components capabilities to the "last-mile" broker, i.e., the broker that actively notifies producers and consumers of the existing match (see Figure 3).

This approach has several advantages. Firstly, we may configure the mediator network to provide a chain of C-GMA components that are compatible and then entitle those components to exchange a specific data type in a second time. Secondly, by limiting the matching at the component level, we reduce the complexity of the matching function implemented at each broker thus keeping the infrastructure lightweight and scalable.

6. Conclusions

The discussed C-GMA architecture offers a general approach to integrate different GMA implementations. The distributed mediator improves the scalability of the C-GMA matchmaking process by leveraging the CBPS communication paradigm. We believe that the resulting architecture could provide highly scalable interoperability framework for various Grid monitoring tools. Performance evaluation as well as exploring other mechanisms for implementing distributed mediator service is subject of further research.

Moreover, the choice of propagating the producer descriptors through the whole network and matching the consumer registrations can be symmetrically replaced by propagating consumer descriptors and matching producer registrations. Assessment of effectiveness of these two approaches should be a subject of further evaluation.

Acknowledgement

The work described in this paper is the result of collaboration enabled through the EU Network of Excellence *European Research Network on Foundations, Software Infrastructures and Applications for large scale distributed, GRID and Peer-to-Peer Technologies*, (CoreGRID, FP6-004265). Part of this work is also supported by the MU Research Intent MSM0021622419.

References

[1] B. Tierney et al., "A Grid Monitoring Architecture", Global Grid Forum Performance Working Group, January 2002.

http://www.gridforum.org/documents/GFD.7.pdf

[2] A. Ceccanti, F. Panzieri, "Content-based Monitoring in Grid Environments", In Proc. of the ETNGrid 2004.

[3] J. Sitera et al., "Capability and Attribute Based Grid Monitoring Architecture", In Proc. of Cracow Grid Workshop 2004.

[4] O. Krajíček et al., "Capability Languages in C-GMA", In Proc. of Cracow Grid Workshop 2006.

[5] R. Raman, "Matchmaking Frameworks for Distributed Resource Management", Dissertation Thesis, University of Wisconsin – Madison, 2001.

[6] Rajesh Raman, Miron Livny, and Marvin Solomon. Matchmaking: Distributed Resource Management for High Throughput Computing. In Proc. of the Seventh IEEE International Symposium on High Performance Distributed Computing, July 28-31, 1998, Chicago, IL.

[7] Křenek, A., et al. C-GMA – Capability-based Grid Monitoring Architecture. CESNET technical report 6/2005. http://www.cesnet.cz/doc/techzpravy/2005/cgma/.

[8] S. Fisher: Relational Model for Information and Monitoring. Technical Report GWD-Perf-7-1, Global Grid Forum. 2001. http://www-didc.lbl.gov/GGF-PERF/GMA-WG/papers/GWD-GP-7-1.pdf

[9] Zoltan Balaton, Peter Kacsuk, Norbert Podhorszki and Ferenc Vajda. From Cluster Monitoring to Grid Monitoring Based on GRM. In proceedings 7th EuroPar2001 Parallel Processings, Manchester, UK. pp. 874-881. 2001

[10] A. Ceccanti, G.P. Jesi, "Building latency-aware overlay topologies with QuickPeer", In Proc. of IEEE ICNS 2005.

[11] I. Stoica et al., "Chord: a scalable, peer-to-peer lookup protocol for Internet applications", in Proc. of ACM SIGCOMM'01, 2001.

[12] P.T. Eugster et al., "Lightweight Probabilistic Broadcast", ACM Transactions on Computer Systems, Vo. 21, 2003.

[13] Antonio Carzaniga et al., "Design and evaluation of a wide-area event notification service", ACM Transactions on Computer Systems Vol. 19, No. 3, August 2001, pp. 332-383.

[14] Patrick Th. Eugster et al., "The many faces of Publish/Subscribe", ACM Computing Surveys, Vol. 35, No. 2, June 2003, pp. 114-131.

USER ORIENTED GRID TESTING* †

Miklós Kozlovszky,[1] Krisztián Karóczkai,[1] István Márton,[1] András Schnautigel,[1] Péter Kacsuk,[1] Gábor Hermann,[1] Ramon Harrington,[2] Danielle Martin,[2] Carsten Winsnes[2] and Thomas Strodl[3]

[1]*MTA SZTAKI Computer and Automation Research Institute, Hungary,* [2]*Worcester Polytechnic Institute, United States,* [3]*Vienna University of Technology, Austria*

Abstract   Grid infrastructures are reaching their production phase but still we miss a well defined and complete infrastructure testing system for such Grids to fulfill the requirements of both end-users. In the beginning of the paper a short overview of Grid infrastructure testing methods is given followed by a discussion about the key issues of these approaches. Later on we are introducing a General Grid Testing Model to show what sort of Grid tests would be very much required by the grid end-users. In the second half of the paper we give an overview about P-GRADE Grid Portal and we describe how can solve some user oriented Grid testing services offered by the P-GRADE Portal.

Keywords: Grid portal, personalized, user oriented grid testing, functional test

1.   Introduction

Grids consist of a very complex network of computers which can provide service to a multitude of different usage scenarios. Nowadays there are many methods and applications available for Grid testing like GridICE, Site map, Inca, WS Core, Real Time Monitor, GStat, MonALISA, VisPerf, Mercury, MDS2 [3-8]. Most of the classical infrastructure status and functional monitoring uses the so called active or automatic site functional tests like GStat, SFTs or SAM [9,10,and 12]. Normal SFTs are working centralized, with a special certificate and only able to test some basic Virtual Organization (VO) dependent functionality. Standalone SFT [11] is using enhanced testing method, the modified version of SFT client can be used to test sites without the need of a dedicated SFT server. Such tests are intended to be used by site administrators or country

---

*This research work is carried out under the FP6 Network of Excellence CoreGRID funded by the European Commission (Contract IST-2002-004265).

†SEE-GRID-2 South-Eastern European GRid-enabled eInfrastructure Development 2, Contract Number 031775

representatives for manually checking their (new) sites. Grid (infrastructure) testing is an active type model of Grid Infrastructure Monitoring. Other very effective testing systems are also available like GridLab Testbed Status Monitoring Tool [13-15]. Grid testing is a real challenge because Grid infrastructure is distributed, dynamic, unreliable, its software multilayered heterogeneous, the technologies used are evolving rapidly, and large scale testing should be executed always carefully, due the high risk of flooding. The main aim of this work was to create and give a generalized and effective grid testing solution for normal users, in a user-friendly easy-to-use manner. We have developed a solution that would allow not only site administrators but normal Grid users to explore and monitor the status of available grid infrastructure with the help of the P-GRADE Portal.

2.   General Grid Testing Model

We can use a layered model (Figure 1) to explore all the relevant error points of the infrastructure from the user point of view. The main four layers in the model are the following: Network layer, Service layer, Security Layer, Application Layer. We can also enumerate the main actors in the Grid system existing as sources and observers of errors:

- Grids - Distributed large scale system with many potential problems
    - Hardware
    - Software /technologies, blocking services(certificates, catalogues,IS)/
    - Network Infrastructure

- Portals - with many potential problems
    - Software implementation
    - Network infrastructure
    - Expiration of host certificates
    - Exhausting of own resources

- Users - with many potential problems
    - "Hardware"
    - Buggy applications
    - Lack of knowledge

We are interested in examining it from the user point of view, because in an unacceptably high number of cases the user is unable to distinguish their own errors from the ones of the Grid environment. From the users' perspective the four layers (with their sublayers) of the testing are transparent, and only the usability of the Grid infrastructure is important. Test scenarios should be able to cover all the layers of the Testing Model, with maximum debugging power and minimum complexity and resource consumption.

Application Layer	Application launchability
	Inter-application communication
	Job requirements (CPU, memory, MPI, etc.)
Security Layer	Layer II: User certificate issues (user certificates, etc.)
	Layer I: Infrastructure certificate issues (Host certificates, etc.)
Service Layer	Service availability (Myproxy, Broker, Information Service, etc.)
Network Layer	Communication network availability

Figure 1. General testing Model of the Grid infrastructure

It is obviously a challenging task to define reliability indicators, and measure such parameters, because these values can be different if we check the system from different perspectives [14]. Even a fully working Grid infrastructure can be seen malfunctioning from user point of view if the user has authentication difficulties. From the usage of P-GRADE Portal by different large Grid communities, we categorized the error frequency of the different layers (Table 1).

Layer	*Function*	*Error Frequency*
Application	Launchability	High
Application-Inter-app. comm.	MPI, etc.	Extremely high
Application-Job requirements	CPU, Memory, Processor, SW	High
Security Layer of User	User cert., VO membership	High
Security Layer of Middleware	Infrastructure sec. issues	Fairly low
Site Services	Access of CE and SE	High
Service (central)	Myproxy, Broker, IS	Rather high
Network	Communication availability	Low

Table 1. Error fequency distribution of layers measured from Portal

Regularly launched Site Functional Tests have been heavily used to capture the status of the Grid infrastructure. The frequency of these tests depends on many parameters, like: the size of the network, amount of resources, and the resource consumption of the tester jobs. It is obvious that the submitted test jobs should contain only the minimum amount of data, and it should not be data or communication intensive application. The general problems with functional tests are the following:

- *Centralized*

    - Functional test applications are using different entry points into the Grid infrastructure as normal user

■ *Independent from the user*

- Functional Test applications are using their own (different) certificates as normal users.

- Functional Tests are checking the system only up to the lower Security Layer (I) usually.

■ *Loosely coupled to services - poor complexity handling*

- The tests are not covering the full complexity and functionality (internal communication, inter-site communication, MPI applications, storage usage, etc.) of the Grid infrastructure.

■ *Problems with accessibility and user level documentation*

- Site test results are difficult to locate by end users. The interpretation of the test result is far from being easy by normal users in many cases due to poor documentation and complex visualization methods.

- Internationalization - documentation is mostly in English

■ *Error codes*

- Huge amount of error codes and other feedback from Grid system is informative only for advanced users [16].

We have extended the P-GRADE Portal user interface and inner architecture to eliminate most of these problems mentioned above.

3.   Description of the P-GRADE Portal

The P-GRADE Grid Portal [1] provides uniform access to underlying grid resources. The Portal Server itself was developed using Gridsphere [2], a grid portal development framework that is responsible for managing security, monitoring and execution visualization. P-GRADE Portal breaks down the barriers between incompatible Grid systems, helping the user to develop parallel code that can be used on both supercomputers, clusters and in various Grids. P-GRADE Portal hides the complexity of the Grid from the user, making it transparent. It is the workflow-oriented Grid portal that enables the creation, execution and monitoring workflows in grid environments through high-level, graphical Web interface [1].Furthermore it can be used as a single access point for a broad range of different Grid technologies, like LCG2, Glite, Nordugrid or GLite3. Components of the workflows can be sequential and parallel (MPI, PVM) jobs.

Users are accessing the Grid through the P-GRADE portal, where they can submit jobs and see the progress of their workflow. PGRADE Portal's main advantages are the close connection to end users and the workflow based, user-friendly interface. The visual feedback is the most important part of the interaction between user and portal. Instead of black-and-white error reports with meaningless, poor documented error codes, users can evaluate the status of the infrastructure simply with the graphical user interface. Users can:

- Test the infrastructure and make decision where to submit the jobs.

- Test their own certificates, or applications, against well defined, error free testing applications.

- Have understanding how the test is built up and functioning.

- Have easy to understand visual feedback about the test results.

Reusable, standardized complex workflows can speed up the exploration of complex Grid infrastructure problems. User oriented testing can help the users to identify what is really wrong in the system from their perspective. Besides the high level graphical visualization the user has the ability to see the error codes and status messages coming from the Grid infrastructure. This feature of the Portal can help to initiate proper action to fix the problem.

Grid protection

Nowadays the Grid does not have automated self protection mechanism against DOS attacks (flooding) or let's say "grand data challenges" initiated by "normal" users. This problem can emerge in the case of user initiated Grid testing as well, because stressing the Grid infrastructure can produce potentially high overhead. Portals (same situation as Grid) are not able to control fully the submission of the users, they can submit a test workflow as many times as they want. However P-GRADE Portal is offering some upper bounds to prevent Grid systems from flooding: like maximum amount of parallel submitted jobs, or the polling rate of the Portal, which can be setup by the Portal Administrator. Besides these indirect protection, an easy to understand and informative web page is shown on a common place of the Portal, offering a wide range of test result done regularly by the portal itself and information of MDS2/LCG2 system. As future plan we would like to make intelligent resource availability visualization based on both prompt and historical data.

4. Offered testing services by the P-GRADE Portal

P-GRADE Portal's testing service is not simple another testing solution implemented on a fancy web portal. The main aim of this development was to cover a much broader testing range of the Grid infrastructure focusing on Grid users. Grid administrators have their own SFTs and P-GRADE Portal can easily work as a platform for the high number of production level Grid tests [9,10], however these tests are only partially suitable for end-users. P-GRADE Portal is offering two main test categories for Grid/Portal Administrators, Application Developers and "normal" users:

- **Infrastructure Tests (IT)**

  - These tests are user specific. The user tests his certificate (and its validity in a given Virtual Organization).

  - The test can be modified by the user as the Infrastructure changes

  - The test can be easily migrated by the user to a new Infrastructure (VO)

  - The test can be submitted at any time by the user

  - The test investigates the most relevant basic functionality features of the Infrastructure (Security, Broker, CE, SE, Grid File Catalogue, Information System)

- **Application Class Category Tests (ACCT)**

  - With its extendable knowledge base (Workflow repository) it may contain a rich set of test workflows.

  - Community specific workflow packages for various user groups.

  - The content of the repository is submitted by a distinguished "Test user" (with the certificate of the Test user) and the success/failure of the tests can be observed by all users.

  - The workflows are submitted periodically finding a proper compromise between the need to be up to date informed and the self restriction refraining from flooding the Portal and Grid Infrastructure.

Both test categories based on workflows, and covering a full range of test scenarios from simple one-job workflows (e.g.: Broker test), towards complex, multi-site tests (e.g.: VO Site functionality test) and user specific application tests. Some workflow templates with large Grid resource consumption are available only for Portal Administrators, and launched on a predefined manner (predefined timing & certificate). However the results are visualized in the common user space of the Portal.

Infrastructure Tests (IT)

VO/Site functionality test. This in-house developed test is one of our key examples from our infrastructure test suit. The aim of such testing is to check the status of the infrastructure from numerous aspects with a single workflow. The user can get visual feedback (by colour codes) how the whole VO is able to serve him. The test workflow is running with the user's certificate. The test involves file transfers ("local" -via gsiftp - and "remote" where one the source / destination of the operation is a Storage Element) and job submissions for each known VO site (executing the same simple mathematical operation) (Figure 2).

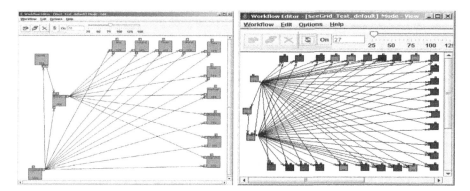

Figure 2.   Complex VO/Site functionality test in starting (a) and in finishing state (b)

The following components are tested by the workflow:

- all Computing Elements (CE) of the VO

- the proper setting of the Grid file catalogue

- the default access to the storage elements (SE)

- the job submission process

For VO scale functional testing the predefined workflow is a great option to speed up and make the testing procedure significantly easier. If every layer is working properly in the VO the workflow terminates successfully. If errors are present in the system, part of the workflow will fail, and the user can see from colour codes which sites are working, and what sort of problems there are. In this complex workflow three types of jobs are combined. Every job contains one executable. The jobs inside the workflow are communicating with each other by input/output files. The number of jobs within the test workflow can be calculated by the number of sites+2 (for synchronization) [17].

Application Class Category Tests (ACCT).   For the Application Class Category test set we have extended P-GRADE Portal with the followings:

- - Test Taxonomy - We have defined taxonomy of the possible test categories.

- - Workflow Repository - We have created a portal specific central storage where the set of tasks (implemented as workflows and uploaded by trained administrators) belonging to these categories are maintained.

- ■ - Automatic Workflow Scheduling - We have implemented a scheduler in the Portal to submit the tasks/workflows automatically

- ■ - Result Visualization - created the test result visualization part on the Portal

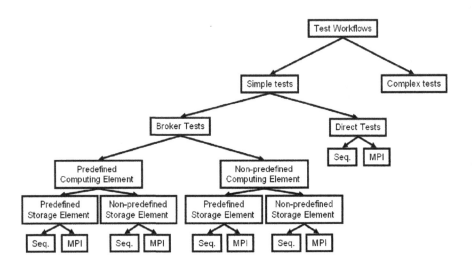

Figure 3.   Test Workflow Taxonomy used in P-GRADE Portal

Test Taxonomy.   We have created a Test Taxonomy to define the different application task categories (Figure 3). Simple test are usable to check simple test cases. Complex tests can be built up from simple test modules, with special test applications to examine special test scenarios on the Grid infrastructure. Besides the predefined test building blocks users are able to create their own test workflows in the Portal. For special job requirements (e.g.: CPU, memory, OS) user needs only to change the appropriate parameters of the predefined workflows. For user specific application testing; reusable predefined workflows can help to create test probes (with changed executable) for the application, or user should create and store his own full application test workflows.

Workflow Repository.   There are many variables involved in defining a VO independent workflow template, including virtual organization, resource, storage and computing elements.

- ■ Regular grid testing. In the name of an in-build user the portal is regularly submitting test jobs into the Grid infrastructure. The results of the specialized test workflows are visualized on a common page of the portal, accessible by all the portal users.

- Personalized testing methods for given or specific users. Users are able to download simple or complex (Personalized VO/Site functional test) workflows from the workflow repository and can submit these workflows in the Grid. The jobs are running in the name of the user.

A workflow repository is created with these various factors in mind, containing specific workflow templates for all the various test scenarios, with standardized naming conventions. From the VO independent workflow templates offline application is creating automatically the VO dependent test workflows. These test workflows are available both for portal administrators and normal users on the P-GRADE portal and can be run through the portal normally as all other workflow.

Automatic Workflow Scheduling. A large set of ACCT like workflows can be submitted automatically into the Grid from the Portal at regular basis. The maximum frequency of the automatic workflow submission is configurable only by the Portal Administrator. Different frequency can be allocated for different tests depending on the complexity. Simple and small workflows can have more frequent submission, than large ones.

Naming Convention. In order to easily determine what the target of the test workflow is, we are using workflow naming convention, based on the previously described Test Taxonomy. The test workflow name encapsulates all the relevant information about the test target. Each segment of the test workflow name begins with a one-letter code, continued by an optional target name and delimited by "_" character. There is a univocal connection between the one-letter codes and the nodes or leafs of the test taxonomy tree (Table 2).

Short name	Node in the Test Taxonomy
U	Simple test (Single job)
X	Complex test
B	Broker test
D	Direct test
C	Predefined Computing Element
F	Non-predefined Computing Element
S	Predefined Storage Element
N	Non-predefined Storage Element
Q	Sequential
M	MPI

Table 2. Used Naming Convention for test workflow names based on the Test Taxonomy

To provide an example, if we define a test workflow containing a single MPI job, submitted by the broker, accessing dedicated SE "AAA" and running on any Computing Element, we should use the following name for the workflow:

U_B_F_S_AAA_M_. We created a java based offline application, which can automatically create from VO independent (abstract) workflow templates and manually created VO descriptor files VO specific test workflow packages. The VO independent workflow template concept makes multi-VO testing an easy task, and increases the portability of the test workflows.

Result Visualization. Generic tests are shown on a common page of the Portal. On this page using predefined naming conventions, the portal creates various visualizations for each type of test. The visualization tries to be as simple and understandable as possible. It contains common information about the workflows, such as time completed and status when finished, but also information specific to the type of test (Figure 4). The results of the personalized tests are shown in the personalized user area.

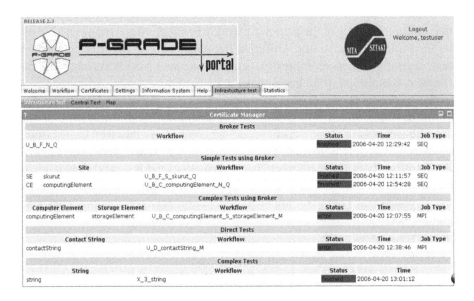

Figure 4. Visualization of ACCT tests on the Portal

5.   Summary

In this paper we showed a user oriented grid testing method offered by the P-GRADE Portal. The extension of P-GRADE Portal is able to overcome many testing problems of the available Grid infrastructure and it can cover all layers of the General Grid Testing Model introduced in this paper. Beside the regular site functional tests, it offers generalized testing methods for all the complexity of the Grid (inter Grid communication, MPI support, etc). Due to the high level workflow based technology used tests are reusable and easily adopted to different VO-s. The user can use their own certificate for the tests, and is informed with visual feedback about the status of the infrastructure. In the future we are planning to connect the test results to an automated ticketing system, improving the reliability of the grid infrastructure. This can enable the support of grids and portals to operate on a higher quality level.

References

[1.] Cs. Nemeth, G. Dozsa, R. Lovas, P. Kacsuk: The P-GRADE Grid Portal. ICCSA 2004: International Conference Assisi, Italy, LNCS 3044, pp. 10-19

[2.] J. Novotny: The Grid portal development kit. Grid Computing - Making the Global Infrastructure a Reality. Ed. F. Berman, A. Hey and G. Fox. John-Wiley and Sons, Ltd. Chapter 12. 2003, pp 657-674

[3.] MonALISA: An Agent based, Dynamic Service System to Monitor, Control and Optimize Grid based Applications, I.C.Legrand, H.B.Newman, R.Voicu, C.Cirstoiu, C.Grigoras, M.Toarta, C. Dobre, CHEP 2004, Interlaken, Switzerland, September 2004

[4.] GridICE: a Monitoring Service for Grid Systems. S. Andreozzi, N. De Bortoli, S. Fantinel, A. Ghiselli, G.L. Rubini, G. Tortone and M.C. Vistoli. In Future Generation Computer Systems Journal, Elsevier, 21(4):559-571, 2005.

[5.] Performance Analysis of the Globus Toolkit Monitoring and Discovery Service, MDS2. X. Zhang and J. Schopf. Proceedings of the International Workshop on Middleware Performance (MP 2004), part of the 23rd International Performance Computing and Communications Workshop (IPCCC), April 2004.

[6.] D. Lee, J. Dongarra, and R. Ramakrishna. Visperf: Monitoring tool for grid computing. In ICCS 2003, Lecture Notes in Computer Science, Springer Verlag, Heidelberg, Volume 2659, pp. 233-243, 2003

[7.] Z. Balaton and G. Gombás. Resource and Job Monitoring in the Grid. In Proceedings of the Euro-Par 2003 International Conference, 2003.

[8.] Matthew L. Massie, Brent N. Chun, and David E. Culler, The Ganglia Distributed Monitoring System: Design, Implementation, and Experience, Parallel Computing, Vol. 30, Issue 7, July 2004.

[9.] http://goc.grid.sinica.edu.tw/gstat/

[10.] http://lcg-sft.cern.ch:8083/sft/lastreport.cgi

[11.] http://wiki.egee-see.org/index.php/SEE-GRID_standalone_SFT

[12.] http://goc.grid.sinica.edu.tw/gocwiki/Service_Availability_Monitoring_Environment

[13.] Grid Management and Monitoring, Matyska L., CGW03, Cracow, Poland, 2003

[14.] P. Holub, M. Kuba, L. Matyska, M. Ruda: GridLab Testbed Monitoring - Prototype Tool. Deliverable 5.6, GridLab Project (IST-2001-32133), 2003.

[15.] P. Holub, M. Kuba, L. Matyska, M. Ruda:Grid Infrastructure Monitoring as Reliable Information Service. In Grid Computing, Second European AcrossGrids Conference, AxGrids 2004. : Lecture Notes in Computer Science 3165, Springer-Verlag, 2004, ISBN 3-540-22888-8. pp. 220-229.

[16.] http://www.cs.wisc.edu/

[17.] http://www.lpds.sztaki.hu/pgportal/v23/includes/VO_functionality_test.html

V

ADVANCED GRID TECHNIQUES

APPLICATION AND MIDDLEWARE TRANSPARENT CHECKPOINTING WITH TCKPT ON CLUSTERGRID

A novel checkpointing approach

József Kovács[1], Rafal Mikolajczak[2], Radoslaw Januszewski[2] and Gracjan Jankowski[2]

[1] *MTA SZTAKI, Parallel and Distributed Systems Laboratory,*
1111 Budapest, Kende 13-17, Hungary,
smith@sztaki.hu

[2] *Poznan Supercomputing and Networking Center,*
61-704 Poznan, Noskowskiego 12/14, Poland
{Rafal.Mikolajczak,radekj,gracjan}@man.poznan.pl

Abstract: This paper introduces a way to transform the existing parallel checkpointing techniques to be applied for software-heterogeneous ClusterGrid infrastructures. While existing solutions are aiming at providing application transparency by building special middleware, this paper aims at targeting both application and middleware transparency at the same time by inserting checkpoint functionality into the application. The compatibility and integrity requirements are identified and corresponding conditions are established. Some of the available checkpointing systems are checked against the conditions in order to examine their conformity. Based on the conditions, a novel checkpointing method is defined and the TotalCheckpoint tool is adapted for ClusterGrid.

Key words: cluster, grid, clustergrid, checkpoint, recovery, parallel, pvm, migration

1.   INTRODUCTION

As the number of resources aggregated by various Grid[1] sites grows very rapidly, there is a need for fault-tolerance and dynamic load balancing support in order to increase the efficiency of resource usage. In a continuously growing Grid the number of failures increases exponentially due to the increasing hardware and software complexity. In these circumstances a job cannot even finish its execution without at least one failure during the execution. Even if it succeeds the job suffers from low performance because of the continuously changing load generated by the calculation in various processes.

In case of a parallel application checkpointing support is even more essential since the number of resources used by the application can be several hundreds or even more at the same time. Therefore migration and fault-tolerance support for these applications is a crucial task in a Grid environment. The basis for both services is creating checkpoints of the application periodically to support fault-tolerance and to provide migration on demand.

Checkpoint is defined as a designated point in an application at which normal processing is interrupted specifically to preserve the status information necessary to allow resumption of processing at a later time. Checkpointing is the process of saving the status information and migration is a checkpoint/restart pair of activities on different resources. To provide checkpoint saving for parallel applications various techniques have been researched in the last few decades [2].

In the checkpointing area two main classes are defined: coordinated and uncoordinated. In the first case a designated component controls the checkpoint saving procedure to ensure the consistency of messages [3] among the processes in the application to avoid message loss or duplication. In the latter case consistency is ensured at time of restarting. During execution, checkpoints must be stored from time to time for each process without removing the ones created previously. At restart checkpoints for each process are searched through and attempted to make a selection in a way that they form a consistent state for the application and represent the latest valid state. While the coordinated version forces the processes to synchronise, uncoordinated checkpointing gives freedom for the processes to create a checkpoint at any time. In coordinated checkpointing only one checkpoint per process is enough to perform a successful resumption of the application, while in uncoordinated version the likelihood of successful resumption increases with the number of checkpoints per process since consistency is not guaranteed when saving. In extreme cases when consistency is not found the application must be started from the beginning in the uncoordinated version. More details about the different checkpointing techniques can be found in [2].

In a computational Grid various resources are collected where one or more broker component performs the mapping of applications to resources based on the application requirements and resource capabilities. In this paper ClusterGrid is defined as a Grid that can contain clusters represented as one compound and undividable resource for the broker. Clusters can be maintained by different organisations, so scheduling and execution policy as well as software environment within a cluster can be different. On clusters various schedulers can handle jobs and at the same time the cluster might be served by different versions of operating systems or message-passing environments. Additionally any kind of service can be installed to support the requirements of the organisation owning and operating the cluster which does not exist in the other ones.

As we can see, the homogeneity of middleware components in a ClusterGrid cannot be expected. Therefore, we are facing a challenge when building a parallel checkpointer that must be able to checkpoint and resume a multiprocess application on different clusters without relying on any support from the middleware running on the clusters. The aim of this paper is to outline the design goals for portable parallel checkpointers operating in a software heterogeneous ClusterGrid i.e. for both application and middleware transparent checkpointers, to define a novel approach fitting to the design goals and to introduce the essential implementation techniques of a prototype called TotalCheckpoint (TCKPT) developed for this kind of ClusterGrid.

The paper is organised as follows. Section 2 details the main requirements a checkpointer tool is facing. Section 3 gives a short overview of the most well-known checkpointing and migration tools while the limitations of these tools are emphasised regarding the ClusterGrid usage. Section 4 introduces an approach described by a set of checkpointing methods and section 5 details the prototype fitting to the requirements. In section 6 standardisation effort for checkpoint interfaces is introduced. Finally, acknowledgement is in section 7 and section 8 concludes the paper.

2.   CHECKPOINTING IN CLUSTERGRID

In case of ClusterGrid infrastructure where clusters can have different software environments installed, the relevant design goals or requirements of a parallel checkpoint tool are *compatibility* (with the encompassing software components) and *integrity* (of the checkpoint information of the application). While the first goal ensures the seamless operation of the checkpointer on clusters with various middleware, the second one is a basis for application migration among clusters.

In order to fulfil the compatibility requirement, we assume the following conditions:

1. Operating system cannot provide checkpointing facility
2. Solution cannot rely on checkpoint support of the job manager

3. Solution must rely on the native version of message-passing system

4. Dependence from external auxiliary process cannot exist

These 4 conditions correspond to compatible operation of checkpointing frameworks. Following these conditions an application can be checkpointed in a way which enables the application to be checkpointed in software heterogeneous ClusterGrid environment, i.e. under the control of any kind of execution environment. Moreover, the application will not be limited to be resumed under the same execution environment where it was checkpointed i.e. it is compatible with the different software environments installed on the clusters.

Checkpointing can serve both fault-tolerance and migration for a parallel application. Since migration itself does not require to checkpoint the state of the entire application including all processes and messages, it might happen that the checkpoint information is not enough to rebuild the application on a different site of the ClusterGrid.

Migration facilities in most of the cases temporarily store checkpoint information about the checkpointed/migrating processes only. In a ClusterGrid infrastructure we assume that an application may not be allowed to be executed using more than one site at the same time, i.e. its processes can only be distributed on the nodes of the same cluster. Therefore, a migration of the whole application from one site to another requires a correct set of checkpoints of the entire application. It is called the integrity of checkpoint.

Based on the previous theory a new requirement is defined as a complementary to the previous 4 called integrity requirement. In order to fulfil that the following condition must be satisfied:

5. Application-wide checkpoint saving must be realised

The 5 conditions together form a framework in which a checkpoint tool must fit in order to provide parallel application checkpoint/restart support on a general ClusterGrid infrastructure. By accomplishing these conditions defined for the parallel checkpoint tools, applications are able to checkpoint and migrate among the different nodes of a cluster and among the clusters.

3. RELATED WORK

The following short overview of the most well-known PVM checkpoint tools addresses the characteristic of each approach that prevents the tool from satisfying the requirements defined in Section 2.

CoCheck[4] is a research project that aims at providing consistent checkpointing for various parallel programming environments like PVM and MPI based on the Chandy-Lamport[3] algorithm. The checkpoint/restart capability of this tool is relying on the replacement of the default PVM resource manager which is equivalent to the modification of PVM. Modification of the message-passing middleware breaks condition no. 3 for the compatibility requirement defined in Section 2.

The goal of the Condor[5] Project is to develop, implement, deploy, and evaluate mechanisms and policies that support High Throughput Computing (HTC) on large collections of distributively owned computing resources. The model they follow is a fault-tolerant execution of Master-Worker (MW) type applications. The user must define the code for the Master process, the Worker processes and the system will distribute the work automatically among the workers in a way defined by the programmer. When a worker process aborts or fails, Condor automatically spawns a new worker with the same workpackage, the failed worker originally owned. Condor does not provide real checkpointing for parallel applications and fault-tolerant execution is limited to a programming framework and a fixed topology. Therefore, it breaks integrity requirement defined by condition no. 5 in Section 2.

Fail-safe PVM[6] has been designed and implemented by the Carnegie Mellon University in the United States of America. The main purpose of the framework is to provide a fault-tolerant PVM environment regarding single-node failures. The main strength of the system is to be capable of detecting failed-nodes and of migrating application processes from the failed nodes to the error-free ones. To do this, PVM daemons are modified which breaks condition no. 3 defined in Section 2 for the compatibility requirement.

Table 1. Classification of existing PVM checkpointing tools based on applied techniques

Tools \ Techniques	Restricted techniques to implement checkpointing/migration				
	Replaced PVM Resource Manager	Modified PVM Daemon	OS level modification	Auxiliary Process	Partial checkpoint of the Application
	Violates condition 1-4.				Violates cond.5
CoCheck	applied				
Condor					applied
Fail-safe PVM		applied			
Dynamite		applied	applied	applied	
MPVM/MIST		applied			
tmPVM		applied		applied	applied
DamPVM		applied		applied	applied
CHARM				applied	
TCKPT					

Dynamite[7] aims to provide a complete integrated solution for dynamic load balancing of parallel jobs on networks of workstations. It contains an integrated load-balancing and checkpointing support for PVM applications. The initial tool focuses on migrating PVM processes but later versions are able to checkpoint the whole application. Dynamite uses its own PVM daemons to maintain routing tables for process communication, which breaks condition no. 3 for the compatibility requirement defined in Section 2.

In Table 1 there is an overview of the examined tools. In the 5 horizontal columns restricted techniques and features are listed. In case a tool is using one of them, application and middleware transparent checkpointing cannot be provided by the tool. Tools are listed horizontally, and for each one applied techniques are signed in the table.

As a consequence, we can say that every examined checkpointing tool is using at least one of the restricted techniques resulting in lack of transparency for application and middleware at the same time. Most of the tools are supporting application transparent checkpointing or migration.

Our purpose is to fulfil the requirements stated in the previous section; therefore TCKPT is not using any of the restricted techniques listed above.

4.   NOVEL APPROACH IN CHECKPOINTING

In this section the main cornerstones of a novel parallel checkpointing approach are introduced. The following 7 key statements form a method which meets the requirements defined in Section 2. The following approach creates a tighter solution range than the compatibility and integrity requirements allow.

1. *Application source code is unmodified* which provides a transparent solution for the application programmer.
2. *Library (system) level checkpointing technique* is used. Alternatives are application and kernel level checkpointing. The first solution conflicts with the previous statement, while using kernel level checkpointing causing incompatibility with clusters having no kernel checkpointer installed.
3. *Application wide checkpointing* is performed in order to generate checkpoints containing state information of every process of the application. In case of partial checkpointing of the application, migration among clusters is not possible due to insufficient checkpoint information for rebuilding the entire application.
4. *Checkpoint information is stored into files* on a stable storage. There are solutions where checkpoint data is temporarily stored in memory to speed-up migration, but these solutions make the delivery of checkpoint information to the targeted cluster impossible.

5. *Parallel checkpointing technique is coordinated* in order to minimise the checkpoint information to be stored i.e. only one checkpoint per process. In case of uncoordinated checkpointing all the checkpoint information generated during the application life-time must be stored (because of the domino effect) until the application finishes its execution causing a huge storage overhead.

6. *Coordination process is part of the application* which lets the application maintain itself and avoids using auxiliary processes for performing the checkpoint or restart mechanisms.

7. *Processes migrate within a cluster without terminating the application,* which causes the checkpointing tool to implement migration within a cluster in a more efficient way. The alternative way would be checkpoint and restart of the entire application with a different resource mapping on the same cluster.

As a summary, we can state that the checkpointer tool must be implemented totally as part of the application, but in a way that the programmer is not forced to change his/her application source code. It is a conflict that must be resolved by using different implementation techniques. A solution is introduced in section 5.

5. THE TOTALCHECKPOINT TOOL

TotalCheckpoint (TCKPT) is a tool to checkpoint, restart and migrate message-passing PVM applications. It performs system (library) level checkpointing providing transparent operation for the application by simply modifying the behaviour of the relevant PVM functionalities.

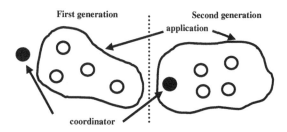

Figure 1. First and second generations of TCKPT

TCKPT executes a consistent coordinated parallel checkpointing algorithm where the coordination process can be an external daemon (first generation) or an internal process (second generation) for the application (see Figure 1).

5.1 First generation

The application is relinked with the tckpt library and all pvm calls in the user code are redirected to those defined in tckpt lib by wrapping the original ones. A start-up procedure is also inserted by the linker automatically before the user code to initiate checkpoint related settings.

Since TCKPT tool is developed based on numerous techniques and solutions the following few paragraphs attempt to point out some of the cornerstones of the applied solutions.

During the execution client processes of the application are connected to the coordinator (see Figure 2). At startup every client registers in the coordinator and continues execution. Checkpoint is triggered by a signal delivered to some clients, about which the coordinator is also notified by one of the clients. Next step is to notify all clients and the checkpoint protocol begins. Clients are synchronising message channels among every processes to ensure consistency. The images of the clients are saved into checkpoint files and finally clients terminate if necessary. The coordinator makes sure that phases of the checkpointing protocol are executed appropriately and distributes the actual pvm identifiers among the clients.

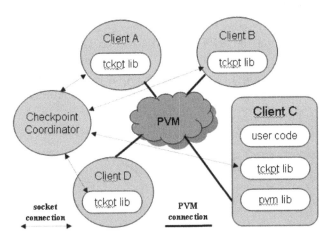

Figure 2. Structure of 1st generation TCKPT

At resumption after the first process of the application is resumed, each process is spawned by its parent and resumption is guided by the coordinator simultaneously. When the entire application is rebuilt, execution continues.

To execute the synchronisation protocol among the clients the coordinator needs to know the accurate number of clients. Clients are created and terminated dynamically. To keep the registered number of clients accurate each client at start-up first builds its own socket connection with the coordinator which also provides the way for the coordinator to detect if a client aborts. When the client is being rebuilt from checkpoint this connection is kept alive.

Further details about the internals of TCKPT can be found in [8] which introduce the various techniques applied by the first generation TCKPT.

5.2   Second generation

The fundamental change in the second generation is that the coordination process became part of the application. While in the first version the coordination daemon must be preinstalled on the cluster where the checkpoint is created or the application is rebuilt, in the second version the coordinator process is created by the application at startup. When the first client process of the application is starting up, coordinator process is spawned. It initiates and the client process attaches to it. Finally, the client process performs necessary preparation and executes user code. All functionalities are the same as it is in the first generation. When the last instance of client processes has left the application the coordinator process terminates.

Resumption of the application depends on the existence of checkpoint descriptor files. In case they are stored in the working directory, a resumption of the application is performed. When the coordinator has been initiated and the first client is performing its start-up phase, the coordinator loads the checkpoint descriptor file. The resumption is done process by process until the entire application is successfully rebuilt.

6.   INTERFACING SINGLE PROCESS CHECKPOINTERS

TCKPT has been originally designed to be capable of integrating various single process checkpointer (SPC) tools. Therefore, a simple API has been defined through which the required functionalities of an SPC library can be utilized by TCKPT. These functionalities are the followings:
- creation of a checkpoint file of the caller process
- resumption of the caller process based on a checkpoint file
- assigning signal for checkpoint activation

- assignment of a callback to be activated before checkpoint saving happens
- assignment of a callback to be activated after a checkpoint saving happened
- assignment of a callback to be activated after a resumption has been performed
- reassignment of filenames and file descriptors at resumption mode

In case an SPC can support these functionalities, TCKPT can utilise that tool. In rare cases it might happen that the operator of a grid infrastructure sticks to use a given SPC. Irrespectively of the type of the checkpointer (library-level or kernel-level) only the predefined SPC API must be implemented.

There is an ongoing work in CoreGRID (FP6 Network of Excellence Project under contract IST-2002-004265) in this direction, where a library-level checkpointer called *psncLibCkpt* [9] and a kernel-level checkpointer called *AltixC/R* [10] (both developed by PNSC) is about to be integrated [11][12] with TCKPT. The aim is to create a proof of concept implementation for generalising checkpoint interfaces and to introduce a concept where high-level checkpointer tools are able to rely on low-level, even kernel-level checkpointer tools.

In case a kernel-level checkpointer is integrated with TCKPT, of course, the application can only migrate among those sites, where checkpointing and recovery are performed in a way which is identical from kernel-level checkpointing aspect.

7. ACKNOWLEDGEMENT

The work described in this paper has been partially supported by the FP6 Network of Excellence CoreGRID funded by the European Commission (Contract IST-2002-004265).

8. CONCLUSION

ClusterGrid with heterogeneous middleware are not able to support parallel checkpointing and migration among the clusters because of the incompatible behaviour of the various tools running on clusters. The key direction is to provide both application and middleware transparency by library-level checkpointing. The necessary step is to insert all checkpoint and resumption capabilities into the application itself. There are two alternatives.

The first is to apply application-level checkpoint/restart mechanism which is trivial but gives an extreme work for the programmer. The second one is to integrate library-level checkpointer with the application using various techniques which make the operation transparent for the application, programmer and middleware.

This paper introduces TCKPT that follows the second way. As a consequence the applied solution has led to a tool which can perform automatic checkpoint/restart functions for the application and migration among the clusters is also supported even if the source and target clusters have different middleware (e.g. job scheduler) installed.

REFERENCES

[1] I. Foster, C. Kesselman, S. Tuecke, "The Anatomy of the Grid. Enabling Scalable Virtual Organizations", Intern. Journal of Supercomputer Applications, 15(3), 2001
[2] Elnozahy E N, Johnson D B, Wang Y M. "A Survey of Rollback Recovery Protocols in Message-Passing System." Technical Report. Pittsburgh, PA: CMU-CS-96-181. Carnegie Mellon University, Oct 1996
[3] K.M. Chandy and L. Lamport. „Distributed snapshots: Determining global states of distributed systems", ACM Transactions on Computer Systems, 3(1):63-75, February 1985.
[4] G. Stellner, "Consistent Checkpoints of PVM Applications", In Proc. 1st Euro. PVM Users Group Meeting, 1994
[5] M. Litzkow, T. Tannenbaum, J. Basney, and M. Livny, "Checkpoint and Migration of UNIX Processes in the Condor Distributed Processing System", Technical Report #1346, Computer Sciences Department, University of Wisconsin, April 1997
[6] J. Léon, A. L. Fisher, and P. Steenkiste, "Fail-safe PVM: a portable package for distributed programming with transparent recovery". CMU-CS-93-124. February, 1993
[7] G.D. van Albada; J. Clinckemaillie; A.H.L. Emmen; J. Gehring; O. Heinz; F. van der Linden; B.J. Overeinder; A. Reinefeld and P.M.A. Sloot: „Dynamite - blasting obstacles to parallel cluster computing", in P.M.A. Sloot; M. Bubak; A.G. Hoekstra and L.O. Hertzberger, editors, High-Performance Computing and Networking (HPCN Europe '99), Amsterdam, The Netherlands, in series Lecture Notes in Computer Science, nr 1593 pp. 300-310. Springer-Verlag, Berlin, April 1999. ISBN 3-540-65821-1.
[8] Jozsef Kovacs: "Making PVM applications checkpointable for the Grid" Proc. of the Microcad 2005 Conference, Section N, pp. 223-228, Marcius 10-11, 2005, Miskolc
[9] http://checkpointing.psnc.pl/Progress/psncLibCkpt
[10] Gracjan Jankowski, Rafal Mikolajczak, Radoslaw Januszewski: "Checkpoint/Restart mechanism for multiprocess applications implemented under SGIGrid Project", Proceedings of the Cracow GridWorkshop 2004, pp.142 149, ISBN: 83-911541-4-5, 2005.
[11] G. Jankowski, R. Januszewski, R. Mikolajczak, J. Kovacs: "Scalable multilevel checkpointing for distributed applications - on the integration possibility of TCKPT and psncLibCkpt ", CoreGRID Technical Report, TR-0019, March 2006
[12] G. Jankowski, R. Januszewski, R. Mikolajczak, J. Kovacs: "Scalable multilevel checkpointing for distributed applications - on the possibility of integrating Total Checkpoint and AltixC/R", CoreGRID Technical Report, TR-0035, March 2006

UML BASED GRID WORKFLOW MODELING UNDER ASKALON*

Jun Qin[1], Thomas Fahringer[1], and Sabri Pllana[2]

[1]*Institute of Computer Science, University of Innsbruck*
Technikerstr. 21a, 6020 Innsbruck, Austria

{Jun.Qin, Thomas.Fahringer}@uibk.ac.at

[2]*Institute of Scientific Computing, University of Vienna*
Nordbergstr. 15/C308, 1090 Vienna, Austria

pllana@par.univie.ac.at

Abstract   Most existing Grid workflow modeling tools are based on user-defined notations. Lack of standards hinders the collaboration among different Grid-related projects. The work presented in this paper introduces a graphical workflow editor Teuta, which has been implemented based on the latest standard UML 2.0 notations and tailored for specifying Grid workflows based on our Abstract Grid Workflow Language (AGWL). In Teuta, Grid workflows are composed by combining predefined UML modeling elements or user-defined constructs in a hierarchical fashion. Teuta can generates the corresponding AGWL representations and submit them to the ASKALON Grid runtime system for execution. We validate our approach for a real world hydrological application.

Keywords: Grid, workflow modeling, UML, ASKALON, AGWL

1.   Introduction

In the recent years, significant research efforts have been involved in the development of tools support for Grid workflow modeling. Compared with textual-based modeling, graph-based modeling allows users to graphically define a Grid workflow through dragging and dropping the modeling elements of interest. However, most of the graph-based Grid workflow modeling tools are based on user-defined notations, which hin-

---

*This research has been partially supported by the Austrian Science Fund as part of the Aurora project under the contract SFBF1104 and the Austrian Federal Ministry for Education, Science and Culture as part of the Austrian Grid project under the contract GZ 4003/2-VI/4c/2004.

ders the collaboration among different Grid-related projects. Much remains to be done to streamline the task of Grid workflow modeling.

In this paper we present our graphical modeling tool Teuta. Compared with our previous work [Pllana et al., 2004], we have customized Teuta for the specification of scientific Grid workflows based on our Abstract Grid Workflow Language (AGWL) [Fahringer et al., 2005b], and integrated it with the ASKALON Grid environment [Fahringer et al., 2005a]. In Teuta, Grid workflows are composed based on the Unified Modeling Language (UML) 2.0 standard. Furthermore, in order to alleviate the complexity of composing large and complex Grid workflows, Teuta supports hierarchical workflow composition. This enables a simple view of the workflow being maintained at each level of abstraction. Teuta has been used as the main user interface to ASKALON, and applied to numerous real world applications.

The remainder of this paper is organized as follows. The related work is described and compared against our approach in the next section. Section 3 provides some background knowledge. Section 4 briefly describes our approach of UML based Grid workflow modeling. Our tool Teuta for modeling Grid workflow applications is introduced in Section 5. Section 6 applies Teuta for a real world application to evaluate our approach. In the last section, we draw our conclusions and outline the future work.

2.   Related Work

GridFlow [Cao et al., 2003] uses Petri Nets to model Grid workflow. Fraunhofer Resource Grid (FhRG) [Hoheisel, 2004], which uses a hierarchical graph definition to model Grid workflows, is also built on Petri Nets. However, Petri Nets may be unable to model workflow activities accurately without extending its semantics [Eshuis and Wieringa, 2003]. And this drawback has been addressed in UML activity diagrams. The work presented in [Bastos et al., 2002] uses UML activity diagrams to model Grid workflows. However, the UML they used is UML1.x, in which the activity diagrams had several serious limitations in the types of flows that could be represented. Many of these limitations were due to the fact that activities were overlaid on top of the basic state machine formalism, and consequently constrained to the semantics of state machines [Bran Selic, 2005]. Rather than following the standard syntax and semantics of Petri Nets and UML, many Grid workflow editor tools create their own graphical representation of workflow components [Yu and Buyya, 2005], e.g. Triana [Taylor et al., 2005] and Kepler [Altintas et al., 2004]. However, lack of standards hinders the collaboration among different Grid-related projects. Much work is thus replicated such as different user interfaces developed by different projects for the same functionality.

In a word, most of existing work suffers from one or several of the following drawbacks: the use of self-defined notations, the use of old UML 1.x activity diagrams, or no adequate tool support. In contrast, we use the latest standard UML 2.0 activity diagram in Teuta to model Grid workflow applications. Teuta can model graphically any Grid workflow application that can be expressed textually using AGWL [Fahringer et al., 2005b]. Moreover, Teuta has been integrated with the ASKALON Grid environment as a user interface for Grid workflow composition, submission, controlling and monitoring.

3. Background

3.1 Abstract Grid Workflow Language (AGWL)

AGWL [Fahringer et al., 2005b] is an XML-based language for descri-bing Grid workflow applications at a high level of abstraction. AGWL allows a programmer to define a graph of activities that refer to compu-tational tasks or user interactions. Activities are connected by control and data flow links.

In AGWL, activities are described by activity types. An activity ty-pe is an abstract description of a group of activity instances deployed in the Grid which have the same input and output data structures. Activity types shield the implementation details of activity instances from the AGWL programmer. A rich set of control flow constructs is provided in AGWL to simplify the specification of Grid workflow appli-cations, for example, `Sequence`, `If`, `Switch`, `While`, `For`, `ForEach`, `DAG`, `Parallel`, `ParallelFor` and `ParallelForEach`. AGWL also supports sub-workflows. Properties and constraints can be defined in AGWL to provide additional information for a workflow runtime environment to optimize and steer the execution of workflow applications.

3.2 UML Activity Diagrams

The UML Activity Diagram is one of the 13 UML diagrams of the UML 2.0 specification and it is used for *flow modeling* of various types of systems independently from their implementation (software or hard-ware). Hierarchical modeling capabilities of the UML Activity Diagram support modeling at arbitrary levels of detail and complexity. An *ac-tivity* is a flow graph, which consists of a set of *nodes* interconnected by directed *edges*. There are three types of nodes: *action nodes*, *control nodes*, and *object nodes*. *Action nodes* are basic units of the behavior

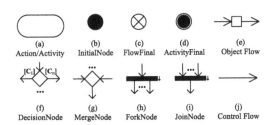

Figure 1.   A subset of modeling elements of UML Activity Diagram

specification (see Figure 1(a)). Actions may contain *pins*, which represent input and output. *Control nodes* steer the control and data along the flow graph (see Figure 1(b,c,d,f,g,h,i)). *Object nodes* contain the data that flows through the graph. An edge of a UML Activity Diagram indicates either a control flow or an object flow. A *control flow edge* specifies the precedence relationship between two interconnected nodes (see Figure 1(j)). An *object flow edge* specifies the flow of objects along interconnected *action nodes* (see Figure 1(e)).

4.   Modeling Grid Workflows with UML Activity Diagram

A Grid workflow Ψ is a pair (A, D), where A is a finite set of activities and D is a finite set of activity dependencies. Every activity dependency d_i, $d_i \in D$, is associated with an ordered pair of activities (a_m, a_n), where $a_m \in A \wedge a_n \in A$. An activity diagram Ω is a pair (N, E), where N is a finite set of nodes and E is a finite set of directed edges. Every directed edge is an ordered pair of nodes (n_k, n_j), where $n_k \in N \wedge n_j \in N$. The relationship between a Grid workflow $\Psi = (A, D)$ and an activity diagram $\Omega = (N, E)$ is defined by relations $R' = \{(a_i, n_i) \mid \text{for all } i, a_i \in A \wedge n_i \in N\}$ and $R'' = \{(d_j, e_j) \mid \text{for all } j, d_j \in D \wedge e_j \in E\}$. This means that each activity a_i of a Grid workflow is associated with a node n_i of a UML Activity Diagram, and each dependency d_j of a Grid workflow is associated with an edge e_j of a UML Activity Diagram.

In order to be able to model different types of systems, the UML specification provides several extension mechanisms to specialize semantics of modeling elements for a particular domain. Based on these mechanisms, we have extended the UML Activity Diagram by defining some new *stereotypes* with associated *tagged values* based on existing elements to model AGWL constructs (see Table 1). Figure 2 depicts an instance of the procedure, where we defined a model element *GridAction* by stereotyping the base class *Action* to model Grid workflow activities. The tagged value *type* specifies the *activity type* (e.g., Fast Fourier Transform

Table 1. Extending the UML Activity Diagram to model AGWL constructs

Base class	Stereotype & Tags	Description
Action	«GridAction» type: string	Indicates that the Action represents a fundmental computation unit in the Grid
SequenceNode	«Sequence»	Indicates that the SequenceNode represents a group of Grid actions/activities that are executed sequentially
ConditionalNode	«If» condition: boolean	Indicates that the ConditionalNode represents a conditional execution of Grid actions/activities in the *if-then-else* fashion
ConditionalNode	«Switch» caseValue: integer	Indicates that the ConditionalNode represents a conditional execution of Grid actions/activities in the *switch* fashion
LoopNode	«While» loopCondition: boolean	Indicates that the LoopNode represents a *while* loop. The loop body is executed zero or more times.
LoopNode	«For» from, to, step: integer	Indicates that the LoopNode represents a *for* loop.
ExpansionRegion	«ForEach»	Indicates that the ExpansionRegion represents a loop that iterates over elements of a data collection sequentially
StructuredActivityNode	«DAG»	Indicates that the StructuredActivityNode represents a group of Grid actions/activities that are executed based on the order specified in the directed acyclic graph
StructuredActivityNode	«Parallel»	Indicates that the StructuredActivityNode represents a group of Grid actions/activities that are executed in parallel
LoopNode	«ParallelFor» from, to, step: integer	Indicates that the LoopNode represents a *for* loop whose iterations are executed in parallel
ExpansionRegion	«ParallelForEach»	Indicates that the ExpansionRegion represents a loop that iterates over elements of a data collection in parallel
StructuredActivityNode	«SubWorkflow»	Indicates that the StructuredActivityNode represents a sub workflow that is invoked at a point of the main workflow

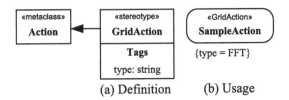

(a) Definition   (b) Usage

Figure 2.   The definition and usage of the stereotype *GridAction*

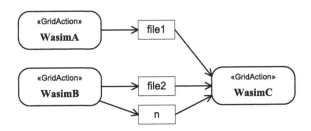

Figure 3.   Modeling data flows

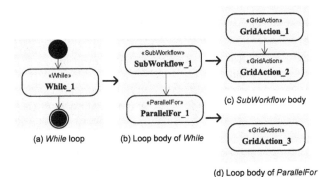

Figure 4.   Modeling Grid workflow hierarchies

(FFT)), which is an abstract description of a group of activity instances (concrete implementations of computational entities) implementing the same functionality and having the same input and output data structure.

We use the *object flow* in UML Activity Diagrams to model the data flow in Grid workflows and *pins* to model input and output data ports, namely, dataIn and dataOut. Connecting one dataOut port of an activity to one dataIn port of another activity constitutes a data flow. Figure 3 illustrates three data flows. The output file *file1* of the GridAction *WasimA* and the output file *file2* and the number *n* of GridAction *WasimB* serves as the input of the GridAction *WasimC*.

Graphical representations of Grid workflows are very intuitive and can be handled easily even by a non-expert user. However, the layout of workflow components on a display screen can become very large and beyond the users control. Similar to [Hoheisel, 2004], our solution is to use hierarchical graph definition. A Grid workflow can be composed through several levels of abstraction, each of which is represented in a separate graph. All AGWL control flow constructs like `While`, `ParallelFor`, `SubWorkflow`, etc. can have lower level workflow graphs. Figure 4 shows three levels of abstraction of a Grid workflow which are represented in four graphs. The workflow contains a while loop *While_1* in the highest level (Figure 4(a)). The *While_1* loop contains two control flow constructs in its loop body: *SubWorkflow_1* and *ParallelFor_1* (Figure 4(b)). The SubWorkflow *SubWorkflow_1* is represented in detail in Figure 4(c), which contains two GridActions: *GridAction_1* and *GridAction_2*. The parallel loop *ParallelFor_1* contains a GridAction *GridAction_3* in its loop body (Figure 4(d)). With the hierarchical graphical definition, users can easily view and evaluate the structure of the entire workflow or change the local part (e.g. a loop body) without being aware of the details and complexity of other parts of the Grid workflow.

By AGWL constructs `subWorkflow`, the hierarchical graph definition directly supports the sub-workflow definition and invocation. The main workflow (caller) provides input data to sub-workflow and gets output data from it. The input data is processed in sub-workflow (callee). The sub-workflow can be saved and reused.

5. Teuta

Teuta is implemented as a platform independent tool in Java based on Model-View-Controller (MVC) paradigm. Teuta comprises three main components: Graphical User Interface (GUI), Model Traverser, and Model Checker. The *Model Traverser* provides the possibility to walk through the model, visit each modeling element, and access its properties. We use the model traverser for the generation of various model representations, e.g. an AGWL representation of a Grid workflow, which serves as the input for the ASKALON Grid environment. The *Model Checker* is responsible for the correctness of the model. Teuta serves for ASKALON as a user interface for workflow composition, submission, controlling and monitoring.

Figure 5 illustrates a Grid workflow model in Teuta which consists of several diagrams. One of the diagrams is *main* diagram, which can be compared to the *main* method in Java/C++ programs, the others are sub-diagrams, e.g. the loop body of the parallel loop *parallelFor1*. These diagrams constitute the hierarchy of the Grid workflow. As shown in Figure 5, the activity types, dataIn ports, dataOut ports and AGWL

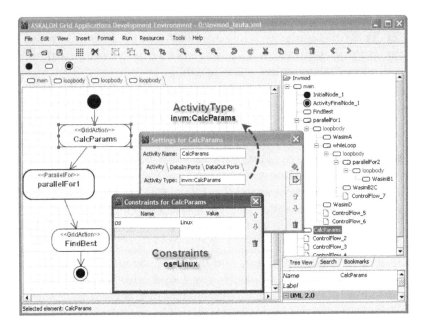

Figure 5. A Grid workflow model and the activity setting dialog in Teuta

properties and constraints can be added through the setting dialog for each modeling element. By specifying the source attributes of the data ports, users can create data flows. The corresponding AGWL representation of the Grid workflow can be generated automatically via the *Model Traverser* component.

6. Modeling a Real World Hydrological Workflow with Teuta

Invmod [Peter Rutschmann Dieter Theiner, 2005] is a hydrological application for river modeling. It has three levels of nested loops with variable number of inner loop iterations that depends on the actual convergence of the optimization process. Figure 6 illustrates the graphical representation of the Invmod Grid workflow application in Teuta. Since we adopt the hierarchical graph definition mechanism, the Invmod workflow looks very simple and can be easily understood: only one parallel loop *parallelFor1* and two atomic activities *CalcParams* and *FindBest* are shown in the *main* diagram of the workflow, because all the other activities are contained in the loop body of the *while* loop.

The code generation, implemented based on the Model Traverser, is done in the following steps: (1) put the activities in the *main* diagram into the object *AGWLWorkflow* as the workflow body; (2) put the acti-

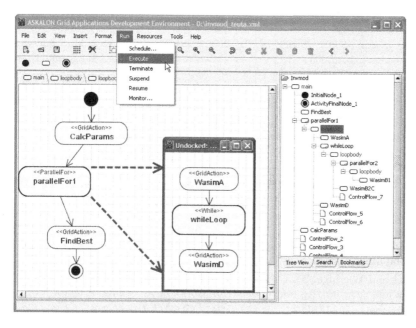

Figure 6.   UML based graphical representation of the Invmod Grid workflow

vities in the other diagrams into the associated parent control flow constructs like the parallel loop *parallelFor1*; (3) invoke the *toXml()* method
of the object *AGWLWorkflow* to generate the corresponding AGWL representation in XML. The workflow then is executed by the ASKALON
enactment engine service, which takes the AGWL representation of the
workflow and executes it based on the execution schedule made by the
ASKALON *meta-scheduler* service. While the workflow is being executed, the *enactment engine* returns the execution status (represented by
different background colors of activities) to Teuta for monitoring.

7.   Conclusions and Future Work

There is a need for streamlining the process of Grid workflow modeling. We have tailored our graphical editor Teuta for the composition
of Grid workflows based on the widely adopted standard UML 2.0. We
have demonstrated our approach for a real world hydrological application, and showed that thanks to the hierarchical workflow composition a
simple view of the workflow is maintained at each level of abstraction.

To further simplifying the specification of Grid workflows, our future
work will focus on improving data flows modeling, e.g. to automatically
fill the source attributes of data ports based on the model checking. We
will also evaluate Teuta for large and complex Grid workflow applications
in the future work.

References

[Altintas et al., 2004] Altintas, I., Berkley, C., Jaeger, E., Jones, M., Ludäscher, B., and Mock, S. (2004). Kepler: An Extensible System for Design and Execution of Scientific Workflows. In *16th Intl. Conf. on Scientific and Statistical Database Management (SSDBM'04)*, Santorini Island, Greece. IEEE Computer Society Press.

[Bastos et al., 2002] Bastos, R., Dubugras, D., and Ruiz, A. (2002). Extending UML Activity Diagram for Workflow Modeling in Production Systems. In *Proceedings of 35th Annual Hawaii International Conference on System Sciences (HICSS02)*, Big Island, Hawaii. IEEE Computer Society Press.

[Bran Selic, 2005] Bran Selic (2005). What's New in UML 2.0. ftp://ftp.software.ibm.com/software/rational/web/whitepapers/intro2uml2.pdf.

[Cao et al., 2003] Cao, J., Jarvis, S., Saini, S., and Nudd, G. (2003). GridFlow: Workflow Management for Grid Computing. In *3rd IEEE/ACM International Symposium on Cluster Computing and the Grid (CCGrid 2003)*, Tokyo, Japan. IEEE Computer Society Press.

[Eshuis and Wieringa, 2003] Eshuis, R. and Wieringa, R. (2003). Comparing Petri Net and Activity Diagram Variants for Workflow Modelling A Quest for Reactive Petri Nets. In *Advances in Petri Nets: Petri Net Technology for Communication Based Systems; Lecture Notes in Computer Science (LNCS)*, volume 2472, pages 321–351, Heidelberg, Germany.

[Fahringer et al., 2005a] Fahringer, T., Prodan, R., Duan, R., Nerieri, F., Podlipnig, S., Qin, J., Siddiqui, M., Truong, H.-L., Villazon, A., and Wieczorek, M. (2005a). ASKALON: A Grid Application Development and Computing Environment. In *6th International Workshop on Grid Computing (Grid 2005)*, Seattle, USA. IEEE Computer Society Press.

[Fahringer et al., 2005b] Fahringer, T., Qin, J., and Hainzer, S. (2005b). Specification of Grid Workflow Applications with AGWL: An Abstract Grid Workflow Language. In *Proceedings of IEEE International Symposium on Cluster Computing and the Grid 2005 (CCGrid 2005)*, Cardiff, UK. IEEE Computer Society Press.

[Hoheisel, 2004] Hoheisel, A. (2004). User Tools and Languages for Graph-based Grid Workflows. In *Grid Workflow Workshop, GGF10*, Berlin, Germany.

[Peter Rutschmann Dieter Theiner, 2005] Peter Rutschmann Dieter Theiner (2005). An Inverse Modelling Approach for the Estimation of Hydrological Model Parameters. *Journal of Hydroinformatics*.

[Pllana et al., 2004] Pllana, S., Fahringer, T., Testori, J., Benkner, S., and Brandic, I. (2004). Towards an UML Based Graphical Representation of Grid Workflow Applications. In *The 2nd European Across Grids Conference*, Nicosia, Cyprus. ACM Press.

[Taylor et al., 2005] Taylor, I., Wang, I., Shields, M., and Majithia, S. (2005). Distributed computing with Triana on the Grid. *Concurrency and Computation: Practice and Experience*.

[Yu and Buyya, 2005] Yu, J. and Buyya, R. (2005). A Taxonomy of Workflow Management Systems for Grid Computing. Technical Report Technical Report GRIDS-TR-2005-1, Grid Computing and Distributed Systems Laboratory, University of Melbourne, Australia. http://www.cis.uab.edu/gray/Pubs/grid-flow.pdf.

A TAXONOMY OF GRID RESOURCE BROKERS[*]

Attila Kertész
Institute of Informatics, University of Szeged,
H-6721 Szeged, P. O. Box 652, Hungary
MTA SZTAKI Computer and Automation Research Institute,
H-1518 Budapest, P. O. Box 63, Hungary
CoreGRID Institute on Resource Management and Scheduling
keratt@inf.u-szeged.hu

Péter Kacsuk
MTA SZTAKI Computer and Automation Research Institute,
H-1518 Budapest, P. O. Box 63, Hungary
CoreGRID Institute on Resource Management and Scheduling
kacsuk@sztaki.hu

Abstract: Grid computing has gone through some generations and as a result only a few widely used middleware architectures remain. Using the tools of these middlewares, various resource brokers have been developed to automate job submission over different grids. Most of the present brokers operate only on a single grid infrastructure, where they have been developed. This taxonomy helps identifying and categorizing the most important properties of brokers within different Resource Management Systems. The result of this work reveals the differences of the examined Resource Brokers, which can enhance a more efficient grid usage and future development.

Keywords: Grid Computing, Taxonomy, Resource Broker, Scheduler, Grid Middleware

[*] This research work is carried out under the FP6 Network of Excellence CoreGRID funded by the European Commission (Contract IST-2002-004265)

1.   Introduction

The Grid was originally proposed as a global computational infrastructure to solve grand-challenge, computational intensive problems that cannot be handled within reasonable time [1]. The first decade of grid research aimed at creating relatively reliable infrastructures to serve researchers and attract users. These attempts have led to the present grid middlewares, and now development is focusing on user requirements.

Executing a job in a grid environment requires special skills such as how to find out the actual state of the grid, how to reach the resources, etc. As the number of the users is growing and grid services have started to become commercial, resource brokers are needed to free the users from the cumbersome work of job handling. Though most of the existing grid middlewares give the opportunity to choose the environment for the user's task to run, originally they are lacking such a tool that automates the discovery and selection. Brokers meant to solve this problem [2]. As resource management is a key component of current grid middlewares, many solutions have been developed up till now. To enhance the manageability of grid resources and users, Virtual Organizations were founded. This kind of grouping started an isolation process in grid development, too. Interoperability among these "islands" will play an important role in grid research. This paper gives a classification of the present Grid Resource Brokers by the most relevant properties and functionalities. Identifying the key features and mapping them to user needs will open a new way for enhancing interoperability among different grids. Although the same services are available in different middlewares, they have been implemented in different ways. This taxonomy reflects the various ways how these brokers are built up and can be accessed. We believe that this paper helps researchers to have a better understanding of the current trends of resource brokerage.

2.   Related work

Regarding taxonomies in Grid Computing, two main papers have been published about resource management systems [3] and workflow management systems [4]. As resource brokers are usually parts of some resource management systems, the first one is closer to our work. That taxonomy introduces an abstract model of resource management in different Grid Systems, then describes and compares the existing architectures. In this paper we are focusing more on smaller entities responsible for brokerage; these can be considered as higher-level tools of resource management systems. While each RMS operates on one middleware, Grid Resource Brokers move towards nearly independent entities and several able to access resources of different middlewares. This taxonomy is needed to clarify the role and usage of these brokers, and to gather and present also those ones that were out of the scope of the RMS taxonomy. We examine the interface and the implementation of these brokers to reveal their main properties.

3. Taxonomy of Resource Brokers

The aim of this taxonomy is to gather the recent Grid Brokers used in Grid Communities, highlighting their main properties and examining the differences and similarities regarding their architecture and operation. We classify the revealed properties to 7 major categories and split into 3 groups. The following subsections comment the categories of these groups.

The first group is middleware oriented (Middleware Support), the second explains the mainly job related categories (Interface, Job Model, QoS and Data Movement), finally the third deals with scheduling features (Information System Support and Scheduling Model).

3.1 Grid Middlewares

The first main category – on Figure 1 – shows the underlying infrastructures of the overviewed brokers.

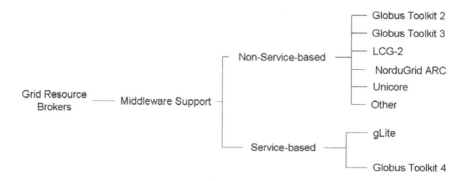

Figure 1. Categories of the Taxonomy: Grid Middlewares group

They usually rely on one of these middlewares [5][6][7][8] and use their functions to discover resources and submit user jobs. We can distinguish between service-based and non-service-based ones. Generally this property determines the architecture of the broker. It can be stated that the most widespread middleware is the Globus Toolkit, since LCG-2 is built upon Globus services and the NorduGrid ARC also uses and extends some of them.

3.2   Job handling

This group contains the mainly user and job related properties and can be seen in Figure 2.

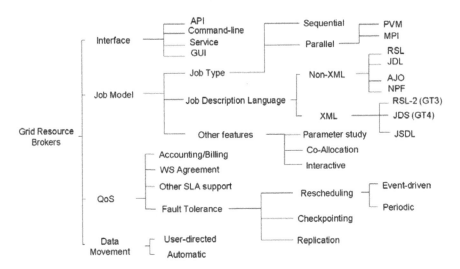

Figure 2. Categories of the Taxonomy: Job handling group

The first thing the user faces is the interface of the broker. Early solutions provided only command-line access, while APIs are important for higher level utilization and management by other applications. Some brokers even have Graphical User Interfaces to facilitate user usage. Service-based brokers offer service access, which is an advanced method and needed by the latest developments. This function can enhance interoperability and provide platform-independent access.

The job model of the broker is also important for users and applications. These properties tell how to describe a user job and what types can the broker handle. There are several non-XML language descriptions, but the latest developments follow the XML syntax. It would be reasonable for the brokers to accept and use XML job descriptions, even if they access middlewares supporting different languages [5][6][7][8]. In this case they would need to translate the request, but this approach leads to better interoperability. The rest of the properties in this subcategory show what type of jobs can be submitted with a specific broker: only sequential or parallel; in the second case co-allocation and advance reservation are handled or not. Brokers can support other special job-handling functionalities such as parameter study and interactive jobs.

Fulfilling user requirements is a critical task of the broker. Quality of Service is the collective expression of the properties to accomplish this task. Accounting is used for the administration of the users and tracking their grid utilization, and billing serves grid economy. Agreements are used to guarantee some level of service during brokering. User requirements can contain special requests, which are crucial for the job or application. On the other hand resource providers would protect sites from flooding by user jobs. In order to find a balance and fulfill requirements these policies appear in the agreements, which are taken into account in scheduling decisions. Various solutions can be developed to make these service level agreements, but this functionality is still an open issue. Basically two types are used: the WS Agreement [9] and the USLA [10]. The third part of QoS is fault tolerance. The dynamic nature of grids lowers the number of successful job submissions. To ensure a higher level of quality, brokers should be fault tolerant. Rescheduling and replication are the basic functionalities, and checkpointing can provide a more reliable brokering, though this is rarely supported, yet. Rescheduling can be event-driven or periodic, and usually choosing a different resource makes sense, retry only time consuming.

Most of the brokers provide automatic centralized data movement for input and output file staging. User-directed utilization can also be supported, when the user copies files to storage elements and tells the broker to use them.

3.3   Scheduling

The third group gathers properties related to resource information, discovery and scheduling. The properties of this group are shown on Figure 3. Several resource brokers use the information system of the underlying middleware. In this case the relevant information from the broker's view is the data store and query. The two main subcategories are the directory-based and service-based implementations. These properties tell us how the brokers access resource data and what kind of information they can use for resource mapping – since this is determined by the information system of the middleware. Some brokers use additional information about the grid gathered by an own information system. Examining historical data (resource availability, job failures, etc.) is one of these approaches. The other type of gathering relies on agents, which provide information about specific elements of the grid.

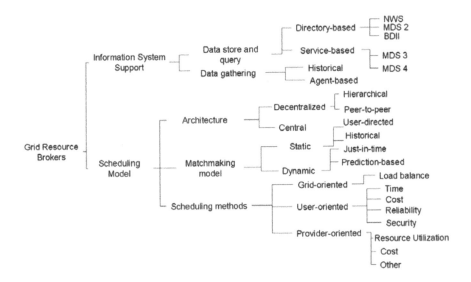

Figure 3. Categories of the Taxonomy: Scheduling group

Matchmaking is the major task of Grid Brokers. The scheduling properties can qualify brokers and determine the goodness of their decisions. In smaller scope of resources like VOs, usually a centralized scheduler component is used to make decisions. In decentralized schedulers the matchmaking process can be split up and queues can be utilized for job requests, or more components can collaborate to utilize a wider range of resources. The first solution is rather used in hierarchical and the second in peer-to-peer architectural models. The decision making can be static and dynamic. When a user fixes a resource for its job, or the scheduler component of the broker uses only static historical information, we are talking about static matchmaking. In a dynamic decision the broker has an up-to-date information about the resources and makes a just-in-time matching, or uses up some additional prediction-based information. The schedulers can take into account specific policies that affect decision making. These methods usually favor the users, but the provider expectations or the balanced state of the grid can also be observed. User policies can tell the broker to submit the job to a resource that completes the request in the shortest time or for the less cost possible. Reliable resource selection can also be a point of view, where less error can occur, or a secure one that ensures the safety of the job. Providers may expect from the broker to utilize more or less a specific resource, or gain as much as they could from the resource utilization. An alternative method is to serve the user requests as to keep the balance of the load on the grid.

4. Survey of the Resource Brokers

The properties of the taxonomy were gathered from 14 Grid Brokers. Table 1. shows the examined brokers, and gives a short description of their architecture and operation. The columns correspond with the groups of categories described in section 3. This survey displays the main properties of the brokers. It indicates how the categories of the taxonomy are implemented and used in different solutions.

Table 1. Survey of Grid Brokers

Grid Broker	Middleware Support	Job handling	Scheduling
AliEn RB [11]	Alice	File transfer optimization, fault tolerance by multithreading	Push and pull task assignment
Apples [12]	GT 2	Parameter study support, event-driven rescheduling	Centralized adaptive scheduling with heuristics, self-scheduled workqueues
EZ-GRID Broker [13]	GT 2, 3	GUI for job handling, transparent file transfer	Own information service with dynamic and historical data, Policy Engine Framework for provider policies
GRIDBUS Grid Service Broker [14]	GT, Unicore, Alchemi	Failure management and application recovery, parameter study, API support (XPML description file)	Economy-based and data-aware scheduling
GridWay [15]	GT	Job migration support (checkpointing, resubmission), API support	Decentralized (or centralized) scheduler, adaptive scheduling
GRIP Broker [16]	GT 2, 3, Unicore	Ontology Engine for translating different job description	Ontology Engine for translating different information service data
GRUBER [10]	GT 3, 4	SLA-based resource sharing in multi-VO environment, disk qouta considerations	Internal site monitoring feature, various user-oriented policies
GTbroker [17]	GT 2, 3	Periodic and event-driven rescheduling, automated file staging	User-oriented policies, additional dynamic information
JSS RB [18]	GT 4, NorduGrid ARC	WS-Agreement for advance reservations, resource filtering by user requirements, file staging and replication support	Scheduling algorithms with benchmark-based execution time and transfer time estimation
KOALA [19]	GT 2, 3	Periodic and event-driven rescheduling, parallel co-allocated job handling, automated file staging	Processor and data co-allocation, own information service, hierarchical scheduling with queues, incremental claming policy

LCG-2 /gLite Broker [6]	LCG-2/gLite	Periodic and event-driven rescheduling, interactive job support	Eager or lazy policies, push and pull models for task assignments, provider-oriented policy support
NIMROD/G [20]	GT 2, Legion	Application level accounting, parameter study support, periodic rescheduling (Nimrod/G plan file)	Deadline and budget-based constrained scheduling, hierarchical and decentralized agent-based scheduler
OGSI Broker [21]	GT 3	User defined ranking in resource selection	User-oriented and provider-oriented resource owner policies, internal agent-based information system

5.   Open issues and future work

From the survey and the taxonomy we can clearly identify, which properties are rarely used and which ones are highly supported. Regarding the whole taxonomy we saw that the Globus Toolkit is used by most of the brokers, therefore the RSL language is still the most widespread. The command-line interface is usual, and most of the brokers use a central scheduling architecture with just-in-time matchmaking optimized for minimal completion time. Rescheduling is widely used for fault tolerance.

On the contrary, the JSDL, which is a uniform standardized language, is rarely supported, yet. APIs, co-allocation, advance reservation and interactive job support should be provided by more brokers. A decentralized architecture could be a better solution in several cases, and own information systems should be built to gather more dynamic data and perform prediction-based matchmaking. As grids are heading towards the markets, provider-oriented policies should be more supported, and economy-based scheduling need to be considered. This solution requires QoS, so agreements must be supported by future brokers. To enhance reliability checkpointing and job migration should be targeted by future developments. Finally the most important thing to do is to provide all these broker properties to the users, making available more services, more middlewares and more resources in a transparent way. Interoperability is the key to achieve this vision.

Utilizing the existing, widely used and reliable resource brokers and managing interoperability among them could be new point of view in resource management. Our future work aims at developing a Meta-Broker that enables the users to access resources of different grids through their own brokers. Designing such an interoperable Meta-Broker, the following guidelines are essential: As standards play an important role of today's grid development, the interfaces must provide standard access. The architecture must be 'plug-in based' – the components should be easily extended by all means. The properties of the underlying components are also important; we need to be aware of the recent Grid Resource Brokers. The presented taxonomy and survey will provide the necessary information: how to interact with these brokers and which broker would provide the best service for a user task.

6. Conclusions

The presented taxonomy helps identifying and categorizing the most important properties of Grid Resource Brokers in various grid environments. We revealed the interfaces and relevant functionalities of the currently used brokers, which can enhance better user utilization and future development. With the presented survey users and scientists can have a better understanding of the operation and utilization of the current brokers. Developers should target issues that missing or rarely used in these solutions, but there is a definite need for them – to achieve this, the properties of the taxonomy give the guidelines. Furthermore, mapping the user needs and these broker categories, meta-brokers can solve the interoperability among Virtual Organizations and grids, which will be the main issue of future generation grids.

7. References

[1] I. Foster, C. Kesselman, "Computational Grids, The Grid: Blueprint for a New Computing Infrastructure", Morgan Kaufmann, 1998. pp. 15-52.

[2] E. Afgan, "Role of the Resource Broker in the Grid", Proceedings of the 42nd annual Southeast regional conference, 2004.

[3] K. Krauter, R. Buyya, M. Maheswaran, "A taxonomy and survey of grid resource management systems for distributed computing", Software: Practice and Experience. vol. 32, 2, 2002, pp. 135-164.

[4] J. Yu, R. Buyya, "A taxonomy of scientific workflow systems for grid computing", SIGMOD Rec., ACM Press, 2005, pp. 44-49.

[5] Globus Toolkit Homepage: http://www.globus.org/toolkit/

[6] EGEE Project Homepage: http://www.eu-egee.org/

[7] D. W. Erwin and D. F. Snelling., "UNICORE: A Grid Computing Environment", In Lecture Notes in Computer Science, volume 2150, Springer, 2001, pp. 825-834.

[8] O.Smirnova et al., "The NorduGrid Architecture And Middleware for Scientific Applications", Springer-Verlag, LNCS 2657, 2003.

[9] A. Andrieux, K. Czajkowski, A. Dan, K. Keahey, J. Pruyne, J. Rofrano, S. Tuecke, and M. Xu, "Web Services Agreement Specification" (WS-Agreement), Internet, 2004, https://forge.gridforum.org/projects/graapwg/document/WS-AgreementSpecification/

[10] C. Dumitrescu, I. Foster, "GRUBER: A Grid Resource Usage SLA Broker", 11th International Euro-Par Conference, LNCS 3648, 2005, pp. 465-474

[11] P. Saiz, A. Buncic, J. Peters, "AliEn Resource Brokers", Conference for Computing in High-Energy and Nuclear Physics (CHEP 03), 2003.

[12] H. Casanova, G. Obertelli, F. Berman, R. Wolski, "The AppLeS parameter sweep template: user-level middleware for the grid", In Proceedings of the 2000 ACM/IEEE Conference on Supercomputing, IEEE Computer Society.

[13] B. Sundaram and B. M. Chapman, "XML-Based Policy Engine Framework for Usage Policy Management in Grids", In Proceedings of the Third international Workshop on Grid Computing, LNCS vol. 2536, Springer-Verlag, 2002, pp. 194-198.

[14] S. Venugopal, R. Buyya, L. Winton, "A Grid Service Broker for Scheduling e-Science Applications on Global Data Grids", Concurrency and Computation: Practice and Experience, Volume 18, Issue 6, 2006, pp. 685-699

[15] E. Huedo, R. S. Montero, I. M. Llorente, "A framework for adaptive execution in grids", Software: Practice and Experience. vol. 34, 7, 2004, pp. 631-651.

[16] J. Brooke, D. Fellows, K. Garwood, C. Goble, "Semantic matching of Grid resource descriptions", UoM. 2nd European Across-Grids Conference (AxGrids 2004), 2004.

[17] A. Kertész, "Brokering solutions for Grid middlewares", in Pre-proc. of 1st Doctoral Workshop on Mathematical and Engineering Methods in Computer Science, 2005.

[18] E. Elmroth and J. Tordsson, "An Interoperable Standards-based Grid Resource Broker and Job Submission Service", First IEEE Conference on e-Science and Grid Computing, IEEE Computer Society Press, 2005, pp. 212-220.

[19] H.H. Mohamed, D.H.J. Epema, "The Design and Implementation of the KOALA Co-Allocating Grid Scheduler", European Grid Conference, Amsterdam, 2005.

[20] R. Buyya, D. Abramson, J. Giddy, "Nimrod/G: An Architecture for a Resource Management and Scheduling System in a Global Computational Grid", The 4th International Conference on High Performance Computing in Asia-Pacific Region (HPC Asia 2000), IEEE Computer Society Press, 2000.

[21] Y. Kim, J. Yu, J. Hahm, J. Kim, et al., "Design and Implementation of an OGSI-Compliant Grid Broker Service", Proc. of CCGrid, 2004.

TOWARDS AN AGENT INTEGRATED
SPECULATIVE SCHEDULING SERVICE

László Csaba Lőrincz, Attila Ulbert, Zoltán Horváth and Tamás Kozsik
*Eötvös Loránd University, Department of Programming Languages and Compilers**
Pázmány Péter sétány 1/c., 1117 Budapest, Hungary
{lesliel|mormota|hz|kto}-@inf.elte.hu

Abstract   The optimization of data access will largely influence the performance of the
current and next generation Data Grid systems. Job finishing times are an important factor in the characterization of Grid performance, as the earlier a newly
submitted job is finished, the more the submitter is satisfied.

   Our focus in this paper is mainly on how the introduction of agents can improve
job finishing time on the Data Grid systems. The strategy takes into account the
way applications access their data and extend the Grid middleware so that earlier
job finishing times can be achieved. The success of this strategy is due mainly to
the following two reasons: (i) the scheduler takes into account the job's behaviour,
(ii) the proposed agents deliver the necessary files earlier, so the job has to wait
less before the execution.

Keywords: DataGrid, scheduling, file replication, agents

1.   Introduction

The scheduling and execution of applications executed several times for
similar input values on the same or similar data files (called parameter sweep
applications) is one of the typical tasks of the (Data) Grid systems. The system
must complete several tasks that determine how soon the execution of the job
can be finished: (i) select the appropriate Computing Element, (ii) prepare the
necessary data files, (iii) execute the job, (iv) deliver the execution results.

In [3] we have already discussed the scheduling of parameter sweep applications in the context of the current Data Grid [8]. The proposed scheduling
strategy is based on the prediction of job finishing times estimated using the
job's behaviour description and the current status of Grid. The job behaviour

This work was supported by GVOP-3.2.2-2004-07-0005/3.0 ELTE IKKK, the National Office for Research and Technology under grant no. RET14/2005, the Bolyai Research Fellowship, and Alvicom Ltd.
(www.alvicom.hu).

description is generated automatically after monitoring an execution of the job. As a continuation of our work the main focus in this paper is still on secondary storage and data access. Based on our previous experiences in this work we extend the Data Grid [8] system with *agents* providing file pre- and postprocessing support, the overall goal being to further optimize the finishing times of data intensive jobs.

Although our ultimate goal is to design and develop services and agents for the next generation Grid, we have opted for an extension of the nodes of the current Grid, with *agent host* functionality using the JADE (Java Agent DEvelopment Framework) [4] framework. Taking as a basis the current Grid systems, our job scheduling method is composed of the following major steps:

1 The user *submits* a new job to the system.

2 Based on the *predicted finishing time* , the Resource Broker *selects* the "best" Computing Element for its execution and the Storage Element(s) (if the chosen Computing Element does not provide enough disk space for the input files) the input files must be replicated to.

3 Agents are *sent* to every source Storage Element, and one to every destination node.

4 The agents will run on the nodes in the background as daemons (the environment for this will be assured by the *agent host*s) and copy the files prior to the execution queue reaching the job requiring them.

The rest of this paper is organized as follows. Section 2 presents the process of automatic generation of job behaviour description. Section 3 presents two scheduling algorithms: the static data feeder scheduler and the agent integrated scheduler and its implementation in Condor-G. Simulation results are presented in Section 4. Finally, Section 5 summarizes the results and contribution of this paper and gives a short overview of related work.

2.   Describing job behaviour

According to our idea, the jobs submitted to the Grid are scheduled based on their estimated termination time, which is calculated by using a description of their behaviour. The description tells the scheduler how the submitted job accesses the resources (files and CPU). The job behaviour description is generated automatically after monitoring the job during execution.

Monitoring

The *monitoring component* is responsible for monitoring the jobs' resource access. It intercepts the IO function calls and their actual parameters (dispatches the IO request to the original IO library function thereafter) and logs the CPU and memory consumption.

The *monitoring component* is implemented as a shared library which must be installed on the Computing Element nodes and the LD_PRELOAD environment variable must be set properly. This is a minimal intrusion, however, platform-dependent solution: it can be used on Linux and Solaris systems, porting them to other operating systems requires further work. After the monitoring component is installed on a Computing Element node it works transparently without any further assistance from the system administrator or the application programmer. Besides, the component does not monitor those applications which are not dynamically linked, therefore the system can be configured to affect (monitor) only the required applications.

The analyser

The data collected by the *monitoring component* is further processed in order to get the desired compact description of the job's resource consumption. The resulting (behavioural) descriptions are utilized by the proposed Grid middleware services to perform scheduling and replication optimization.

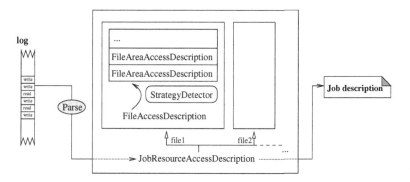

Figure 1. The Analyser

The job behaviour description generated by the analyser (see Figure 1) contains information about the input and, additionally, output file usage of the job. This information is called the Data Access Pattern of the application, and it is composed of:

- Type of the file (input or output).

- What fraction of the file is used (access_ratio).

- The file usage redundancy (intersection_ratio). This value will describe the average overlapping that exists between the data accessed by a predefined (and configurable) number of consecutive read or write operations on this file.

- A list of the datablock information. Each datablock contains:

  - The file access method (*sequential*or *random*) used in the section.
  - The starting and ending positions defining the current datablock through four values (two of them representing the absolute and two of them the relative file positions).
  - The distance (step) between starting positions of two successive data access operations (in the case of sequential file access). This number can also be negative if the job steps backward between these operations.
  - The size (in bytes) of the data processed in a single operation.
  - The frequency of the data access operations: the minimum and the average system time (in milliseconds) and CPU time (in mips) between two consecutive operations.

The following example depicts the behaviour description of the `gzip` program compressing file `test.avi`. According to the description, gzip read 16384 byte-length chunks from `test.avi` sequentially, and wrote 65536 byte-length blocks to file `test.avi.gz`:

```
<file_out name="test.avi.gz" access_ratio="1" intersection_ratio="0">
 <sequential>
  <datablock min_pos_absolute="0" max_pos_absolute="116162560"
   min_pos_relative="0" max_pos_relative="0.999894"
   step="16384" size="16384" />
  <timing op_time="0" op_mips="0"
   avg_op_time="0.00334029" avg_op_mips="6.35532" />
 </sequential>
</file_out>
<file_in name="test.avi" access_ratio="1" intersection_ratio="0">
 <sequential>
  <datablock min_pos_absolute="0" max_pos_absolute="117440512"
   min_pos_relative="0" max_pos_relative="0.999634"
   step="65536" size="65536" />
  <timing op_time="0" op_mips="0"
   avg_op_time="0.00659522" avg_op_mips="17.5861" />
 </sequential>
</file_in>
```

3.   Scheduling strategies

This section presents two scheduling strategies: the static data feeder [3] and the agent integrated scheduler. The scheduling decision of both schedulers is based on the job finishing time estimate: the scheduler takes a trial run through the suitable Computing Elements and estimates the time the job would finish its execution if it ran on the selected Grid component. The scheduling strategies presented differ in two aspects: the estimation of job finishing time and the used data delivery/replication service.

Static data feeder scheduler

The output of this strategy is a list of Computing Elements the job can be run on, ordered by the estimated termination time of the job and optional commands for the *Replica Manager* [7] specifying those files that need to be copied to or in the vicinity of the Grid element on which the job will run.

The finishing time estimate of a job running on a given Computing Element is calculated as the sum of the following:

1 The estimated termination time (which includes the delivery of output files) of the last job in the Computing Element queue.

2 The estimated input file transfer time, which is a function of the size of the files and the average network bandwidth.

3 The estimated job execution time calculated based on the extended job description (see Section 2).

4 The estimated output file transfer time calculated similarly as in the case of input files.

After calculating the ordered list of jobs, the scheduler will try to schedule the actual job to that Computing Element on which its execution would be finished as early as possible.

The agent integrated scheduler

According to the static data feeder scheduler, a job cannot be started until the output files of the previously executed job are copied to the desired destination. The agent integrated scheduler introduces - and as a result considers - agents that allow the jobs to be executed earlier by copying files during the running of a job.

Introducing agents. In order to improve the job finishing time, we have introduced agents, called FileAccessAgents, transferring files among Storage Elements and the hosts of the Computing Elements in such a way that allows the jobs to be started earlier. The FileAccessAgents provide additional functionalities over the Replica Manager: a) they execute the copy operations taking into account the status of multiple jobs; b) they can duplicate files also to CE-s;

c) and they can be enabled to support filtered data transfer copying only the required parts of the files. The `FileAccessAgents` run on the agent hosts on every Storage and Computing Element, and interact with each other in order to implement the required functionalities. The *source agents* (agents *sending* files) are always located on Storage Elements. A *source agent* can serve several *destination agents* (agents *receiving* files), and every *destination agent* can collect the required files from several sources.

The execution of a job on a CE is managed by a `JobManagementAgent`. For each job these agents coordinate the *destination* `FileAccessAgents` required by the job associated to them: start the `FileAccessAgents` according to the queue order of the jobs; collect status information from them; inform other `JobManagementAgents` about the termination of the copy operations. Currently `JobManagementAgents` are implemented only in the OptorSim simulation (see Section 4).

The agent integrated scheduler. The `FileAccessAgent` implements file sending and the file receiving functionalities. This simplifies the process of job data resource management, since at the end of their execution some jobs could require the copying of some files back to a given server.

The termination time of a job is estimated as the sum of its execution time (which is calculated based on its behaviour description) and the time when its execution can be started on the given CE. By using `FileAccessAgents`, the job's execution can be started earlier, as the agents copy the necessary input files of the jobs waiting in a CE queue parallel to each other, therefore a job does not have to wait until all the previous jobs have been processed. Besides, the `FileAccessAgent` can transfer files in parallel on a CE node after the execution of a given job is terminated. While the output files of the terminated job are being copied to the destination node, the corresponding `FileAccessAgent` prepares the input files for the next job scheduled on the given node. This allows the next job to be started, and therefore to be finished earlier than in the case of the static data feeder strategy.

The new scheduling method integrates the static data feeder-based scheduler (see Section 3) with the `FileAccessAgent` (see Figure 2). The following scenario describes the life-cycle:

1 The user submits the job and its description. The job description file can contain the description of the job behaviour.

2 If the user had provided the job behaviour description, the scheduler uses the proposed scheduling algorithm, which calculates the estimated job finishing time for every Computing Element (CE) and schedules the job to that CE where the job would be finished the earliest (according to the job behaviour description and the current state of the Grid reported by

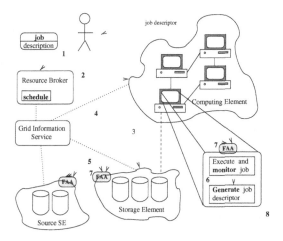

Figure 2. Scheduling and Agents

the Grid Information Service). If no behaviour description is provided, then another (default) scheduling algorithm is used.

3 If the chosen Computing Element does not provide enough disk space for the input files, the scheduler will also collect the best Storage Element (or Elements if disk space requirements cannot be satisfied by a single SE) to which the input files should be mirrored (if no replica of the files exists there already).

4 The scheduler will send FileAccessAgents to every source SE and one to every destination node. If there is already a FileAccessAgent on the targeted node, the system can either mirror it and send only the information about the claimed copy operation there, or it can send the whole agent with the mirroring information (note that compared to the input files, the size of the agent itself is negligible).

5 Upon arrival at its destination node, if another FileAccessAgent is running, the new agent will be placed into a queue. Once started, it will run in the background (the environment for this will be assured by the agent hosts) and will start copying the required input files. If the job the FileAccessAgents are connected to is started before the agents can finish their operation (e.g. there is no other job in the execution queue of the CE) it will wait until all of the files have been copied to the specified destination.

6 The job is executed on a computer belonging to the chosen CE. The job's resource consumption is monitored, and after the job is terminated a new re-fined job description is created.

7 The `FileAccessAgent` starts copying back the result (output) files (if any) of the job execution (and the behaviour description) to the specified SE-s. This operation is also performed in the background, so the next job from the queue of the CE can be started without having to wait for the file copy operation to finish.

8 The new behaviour description of the job is copied to the specified target node.

Note that the introduction of `FileAccessAgents` does not increase the execution time of the jobs, even if the jobs are suspended until the agents finish their copying operation, since these duplications would have been done either way, the only difference is the source requesting them (e.g Replica Manager, the job execution environment).

Implementation in Condor-G

Since the next generation Grid systems are only in development phase [9], we have opted for an extension of a Condor-G based system with agent host functionality. The JADE [4] framework provides a suitable platform for our goals:

- it can be distributed across machines,

- it is implemented in Java language and it is platform independent, thus allowing easy installation on almost any type of grid node,

- its communication model complies with the FIPA [5] specifications,

- and its transport mechanism has built-in support for the HTTP protocol.

Running agents in the JADE framework over multiple computers is possible through the usage of *containers*. Once the Main Container is active, the `FileAccessAgents` can be inserted into the system by adding them to containers that are connected to the Main Container (the Main Container can be identified by the address of the host it is running on).

The agents are submitted by Condor jobs to the desired Computing and Storage Elements as an *attachment* (or more precisely, as an input file) of the given job along with a *simple shell* script. Once the job arrives at its target, the underlying Condor system executes the shell script that will start the JADE environment (providing the agent host functionality), and will run the specified agents inside this environment.

Since the agents should be executed in the background as daemons without hindering the given Condor node in running other jobs, all of the jobs used to submit them in the system should start the containers in the background, and then exit. The closure of the containers must be assured then by their agents.

The necessary JADE libraries as well as the jar files containing the classes of the agents are specified as input files to be transferred upon job submission. The following Condor submit file creates a new *container* on node n02 containing an instance of agent A1 with the name a1. The Main Container is running on host n01:

```
universe       = vanilla
executable     = runjade
output         = jadesend.out
error          = jadesend.err
log            = jadesend.log
arguments      = -host n01 -container a1:A1
transfer_input_files = agent.jar,jade.jar,jadeTools.jar,iiop.jar, \\
commons-codec-1.3.jar
WhenTOTransferOutput = ON_EXIT
requirements   = (machine == "n02")
queue
```

The agents are using the integrated FIPA [5] *communication model* along with a well defined ontology that validates the information to be converted from a semantic point of view. The Content Manager transforms the objects representing the information in the source agent into a machine-readable byte sequence according to the syntactic rules of the related content language. Thereafter the generated byte sequence is transported to the destination agent over the HTTP protocol. Upon arrival the Content Manager (using the same codec) converts the byte sequence back into objects representing the given information for the destination agent (the representation of this information can differ from one agent to another).

The agent communication is completely *transparent*. In order to fulfill their security requisites the only requirements are to implement the chosen (secure) protocol in the agent host framework and select it as the default protocol for inter-domain data-exchange. Besides, the standard FIPA communication model along with the defined ontology allows the actual implementation of the agents to be changed at any time without the need to redesign and rewrite the entire model.

4. Simulation results

In order to evaluate the efficiency of the presented approach simulations were performed. OptorSim v2.0 [2] was extended with the addition of the *static data feeder* scheduler and the *agent integrated scheduler* implementation. Besides the new scheduling strategies, the simulation environment was also extended with FileAccessAgents running on every Storage Element of the Grid (the Computing Elements in the simulation do not have their own disk storage), and with JobManagementAgents running at every Computing Element.

The simulation follows the proposed scheduling and file management strategies closely: if the agent integrated scheduler is used, the Resource Broker selects the best CE for running the job (based on the estimated CE queue and job finishing time) and also the best SE (or SE-s if disk space requirements can not be satisfied by a single SE) to which the input files should be transferred (if no replica exists there already). The job is started after all preceding jobs in the CE queue have been terminated and the input file copy operations have been finished.

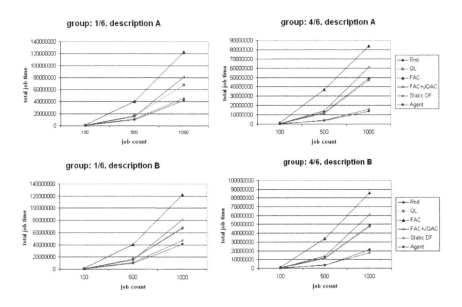

Figure 3.   Simulation results

The extended OptorSim was configured to use the EDG topology specified by the configuration file shipped with the simulator. The CEs of the configuration were extended with MIPS values. The group of jobs submitted to the Grid was extended with further *test jobs* that simulate the *single source shortest path searching algorithm in a graph*. The job first parses the graph description loaded from a 300 MB input file then it starts to calculate the shortest path from the given parameter node to every other node in the graph. After monitoring multiple executions of the application, *two job descriptions* have been chosen for further testing, the main difference between them being the consumed CPU time. The jobs provided by OptorSim are using input files of 10 GB each.

For each job description 2-2 simulation groups were performed: in one simulation group $\frac{1}{6}$ of the jobs submitted to the Grid had a job description, in the other simulation group $\frac{4}{6}$ of the jobs had a behaviour description. Each simulation group was executed with different job numbers: 100, 500, and 1000.

According to the simulation results (see Figure 3), using the *static data feeder* scheduler (Static DF) the mean job time of all jobs on Grid is about 29% lower than in the case of the scheduler which considered the file access cost and the job queue access cost (FAC + JQAC). The *static data feeder* strategy outperforms the *random* (Rnd), the *queue length* (QL) and the *file access cost* (FAC) strategies as well.

Due to the more sophisticated file transferring approach, using the *agent integrated* (Agent) scheduler leads to even better (about 16% lower) mean job times. Besides, compared to the *FAC + JQAC* scheduler, the jobs scheduled by *Agent* are finished 39% sooner.

5.   Summary and related work

This paper presented a new approach in scheduling regarding job execution optimization on Data Grid systems. The goal is to optimize the finishing time of data intensive jobs [10]. The basic idea is mainly to take into account the job's behaviour (file and CPU access) and reduce the time the jobs have to wait for data related operations. The former is done through scheduling using the job behaviour description in order to estimate the job completion time. The latter is achieved through the introduction of FileAccessAgents, that will run on an agent host on every SE and CE. These agents add support for file pre- and postprocessing functionalities, all of which include additional possibilities over those provided by the Replica Manager.

Many different scheduling and data replication algorithms exist and are used by the Data Grid systems. Nabrzyski et al. [12] gives an excellent overview of Grid resource management presenting state of the art research and experiences. Kunszt et al. [11] focuses on the data replication, and presents the replica management middleware developed within European DataGrid Project [8].

Similar to our approach, Y. Gao et al. [6] introduces models for estimating the completion time of jobs in a service Grid and proposes scheduling algorithms minimizing the average completion time of all jobs. The prediction of the completion time of an impending job is partially based on the number of jobs running on the Grid nodes and historical execution time of already completed jobs. Bell et al. [1] make use of sophisticated economy-based decision algorithms. The file replication strategy presented here does not, however, take into account the behaviour of the submitted job.

The major weakness of the current solution is that the proposed services cannot consider different behaviours of a given job. For example, if a job processes large files once with little CPU consumption and another time the job completes computation intensive tasks the generated behaviour description reflects only one of the operation modes. As a result, the scheduler cannot consider the actual complex job behaviour. The introduction of complex job behaviour descriptions and the adaptation of the scheduling algorithms will be the subject of our future research.

We performed simulations using OptorSim v2.0 [2]. The simulation results show that the introduction of the `FileAccessAgent` agent lead to earlier job finishing times compared to the "pure" static data feeder strategy [3] and the other replica management and scheduling strategies presented in [2]. Besides the simulations, we also implemented a prototype of the `FileAccessAgent` in a Condor-G based system.

Acknowledgement

We would like to express our thanks for the work of the following students: Csaba Kós for implementing the new scheduling algorithm in OptorSim, and Zoltán Takács for his work in testing the agent host capabilities.

References

[1] William H. Bell, David G. Cameron, Ruben Carvajal-Schiaffino, A. Paul Millar, Kurt Stockinger, Floriano Zini: Evaluation of an Economy-Based File Replication Strategy for a Data Grid. In: International Workshop on Agent based Cluster and Grid Computing at CCGrid 2003, Tokyo, Japan, May 2003. IEEE Computer Society Press.

[2] David G. Cameron, Ruben Carvajal-Schiaffino, A. Paul Millar, Caitriana Nicholson, Kurt Stockinger, Floriano Zini. Analysis of Scheduling and Replica Optimisation Strategies for Data Grids using OptorSim, International Journal of Grid Computing, 2(1): 57-69, 2004.

[3] László Csaba Lőrincz, Tamás Kozsik, Attila Ulbert and Zoltán Horváth: A method for job scheduling in Grid based on job execution status.
Multiagent and Grid Systems - An International Journal 4 (MAGS) Volume 1, Number 2, pp. 197-208, ISSN: 1574-1702/05, 2005.

[4] Java Agent DEvelopment Framework. http://jade.tilab.com/index.html

[5] FIPA: Foundation for Intelligent Physical Agents. http://www.fipa.org/

[6] Yang Gao, Hongqiang Rong, Joshua Zhexue Huang: Adaptive grid job scheduling with genetic algorithms. Future Generation Computer Systems 21, pp. 151-161, 2005.

[7] Foster, I.: The Grid: Blueprint for a New Computing Infrastructure. Morgan-Kaufmann, July 1998.

[8] The DataGrid Project. http://eu-datagrid.web.cern.ch/eu-datagrid/

[9] Foster, I., Kesselman, C., Nick, J. and Tuecke, S., The Physiology of the Grid: Open Grid Services Architecture for Distributed Systems Integration, presented at GGF4, Feb. 2002.

[10] Balázs Ugron, Szabolcs Hajdara, and László Kozma, Synthesis of the synchronization of general pipeline systems, Acta Cybernetica, 17, pp. 123-151, 2005.

[11] Peter Kunszt, Erwin Laure, Heinz Stockinger, and Kurt Stockinger. File-based Replica Management, Future Generation Computer Systems, 22(1):115-123, 2005, Elsevier.

[12] Jarek Nabrzyski (ed.), Jennifer M. Schopf (ed.), Jan Weglarz (ed.). Grid Resource Management : State of the Art and Future Trends, 2003.

[13] Thomas Erl. Service-Oriented Architecture (SOA): Concepts, Technology, and Design. Prentice Hall PTR, ISBN 0-13-185858-0, August 2, 2005.

Author Index